Youth Justice and Social Work

Youth Justice and Social Work

Second Edition

JANE PICKFORD AND PAUL DUGMORE

Series Editors: Jonathan Parker and Greta Bradley

Los Angeles | London | New Delhi
Singapore | Washington DC

Learning Matters
An imprint of SAGE Publications Ltd
1 Oliver's Yard
55 City Road
London EC1Y 1SP

SAGE Publications Inc.
2455 Teller Road
Thousand Oaks, California 91320

SAGE Publications India Pvt Ltd
B 1/I 1 Mohan Cooperative Industrial Area
Mathura Road
New Delhi 110 044

SAGE Publications Asia-Pacific Pte Ltd
3 Church Street
#10-04 Samsung Hub
Singapore 049483

Editor: Luke Block
Development editor: Kate Lodge
Production controller: Chris Marke
Project management: Deer Park Productions
Marketing manager: Zoe Seaton
Cover design: Code 5 Design Associates Ltd
Typeset by: Pantek Media
Printed by: MPG Books Group, Bodmin, Cornwall

Library of Congress Control Number: 2011944210

British Library Cataloguing in Publication data

A catalogue record for this book is available from the British Library

ISBN: 978 0 85725 319 4

This book is also available in the following formats:
Adobe ebook ISBN: 978 0 85725 321 7
ePUB ebook ISBN: 978 0 85725 320 0
Kindle ISBN: 978 0 85725 322 4

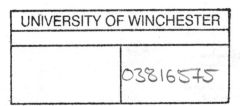

Contents

Series editors' preface

The Western world including the UK face numerous challenges over forthcoming years, many of which are perhaps heightened following the 2007 fiscal crisis and its lasting ramifications. These include dealing with the impact of an increasingly ageing population, with its attendant social care needs and working with the financial implications that such a changing demography brings. At the other end of the life-span the need for high quality child care, welfare and safeguarding services have been highlighted as society develops and responds to a changing complexion. National and global perturbations have continued to influence and mould social policy developments, which often determine the ways in which they are applied in social work practice.

Migration has increased as a global phenomenon and we now live and work with the implications of international issues in our everyday and local lives. Often these issues influence how we construct our social services and determine what services we need to offer. It is likely that as a social worker you will work with a diverse range of people throughout your career, many of whom have experienced significant, even traumatic, events that require a professional and caring response grounded, of course, in the laws and social policies that have developed as a result. As well as working with individuals, however, you may be required to respond to the needs of a particular community disadvantaged by world events or excluded within local communities because of assumptions made about them, and you may be embroiled in some of the tensions that arise from implementing policy-based approaches that may conflict with professional values. What is clear within these contexts is that you may be working with a range of people who are often at the margins of society, social excluded or in need of protection and safeguarding: the social policy responses designed to work with people marginalised within or excluded from society are dealt with in this book. This text provides important knowledge and information to help you become aware of these issues, and to respond appropriately when faced with challenging situations.

The importance of social work education came to the fore again following the inquiry into the death of baby Peter and the subsequent report from the Social Work Task Force set up in its aftermath. It is timely, also, to reconsider elements of social work education as is being taken forward by the Reform Board process in England and its implementation – indeed, we should view this as a continual striving for excellence! Reflection, revision and reform allow us to focus clearly on what knowledge is useful to engage with in learning to be a social worker. The focus on 'statutory' social work, and by dint of that involuntary clients, brings to the fore the need for social workers to be well-versed in the mechanisms and nuances of legislation that can be interpreted and applied to empower, protect and assist, but also to understand the social policy arena in which practice is forged. This important book provides readers with a beginning sense of the realities of practice and the importance of understanding the history of social protection, welfare and policy as it impacts on the lives of individuals in the UK.

The books in this series respond to the agendas driven by changes brought about by professional body, Government and disciplinary review. They aim to build on and offer introductory texts based on up-to-date knowledge and social policy development and to help communicate this in an accessible way preparing the ground for future study as you develop your social work career. The books are written by people passionate about social work and social services and aim to instil that passion on others. The knowledge introduced in this book is important for all social workers in all fields of practice as they seek to reaffirm social work's commitment to those it serves.

Professor Jonathan Parker, Bournemouth University
Greta Bradley, University of York

Introduction

Social work practice within the youth justice setting can be complex, challenging and laden with ethical dilemmas. However, it is also one of the areas in which social workers can really engage in significant work with young people in order to effect positive change. This can involve working with a wide range of service users aged from 10 to 17 (inclusive), as well as working closely with parents and carers all from a variety of social and cultural backgrounds. Young people will also present with many diverse experiences and needs and engage in a whole host of offending behaviour from first-time, trivial criminality to persistent and serious offences. Social workers in this area have to work closely with a wide group of professionals including those making up multi-agency Youth Offending Teams (YOTs) such as the police, health and education staff to solicitors, judges, magistrates and prison officers. Working within youth justice can be both difficult and incredibly rewarding as often you will be able to build important relationships and make a difference to the lives of young people.

In order to be able to carry out the roles and responsibilities in this area of social work practice, social workers need to employ a range of skills as well as acquire the relevant knowledge and display appropriate values and qualities in order to work effectively with young people who find themselves in trouble as a result of criminal behaviour. This includes:

- The National Occupational Standards for Social Work.

- The General Social Care Council's (GSCC) Code of Practice for Social Care Workers.

- Philosophical and theoretical standpoints in social work and criminology in relation to youth justice work.

- The relevant legislative frameworks in relation to children and criminal justice.

- The ever-changing social and political context that generates debates about young offenders within the media.

- Inter-agency and inter-professional working.

- Working with difference.

- Being aware of policy reform and new laws on youth justice.

This book considers all of these areas of knowledge in relation to working within youth justice social work practice.

The subject benchmark statement for social work identifies four key areas in which students need to acquire knowledge, understanding and skills:

- Social work services and service users.

- Values and ethics.

- Social work theory.

- The nature of social work practice.

Working within youth justice requires a wide range of transferable skills. These include communication, gathering information, preparation, engagement, assessment of need and risk, record-keeping, analysis, report writing, time management, team working, decision-making, problem-solving, and intervention. These skills will be considered over the next eight chapters. Instrumental to these skills being employed effectively is the ability to practise in an anti-oppressive way that takes into account difference.

Youth justice has been the subject of considerable change over the last 15 years and it seems highly likely that this will continue to be the case as the coalition government introduces and implements a raft of new legislation in relation to children and criminal justice.

This book is designed for criminology, law and social work degree students as well as those studying for youth justice qualifications. Those involved in the education of social work and youth justice and practitioners within the youth justice system will also find the content of this book useful.

Book structure

Chapter 1 discusses the values and ethics involved in working in youth justice. It considers some of the issues social workers have to wrestle with in this area of practice and places these within the context of the regulatory bodies involved in social work and youth justice. The first part of this chapter will examine ethical conflicts between legal and social work practice within the youth justice system. It examines trends in youth offending and looks at international legal conventions and human rights issues. In part two you will be encouraged to explore the value base from which you approach your social work practice and how your beliefs and prejudices might impact upon your practice with young people who offend.

Chapter 2 examines the development of youth justice theory, policy and practice. In order to understand the rationales underpinning any area of social work practice, it is vital to have an insight into the way your area of practice has been shaped by its history. The structure of the youth justice industry has been imbued by dominant philosophies that have seeped into the roots of the foundations of youth justice practice and govern contemporary practice. This chapter analyses the bedrock of youth justice theory, reviews the many developing perspectives of youth justice practice and traces the evolution of our unique youth justice system.

Chapter 3 analyses theories of criminality that may be useful for practitioners within the youth justice system. These theories relate to understanding why young people commit crimes and take part in anti-social or delinquent behaviour. In this chapter we undertake a basic theoretical tour of some of the mainstream criminological theories.

Chapter 4 goes into some detail about the policy discussions and legislation that shape contemporary youth justice practice. As a social worker within the youth justice industry, you will need to be familiar with the law underpinning your practice and the rationales that justify the current legal framework. We will examine the contemporary legal framework governing youth justice and set out the current risk assessment strategy and sentencing options for young offenders. We will also analyse non-criminal orders, which have the force of civil law constraints on young people who take part in anti-social and disorderly behaviour.

Chapter 5 considers the professional context that social workers practise within. This includes an examination of the youth justice system and the process a young person who commits an offence goes through, from arrest to sentence. We will look at the role of each of the key agencies in the youth justice system: the police, Crown Prosecution Service (CPS), courts and secure estate. The role and function of the multi-agency YOTs will also be explored, including each of the main professionals: social workers, probation officers, police officers and education and health officers. It will consider some of the issues social workers face when working within the same team as a wealth of other different professionals.

Chapter 6 focuses on the purpose, nature and process of assessment within youth justice. The assessment tool, Asset, used by YOTs is discussed and the interrelation between Asset and pre-sentence reports (PSRs) and risk assessments is considered. The chapter also looks at the relationship between assessment, risk and need, specifically in relation to safeguarding and mental health.

Chapter 7 addresses the different types of work that YOT social workers undertake with young people who have offended or are at risk of offending. This will include issues of diversity, equality and working with difference. This chapter considers the importance of planning, reviewing, ending and evaluating interventions with young people and the frameworks in place for achieving this, all of which follow from assessment. Finally, consideration is given to the different approaches to working with young people, such as one-to-one work, group work, restorative justice and what are effective methods of intervention.

Chapter 8 examines two key areas relating to effective future practice as a youth justice professional. The first part covers transferable skills and continuing professional education. Part two discusses the possibilities for future legislation in the youth justice arena. As a youth justice practitioner you will become aware that laws and procedures are regularly subject to change. In order to face the challenges of change within your professional environment, you must keep abreast of contemporary policy debates, reports, reviews and proposals. This chapter informs you of future proposed reforms and of ways of keeping on top of professional and legal changes.

Throughout the book, each chapter refers to the relevant National Occupational Standards and subject benchmark statement for social work and contains activities, case studies and research summaries to assist you in reflecting upon your values, beliefs and practice with young people who offend.

Chapter 1

Values, ethics and human rights issues in youth justice social work

Jane Pickford and Paul Dugmore

A C H I E V I N G   A   S O C I A L   W O R K   D E G R E E

This chapter will help you begin to meet the following National Occupational Standards.
Key Role 6: Demonstrate professional competence in social work practice.
- Work within agreed standards of social work practice and ensure own professional development.
- Manage complex ethical issues, dilemmas and conflicts.

It will also introduce you to the following academic standards as set out in the social work subject benchmark statement:
5.1.1 Social work services, service users and service carers.
5.1.3 Values and ethics.
Problem-solving skills.
5.5.3 Analysis and synthesis.
5.6 Communication skills.
5.7 Skills in working with others.

Part one: Understanding ethical dilemas between legal and social work practice in youth justice

Jane Pickford

Introduction

The youth justice system in England and Wales caters for young people who get into trouble with the police who are aged between 10–17 (inclusive). Youth justice practice is unlike any other area of social work because your client, no matter how harsh their background, will be viewed primarily as a wrongdoer who deserves to feel the weight of legal powers pressing against them. When this force is applied, you may find that some of the caring precepts of your profession become challenged, diluted and on occasion, negated.

Consequently, the discord between social work ethics and legal principles is perhaps no more keenly felt than in work with juvenile suspects and law-breakers. In some instances welfare instincts that practitioners are trained to develop within a culture of safeguarding and child protection, hit a legal brick wall when confronted with principles of justice and victims' rights.

In the first part of this chapter, you will be introduced to the ethical conflicts involved in youth justice social work. This will include examining dominant concepts of childhood that have undoubtedly impacted upon our juvenile justice system, explaining the traditional conflicting theories of youth justice and of criminology, as well as analysing how our youth justice system fares when faced with moral and legal standards imposed by international conventions and human rights legislation. In addition, it will be useful to outline statistics in relation to trends in youth offending, risk factors and custody rates, in order to contextualise our investigations.

The second part of the chapter provides an examination of the values and ethics underpinning social work practice and the regulatory frameworks in place to ensure practice is in accordance within the values and ethics fundamental to the social work profession. It considers the application of social work values to practice and potential ethical dilemmas facing social workers in their practice with children and young people who offend.

But first, let's introduce the nature of the big ethical problem for youth justice practitioners.

The 'big dilemma' in youth justice

Are children born innocent and become corrupted by exposure to the adult world and so need protection, or are children born with the potential for evil and so need to be controlled and civilised by adults? This fundamental question that is at the core of the nature *vs* nurture debate (which perhaps cannot be answered, even with the wealth of biological, psychological and environmental research gathered over the history of criminological investigation) is one of the most potent ethical dilemmas you will encounter in youth justice practice. It relates to the divergent approaches that have developed in relation to models for dealing with young offenders.

Though many academics assert that it might now be old fashioned to analyse tensions between the two historically dominant perspectives of welfare *vs* justice, it is evident to practitioners that these tensions are at the root of differences of opinion in public, professional and political arenas, when deciding how to deal with children and young people who come before the criminal justice system. Though these approaches (and others that have developed) will be examined later in this chapter and in detail in Chapter 2, it is useful to briefly outline them here and analyse how they interact with models of childhood (see Hendrick, 2002) and two mainstream criminological theories. Figure 1.1 attempts to simplify the polemic dominant theories of childhood, youth justice and criminology and highlight how they interact and overlap.

Figure 1.1 Overlaps and tensions in theories of childhood, youth justice and criminology

Children are born innocent	Children are born with the potential for evil
Romantic model of childhood	*Evangelical model of childhood*
• From the ideas of Rousseau. • Concept of 'original innocence'. • Children are born good and corrupted by the adult world. • Childhood should be respected as an important stage. • It is precious – a separate period of life that is distinct (opposite) from adulthood. • Children should be protected.	• From the religious ideas of Wesley and More. • Children are born with 'original sin'. • Children need discipline and education to civilise them. • Under this model children need to be strictly controlled. • Children are naturally self-seeking (see Hendrick, 2002).
Welfare approach to young offenders	*Justice approach to young offenders*
• Delinquent kids are a product of an adverse environment. • Delinquency is pathological – a manifestation of a deeper problem. • Delinquents are not fully responsible for their actions. • Delinquents are better dealt with by a system designed around need – by social workers and other professionals trained to work with young people. • Treatment and rehabilitation is possible if disadvantage is alleviated. • Discretionary powers are necessary. • Informality and flexibility is required.	• All people (inc young people) commit crime due to choice and opportunity. • Young people should be held fully responsible for their actions. • Sanctions are justifiable as deterrents. • Rigorous legal procedures and standards of proof should be adhered to. • Punishments should be proportionate and commensurate to the seriousness of the crime they have committed. • Sanctions should be based on the nature of the crime, not on the nature/circumstances of the criminal. (see Muncie 2009)
Criminological theory of positivism	*Criminological theory of classicism*
• Various factors cause criminality – positivists investigated biological/genetic triggers, psychological triggers and social/environmental triggers. • Causational factors can explain criminality and function as mitigations to full culpability. • Youth itself can count as a mitigation – the younger the culprit the less likely they are to be aware of the full consequences of their actions. • Causes need to be located and risk factors addressed. • Individualised treatment is required in order to address the problems that precipitated the criminal behaviour.	• Crime is committed out of choice. • Humans are rational beings but by nature self-seeking and hedonistic. • They are concerned with the pursuit of pleasure and avoidance of pain. • The would-be offender will undertake a cost-benefit analysis of the proposed deviant action. • The offender knows that their act is wrong, so should take full responsibility for crime and deserves to be punished. • Punishment should be proportionate to the wrong caused. • Personal circumstances don't excuse bad behaviour.

Examining Figure 1.1, it is clear that (i) the main perspectives of childhood, (ii) the dominant theoretical approaches to young offenders, and (iii) mainstream criminology, all share characteristics and are mutually supporting. The romantic model of childhood has a lot in common with the welfare approach to youth justice which in turn shares similarities with the school of positivism within criminology. Whereas, the evangelical model of childhood is reflected in the justice perspective of youth offending, which is in turn supported by the classical school of criminology. However, it is also clear that these two sets of three mutually supportive approaches are arguably oppositional polemic positions, and herein lies the 'big dilemma' in youth justice practice. The inability of successive governments (and indeed public opinion) to clearly recognise this dilemma and choose between these fundamentally different ways forward, continues to cause tensions within youth justice practice. Due to the elemental nature of this question, the polemics it raises and the fact that it taps into deep-seated and perhaps irresolvable academic arguments surrounding the nurture *vs* nature debate, it is doubtful that we will find any resolution to this issue.

Trends in youth offending

In order to conceptualise the youth crime problem, it is useful to examine the nature and extent of juvenile law breaking. Statistics indicate that during the period 1992 until 2003, there was a significant decline in detected juvenile criminality. Over that period, the total youth offending dropped by 27 per cent, despite public perceptions to the contrary (NACRO, 2009). However, the period from 2003–2007/8 witnessed an apparent reversal of that trend, with overall youth crime rising.

The apparent rise in detected youth crime over those years was probably influenced by issues other than the actual rate of youth criminality. It has been acknowledged by academics and practitioners that changes in police practice probably impacted on crime figures, creating misleading statistical data about seeming rises in juvenile law breaking. In 2002, the Labour government set a target (eventually of 1.25 million) for the police to narrow the 'justice gap' (between offences recorded and those 'brought to justice') by increasing the number that result in 'sanction detection' (i.e. by obtaining convictions **or** by issuing penalty notices for disorder (PNDs) **or** obtaining confessions from existing offenders of previous offences to be taken into consideration (TICs) when sentencing a current offence or by issuing reprimands and final warnings). One possible consequence is that offences which would previously have been dealt with informally (and go unrecorded) might have received a formal response over that period and so be reflected in the recorded figures for youth crime. Further, the increased use of anti-social behaviour orders (ASBOs) and the consequent criminlisation of those who breached orders arguably similarly and misleadingly inflated the statistics (NACRO, 2009).

The increase in 'sanction detections' was not followed by a concomitant increase in the police clear-up rate. Bateman's analysis of the seeming rise in detected youth crime was that it was a *function of sanction detections being imposed for behaviour that would previously not have attracted such an outcome* (Bateman, 2008).

The target was, in other words, met at the expense of those populations of offenders who might otherwise have received an informal response for minor transgression against the law (NACRO, 2009).

These would include:

- offences committed by younger people;
- less serious offending;
- offences committed by girls.

Analysis of the data confirms that the apparent rise in juvenile criminality 2003–2007 can be substantially explained by disproportionate rises in each of the above categories. It seems that the police were picking low-hanging fruit – those easiest to pursue – when attempting to meet government targets over this period. Once the targets were removed, declines in overall youth crime, particularly in relation to first offenders, were notable.

Youth crime figures peaked in 2007/8 and since that period total offences committed by young people has notably declined, largely due to a reduction of first time entrants into the youth justice system (i.e. those receiving their first reprimand, final warning or conviction (Department of Education, 2010; Youth Justice Board/Ministry of Justice, 2011)).

ACTIVITY **1.1**

Take a look at the most recent statistics relating to youth crime at the Ministry of Justice website: www.justice.gov.uk and outline the current trends in youth crime. Has the crime rate for 10–17 year olds risen or fallen over the last few years? What factors might have precipitated recent trends? Have there been any noticeable patterns in increases or decreases of particular types of crime?

If we analyse some of the key data published jointly by the Youth Justice Board and the Ministry of Justice early in 2011, the downwards trend is clear:

- There were 198,449 proven offences committed by young people aged 10–17 which resulted in a disposal in 2009/10 – this is a decrease of 19% from 2008/09 and 33% from 2006/07.
- The most common offences resulting in a disposal in 2009/10 were:
  - theft and handling – 21% of all offences;
  - violence against the person – 20% of all offences;
  - criminal damage – 12% of all offences.
- In 2009/10 most youth offending in England and Wales was committed by young men – 60% of all offences were committed by young men aged between 15 and 17 years. Young males were responsible for 78% of the offences committed by young people.

- There were 155,856 disposals given to young people in 2009/10. This is down 28% from 2006/07.

- These falls followed a period of rapid growth from 2003/04 to 2007/08, when out of court disposals almost trebled.

- This increase was due to the introduction of Penalty Notices for Disorder (PNDs) which coincided with the introduction of a public service agreement target, which took effect in 2002, to increase the total number of offences brought to justice (OBTJ). This target has now been removed.

- Females accounted for 22% of all disposals given to young people in 2009/10. They accounted for 32% of all pre-court disposals given, and 17% of all first-tier disposals. They accounted for 15% of all community disposals and only 8% of custodial disposals.

(Youth Justice Board/Ministry of Justice, 2011)

Trends in custodial sanctions

In England and Wales we lock up more children and young people than almost any other Western society. NACRO (2010) in a policy position paper recommending further reductions to the amount of children and young people being sent to the secure estate, made the following comments on custodial remands and disposals:

- Between 1992 and 2002, the number of young people sentenced to custody rose by more than 85% while the level of detected youth crime reduced by more than a quarter.

- During the early months of 2009, the population of the secure estate fell for the first time since 2000 – this trend has continued and early 2011 there are approx 2,100 young people in the secure estate – at its peak it reached approx 3,000.

- In England and Wales we incarcerate four times more under 18s than France, ten times more than Spain and 100 times more than Finland.

- Custody is costly but has an appalling success rate (75% are reconvicted within one year) and academic evidence suggests that for many young people the use of custody actually increases the risk of reoffending.

- *Reoffending following release from custody is inversely related to age: younger children are more likely to be reconvicted than older teenagers, who in turn are more likely to be reconvicted than adults* (NACRO, 2010, p2).

- A large number of young people who are detained in custodial facilities do not pose a serious risk to the public.

- Of young people aged 16 to 17 convicted of non-violent offences, 12% are given custodial sentences, while over a third of younger children below the age of 15 in custody do not seem to meet the statutory criteria for incarceration.

- Around 40% of the population of the secure estate for children and young people are classified as vulnerable and one third of children have no educational provision on entering those establishments.

(NACRO 2010)

Risk factors and youth offending

The Youth Justice Board highlighted the following four risk factors as being the most influential on youth offending:

- *Family* e.g. inadequate, harsh or inconsistent parenting.

- *School* e.g. low achievement, disaffection, truancy or exclusion.

- *Community* e.g. residence in areas of low community cohesion, crime hot spots or easy access to drugs.

- *Personal* e.g. being male, mixing with offending peers, poor physical or mental health or misuse of drugs or alcohol.

(Youth Justice Board, 2005b)

To these four major influences, Pitts (2008) possibly adds a fifth (though linked to the factor of community) namely, physical area. When investigating gang activity, Pitts discovered that youth involvement in serious criminality correlated more strongly with habitation in deprived neighbourhoods than with the other factors noted above.

These vulnerability/susceptibility factors are at the centre of risk assessments undertaken by Youth Offending Teams (YOTs) across England and Wales. The Youth Justice Board designed a risk assessment tool – Asset – which is used to *'score' a young person's risk of further offending* using the *'scaled approach'* introduced in November 2009.

Some academics and practitioners have been highly critical of this move, because:

- it could 'up-tariff' a YP for welfare issues;

- its focus is on individual rather than structural factors such as government policy, unemployment, poverty, etc. (Smith, 2007);

- some people who are predicted as high risk do not re-offend and vice versa;

- calculating the risk of a young person committing further offences cannot be reduced to an actuarial or mathematical equation because young people often do not act predictably and their lives are often varied and complex. The process is totally oversimplified and this experiment in actuarialism amounts to treating young people who come before the criminal justice system like *crash test dummies* (Case and Haines, 2009) (see Chapter 4 for a further critique).

The interface between law and ethics

In this section we consider our youth justice system in relation to international legislation and conventions, as well as examining how it may stand up to the provisions of our own Human Rights Act 1998.

International conventions, guidelines and rules relating to youth justice

Is the way we treat young people who come into contact with the criminal justice system comparable to juvenile justice systems in other legal cultures? How well do we fare when we scrutinise our brand of youth justice and test its compliance with international legal requirements? We analyse how the implementation of human rights legislation into our domestic law has impacted upon our practice of youth justice. Do some of the practices within our youth justice legislation breach fundamental principles of human rights?

But first we must examine international law on the rights of the child and the many protections that have developed over the past few decades. Some countries have taken international provisions about minimum requirements in relation to youth justice systems more seriously than others. How does our system fare when we put it to the test of international conventions? Have we developed a child-oriented system when we deal with young people who are accused of breaching our criminal law?

International human rights law should offer protections for young offenders, if provisions are adhered to at a domestic level. You should be aware of them to check whether procedures your client has been subject to might be in breach of these safeguards. The most significant examples include:

- United Nations Convention on the Rights of the Child (1989).

- United Nations Rules for the Administration of Juvenile Justice (1985) (Beijing Rules).

- United Nations Rules for the Protection of Juveniles Deprived of their Liberty (1990b).

- United Nations Guidelines for the Prevention of Juvenile Delinquency (1990a) (Riyadh Guidelines).

and also:

- Article 5 of the European Convention on Human Rights – the right to liberty and security (now part of our Human Rights Act 1998).

- Article 6 – the right to a fair trial (now part of our Human Rights Act 1998).

- International Covenant on Civil and Political Rights (ICCPR) (1966) – Article 14 (4): . . . *in the case of juvenile persons, the procedure shall be such as will take account of their age and the desirability of promoting their rehabilitation.*

The most far-reaching is the Convention on the Rights of the Child; this is due to its binding character and the fact that it has been ratified by 191 states/countries. The convention acknowledges that distinct legal procedures are necessary when dealing with under 18 year olds who are accused of criminal activities.

Article 40 is one of the most significant parts. It states that:

> *State Parties recognise the right of every child alleged as, accused of, or recognised as having infringed the penal law to be treated in a manner consistent with the promotion of the child's sense of dignity and worth . . .*

This includes minimum due process guarantees, including:

- The presumption of innocence.
- The right to be informed promptly of the charges against him or her.
- The right to have legal assistance in the preparation of his or her defence.
- The right to be tried without delay by a competent legal authority.
- A requirement to set a reasonable minimum age of criminal responsibility.
- The need to provide non-judicial methods of dealing with children in conflict with the law.
- The need to establish alternatives to institutional care.

These provisions are supplemented by Article 37, which prohibits the death penalty and life imprisonment without the possibility of release. Article 37 also requires that imprisonment 'shall be used as a measure of last resort' and where children are imprisoned it must be for the shortest possible period of time.

Article 39 requires the countries to promote physical and psychological recovery and reintegration of child victims.

The Convention also has general principles, which should be considered in addition to specific principles. These include:

- All procedures should be in the best interests of the child (Article 3).
- Judicial bodies/tribunals must take into account the evolving capacities of the child (Article 5).
- Judicial bodies/tribunals must give due weight to the views of the child (Article 12).
- Procedures must be free of discrimination (Article 2).

The United Nations Committee on the Rights of the Child monitors countries who have ratified the Convention on the Rights of the Child to test for compliance and publishes periodic reports. Our youth justice system has been scrutinised by the Committee on three occasions: 1995, 2002 and 2008. On each occasion the Committee has raised serious concerns. Most notably, there was concern expressed about the fact that the government in England and Wales had not encoded the principles of the convention into domestic law. The result of this is that, while there is an obligation to comply with the convention, there is no domestic sanction for non-compliance! It is arguable that public opinion in our country (often prompted by tabloid coverage of young offenders) has not been conducive to the idea of promoting suspect's and offender's rights generally. (Indeed, the coalition Conservative/Liberal Democrat government has adopted this tone in its proposal to abolish the Human Rights Act). Monaghan (2005, p47) asserts that,

> . . . with regard to youth justice, there remains considerable ambiguity of commitment to rights and a significant level of infringement and outright denial . . . respect for children's rights is selective and, arguably, discriminatory.

The 2008 report of the committee on the Rights of the Child echoed these concerns, commenting on a popular intolerance for adolescents and asserting that the media attitude towards youths could encourage further human rights infringements. This negative characterisation was also observed by a YouGov survey in 2008 when over half of those surveyed said that children were behaving like animals and just under half said that children were potentially a danger to society. These populist attitudes are reflected upon in the Committee's conclusions, below.

The Committee noted that, while there had been some positive interventions since their 2002 report (e.g. the government's development of the Children's Plan, the creation of Children's Commissioners, the segregation of youths from adults held in custody and the establishment of the Equalities and Human Rights Commission) overall, many serious deficiencies remained. Their main concerns regarding youth justice can be summarised as follows:

1. *The age of criminal responsibility in England and Wales*. The Committee criticised our threshold of ten years old and stated that we were out of line with most other countries, recommending that this be raised substantially. The table below illustrates the differences of acceptable ages of criminal culpabilities between countries.

Table 1.1 International comparisons of minimum age of criminal responsibility

Age of criminal responsibility	Country
7	Switzerland, Nigeria, S Africa
8	Sri Lanka
10	England, Wales, Northern Ireland, Australia, New Zealand
12	Scotland, The Netherlands, Canada, Greece, Turkey, Southern Ireland
13	France
14	Italy, Germany, Bulgaria, Romania, China
15	Denmark, Sweden, Norway, Finland, Czech Republic, New York (US), South Carolina (US)
16	Spain, Japan, Texas (US), Poland
18	Belgium, Luxembourg, many US states

In March 2010, England's children's commissioner Maggie Atkinson called for the age of responsibility to be raised, stating that most criminals under the age of 12 did not fully understand their actions (www.guardian.co.uk/uk/2010/mar). However, the Ministry of Justice said those aged 10 and over knew the difference *between bad behaviour and serious wrongdoing* and that the age should not be raised (http://news.bbc.co.uk/1/ni/uk/8566591.stm). Her timing was perhaps unfortunate, as her plea followed soon after the trial of two boys from Edlington who, at the age of 11 and 12, seriously tortured two younger children, a case which bore strikingly similar characteristics to the killing of James Bulger some 16 years earlier. Later that year, in May 2010, a trial at the Old Bailey of two 10-year-old boys who were found guilty of the attempted rape of an 8-year-old girl, re-ignited the debate about the age of criminal responsibility. Article 40 (c) of the Convention on the Rights of the Child says that it is for states to set a reasonable minimum age, but declares that it considers that a minimum threshold that is below the age of 12 is *not internationally acceptable*. Echoing these concerns and noting the very low age of criminal responsibility in England and Wales, Thomas Hammarberg, Commissioner for Human Rights of the Council of Europe (Council of Europe, 2008) recommended in 2008 that the Government considerably increase the age of criminal responsibility to bring it in line with the rest of Europe, where the average age of criminal responsibility is 14 or 15 years.

2. *The use of adult courts for juveniles.* The Committee reiterated its previous opinion that crown courts are adult courts and unsuitable for children and young people and that a youth court that deals with serious crimes should be established. Similarly, though a young person who is tried with an adult co-defendant at an adult magistrate's court is usually referred to youth court for sentence, the committee deemed it inappropriate to hold trials of juveniles at adult courts. Further, the practice that many young suspects have bail and remand decisions adjudicated at adult courts after arrest because youth courts usually sit only for one day each week in most areas, was also viewed as unacceptable.

3. *The use of detention.* The Committee stated that detention levels both for sentenced and remanded juveniles were objectionably high and indicated that the 'last resort' principle of youth custody enshrined in the Convention was not being adhered to. The Committee found it noteworthy that there is no simple guidance relating to the classification of a 'persistent young offender' and that assessments of dangerousness are often subjective. The Committee also expressed concern regarding deaths in custody and the high levels of self-harm among detainees.

4. *ASBOs for children should be abolished.* The Committee was concerned that:
   - ASBOs are civil orders that attract criminal sanctions on breach;
   - orders often prohibit a wide range of behaviour/activities;
   - that there exists a culture of *ease of issuing such orders*;
   - ASBOs facilitate early contact with the criminal justice system, which is detrimental to young people;
   - they are primarily targeted at adolescents from disadvantaged backgrounds.

   (Note: specific human rights law implications of ASBOs will be examined under the sub-heading Human Rights Act, below.)

5. *The use of dispersal orders and methods to curtail peaceful assembly.* The Committee condemned the use of dispersal orders and the use of the 'mosquito' high pitched electronic device against young people who assemble in public places.

6. *The right to privacy.* The Committee was concerned about the climate of zero-tolerance towards youth disorder as reflected in the trend in some areas to publicise details and pictures of youths subject to ASBOs and the proposal in the Youth Crime Action Plan 2008 to drop the reporting restrictions in relation to those aged 16 and 17. Further, disquiet was expressed about the growth of the taking and retention of DNA samples of young suspects.

7. *The use of restraint techniques.* The Committee urged a more reticent attitude to the use of restraining methods, which should be used as a last resort and only when the young person is a danger to themselves or others.

In a review of the Committee's findings, NACRO (2008) concluded that, not only had our government failed to address ongoing concerns such as the high levels of detention and the low age of criminal responsibility, but that human rights infringements were of growing concern in relation to the flourishing use of ASBOs and other civil measures that restricted freedom and privacy. Additionally, the growth of a popular, perhaps media provoked demonisation culture regarding youths, *should be viewed with dismay*. While it is up to the government to implement the Committee's recommendations, youth justice practitioners should

> *. . . consider and defend children's human rights with vigour . . . Ensure that they are familiar with children's human rights, and frame practice around the principles and provisions of the Convention on the Rights of the Child.*

> (NACRO, 2008, p8)

The Human Rights Act 1998

The Human Rights Act 1998 incorporates the European Convention on Human Rights into domestic law so that all current and planned legislation must be implemented in a manner consistent with the rights and freedoms set out in the Convention. Additionally, the Act includes the adoption into domestic law of the United Nations Convention and linked protocols including (very significantly from a youth justice standpoint) the Beijing Rules (the United Nations Standard Minimum Rules for the Administration of Juvenile Justice 1985).

Has the inclusion of these international provisions affected the practice of youth justice in this country? Could legal challenges be mounted under the Human Rights Act about the way we treat young people who are deemed to be anti-social or who are suspected of or convicted for a criminal offence? You should be aware of these protections in your work with clients and be prepared to challenge any breaches.

In 1999 the European Court of Human Rights, in the case of Thompson and Venables (the killers of toddler James Bulger), (prior to the implementation of the Human Rights Act) ruled that:

*   The process in the Crown Court was unfair because it was unsuitable for the two defendants (aged 11 at the time) in that it was intimidating and incomprehensible for the boys. This ruling has yet to be acted upon.

*   Sentencing should be left to judges to decide and recommendations should not be overruled by politicians (the boys were originally sentenced to eight years by the trial judge; this was raised to ten years by the Lord Chief Justice and then to 15 years by Michael Howard, the then Home Secretary).

*   Decisions about release should not be decided by the Home Secretary but by an independent judicial body such as the Parole Board.

Following this ruling, Jack straw the Labour Home Secretary in 2000 referred the issue to the Lord Chief Justice who declared that the boys had served their minimum tarrif. This paved the way for a parole application and a successful injunction to protect their anonymity. They were released with new identities in 2001. The sentencing of juveniles convicted of the gravest crimes will be set by the Lord Chief Justice on recommendation of the trial judge.

It is noteworthy that the European Court's ruling regarding Crown Courts being unsuitable places for dealing with young people (the Crown Court is essentially an adult court) has been ignored by the government. Young people who are alleged to have committed serious offences are still tried in this unsuitable and confusing environment. The implication seems clear: children should not be subject to adult court procedures. Changes must be made to the system of trial of children and young suspects in the crown court, especially those at the youngest end of criminal responsibility (i.e. 10 to 13 year olds). As noted in the last section, the United Nations Committee on the rights of the child has consistently urged our government to reform this area of youth justice procedure.

The above decision highlights how the government can be challenged for breaches of human rights and international protections in relation to young offenders. There are other possible breaches that could impact upon your social work practice in advising young people and their parents. Further challenges that could possibly be taken in relation to the provisions in our contemporary youth justice law and practice include:

- *Anti-social behaviour orders (ASBOs), anti-social behaviour contracts (ABCs) and local child curfews*. A magistrate can order an anti-social behaviour order in respect of any person over the age of 10. The police, in conjunction with the local authority, make the application for an ASBO. The local authority can also impose ABCs on young people (and adults) before an ASBO application is made. Young people may feel pressurised to accept the terms of an ABC, for fear that a formal ASBO application might be made to the court if they decline. (See Chapter 4 for more information about ASBOs and ABCs and other civil orders.) Although an ASBO is civil in nature, its breach can involve criminal sanctions. Such an order can now be made for beyond the original two year limit and its potential for constituting an intrusion of individual and family privacy seems clear. Furthermore, the local child curfew, which can be imposed on a group of children under the age of 10 for an extendable period of 90 days, appears similarly intrusive. As with the anti-social behaviour order, no criminal behaviour need be proved before a curfew is imposed.

The growth of other civil orders such as dispersal orders, the introduction of wider powers against parents and broader control measures within the parenting order alongside the development of the anti-social behaviour injunction (in 2010) all provide evidence of wider and deeper tactics of government control of those perceived to be unruly within our society. The danger of human rights infringements has grown in tandem with this increase in state interventions, interventions that appear to be targeted disproportionately against young and marginalised communities (UN Committee on the Rights of the Child Report, 2008).

It is noteworthy that Alvaro Gil-Robles, the Human Rights Commissioner for the Council of Europe, alleged in his report back in June 2005 that the UK was already suffering from 'asbomania'. Also, Shami Chakrabarti, the current director of Liberty, when asked to comment on the practice of some local authorities to 'name and shame' young people subject to ASBOs said that this practice was: *More akin to the medieval stocks than a 21st century law and order strategy. We are in danger of transforming Britain into Asboland* (*Observer*, 12 June 2005).

Successful challenges have been mounted by individual 'defendants' to allegedly unreasonable ASBO restrictions. In May 2005, a 16 year old from Collyhurst Village near Manchester became the first person to be banned under an ASBO from wearing a hooded top. However, in August 2005 a youth in Portsmouth, who was banned from wearing a hooded top or a baseball cap under the terms of an ASBO, had this part of the order set aside by a district judge when his solicitor successfully argued that this restriction breached his human rights. Similarly, in July 2005 the High Court backed a 15 year old's claim that ASBO powers that sanctioned the police to remove him from curfew zones breached the Human Rights Act in that it unreasonably interfered with his freedom of movement. Also, magistrates might be wary of breaching basic freedoms under the Human Rights Act, as was seen in May 2010 when a Bench in Bedford refused to impose an ASBO condition requested by the police and CPS against an 18 year old, which purported to ban him from wearing his trousers so low that his underpants were visible.

As Muncie (2009, p321) has noted:

> *The unintended consequences of raising anxiety and fear of the 'disrespectful' is to encourage a greater mistrust not only of 'the irritating' but also of 'difference'.*

- *Article 8 of the European Convention on Human Rights, which is incorporated into domestic law by the Human Rights Act 1998, states that every person has the right to respect for their individual, private and family life*, unless an intrusion is necessary for (among other things) the prevention of crime. It may be difficult to justify severe restrictions on the liberty of a child who has not yet been convicted of committing any criminal act. Article 8 may also cover situations where a young person has been remanded into local authority accommodation and, due to shortage of specialised places (especially of secure accommodation), they are placed some considerable distance from their family, possibly for a number of months while awaiting trial.

- *Article 6 of the Convention covers the right to a fair trial*: possible issues arising under this provision are threefold.

First, it has been noted earlier that criminal sanctions can be applied for breaches of civil orders (e.g. anti-social behaviour and local child curfews, etc). For a civil order to be made, the standard of proof is on the balance of probabilities – a much lower standard than the criminal law requirement of proof beyond reasonable doubt. Furthermore, parental bind-overs are deemed to be civil in nature and criminal sanctions can accrue for breach. Additionally, the referral order established by the Youth Justice and Criminal Evidence Act 1999 enables a court to refer a young person to a Youth Offender Panel, a body outside the 'official' criminal justice system, where there is no right to legal representation, yet which is authorised to pass criminal sanctions. Arguably, as such provisions and procedures are either in reality criminal in nature or have criminal consequences, they legitimately fall into the ambit for scrutiny by Articles 6 and 8 of the Convention (particularly as no rights of appeal are set out in either the Crime and Disorder Act 1998 or the Youth Justice and Criminal Evidence Act 1999).

Second, Section 35 of the Crime and Disorder Act 1998 permits an adverse inference to be drawn from a defendant's silence at interview or trial stage: this provision applies from the age of ten. Article 6, in its assertion of the presumption of innocence and the right to a fair procedure, arguably sits uneasily with Section 35 in relation to young suspects. Also, it can perhaps be implied that Article 6 requires that an appropriate adult be present when the young person is cautioned about their 'right' to silence, so that they can be properly instructed as to the full implications of their silence.

The third possible challenge in relation to Article 6 concerns reprimands and final warnings under Section 65 of the Crime and Disorder Act 1998 and the recently introduced youth conditional caution. Issues about proportionality in relation to such sanctions, coupled with the continued debate about the possibility that young people, in eagerness to rid themselves of any further involvement with the criminal justice process, may confess to things they might not be found guilty of in a court of law, may be open to question in relation to fairness of procedure. Additionally, any failure to co-operate with the requirements of a conditional caution may result in the breach being cited in court and possibly lead to a harsher sentence being given in any future court appearances.

- *Article 3 of the European convention covers the prohibition of torture*, which includes degrading treatment or punishment. Linked to this, the Beijing Rules state that when a young person is sentenced it should amount to a *fair reaction* – in other words, it should adhere to the principle of proportionality. It could possibly be argued that the Crime and Disorder Act 1998 implicitly sanctions the use of deterrent sentences in order to dissuade others from certain behaviours and that such sentences may, therefore, fall foul of the Human Rights Act 1998. Further, the 18 options available to a sentencer when sanctioning a youth rehabilitation order could result in some young people being given a range of requirements which might be disproportionate to the crime(s) they committed.

- *The consequences of being a young person refused bail*. This may mean that their relationship with their parents is severely affected. In an adversarial process where there may have been only a short time to respond to an application to refuse bail, the parent may not be involved at all in the decision-making process. Certain decisions to refuse bail may possibly breach Article 8 (noted above) and Article 5 of the Convention, which covers the right to security and liberty.

So it appears that there is potential for a number of challenges to our youth justice system that could be mounted under the Human Rights Act. Lawyers representing young offenders and Youth Offending Teams should perhaps have made such challenges a priority but unfortunately we still await the formulation of firm legal guidelines via case law challenges of many of these possible Human Rights Act breaches. As a well-informed, proactive practitioner, you must be aware of any potential challenges.

ACTIVITY **1.2**

Legal case study

Karim (aged 12) and Simon (aged 11) decide not to return to school after lunchtime but instead go to their local shopping mall in Kenchester. They enter a shop and Simon suggests that they steal some sweets from the pick 'n' mix counter. While they are stuffing confectionery into their rucksacks, Ken, a security guard, approaches them and asks them to open their bags. Karim complies with this request and reveals the chocolate he has stolen. Simon refuses to open his bag, and when Ken tries to take it from him Simon takes a baseball bat from the side pocket of the bag, hits Ken on the head and runs out of the shop. The police are called and Simon is apprehended while running from the shopping centre and arrested. Karim is also arrested and both boys are taken to the police station for questioning. Ken goes to hospital suffering from a split lip and a broken nose.

Simon is charged with grievous bodily harm (under Section 20 of the Offences Against the Person Act 1861) and theft (under S1 of the Theft Act 1968) and Karim is charged with theft.

Karim already has a previous final warning for another matter of shoplifting six months earlier and Kenchester Youth Court sentence him to a four-month referral order. At the Youth Offender Panel meeting, the panel state that Karim must sign a contract that requires him to attend community reparation sessions for six hours every other Saturday for the duration of the order. In addition he must attend two one-and-a-half hour meetings with the YOS worker on Mondays and Wednesdays at 2.30 p.m. Karim's mother tells the panel that this will interfere with his school attendance, his extra-curricular sports activities, his homework time and family social time and that she feels that the requirements seem to be quite harsh for the theft of sweets worth £2.50. The panel tell Karim's mother that if he does not sign the contract the matter will be referred back to court for non co-operation and that if this happened Karim could be sentenced to a custodial sentence. Reluctantly, Karim signs the contract. After the court hearing the police and the local authority successfully obtain an ASBO on Karim that bans him from the shopping mall and from anywhere within a two-mile radius of the mall, and prevents him from wearing a hooded top. Karim usually attends a youth club half a mile from the mall on Friday evenings. Also, Karim was scalded as a child and is embarrassed of a large red scar on his neck. He regularly wears hooded tops to cover this mark.

Simon, who has previous convictions for shoplifting and robbery of a mobile phone, has learning difficulties. He initially goes to the Youth Court, but as the injuries to Ken were serious his case is referred to the Crown Court. He is refused bail as it is argued by the prosecution that he is a persistent offender, that this is a serious offence and that he might offend again. As there are no secure remand placements in Kenchester, he is placed in a centre in Durham, 300 miles away from his family. As his parents are on benefits, they can't afford to go to see him. The trial takes place six months later. At the trial, Simon is very worried and confused. He tells his lawyer that he doesn't understand the legal jargon or the procedure.

Advise Karim and Simon regarding legal challenges that might be brought in relation to any possible breaches of their rights.

COMMENT

As a practitioner dealing with these youths the issues that you might raise include:

Regarding Karim

- *Karim's referral order seems to breach Article 6 of the European Convention on Human Rights (ECHR) as it is questionable whether he has had a fair hearing and there is no appeal.*

- *The level of restriction in the referral order on his liberty seems to breach Article 3 of the ECHR as it arguably is not a 'fair reaction' to the crime, as is required.*

- *The many requirements of the referral order arguably breach Article 8 of the ECHR as they seem to unnecessarily interfere with his private and family life, preventing him from undertaking his educational, sporting and social activities.*

- *In relation to Karim's ASBO, this is a civil order and if he breaches it he could receive a criminal sanction. This too is possibly a breach of Article 6, above.*

- *There have been some recent successful court challenges in relation to very restrictive ASBOs that the courts have held have breached the human rights of recipients. The two-mile radius ban and the subsequent impact upon his attendance at the youth club is arguably unreasonable, given the nature of the offence and that he has no other record of anti-social behaviour. The hooded top ban is also possibly a breach of his human rights.*

Regarding Simon

- *His placement in Durham is possibly in contravention of Article 8 of the ECHR as it interferes with his private and family life.*

- *The length of detention is also an issue under Article 8 as this is a young man who is on remand and has not yet been convicted of the offence.*

- *As Simon is only 11 years old and finds the trial in the Crown Court (an adult court) confusing, this seems to contravene one of the decisions of the European Court of Human Rights in* Thompson and Venables [1999] *which stated that a Crown Court was an unsuitable place for the defendants (who were aged 11 at the time of the case) to be tried.*

The dual agenda of youth justice and social work: Justice vs welfare

Are young people who come before the criminal justice system offenders, who have chosen to break society's rules and so deserve to be punished, or are they (as the Children Act 1989 asserts) children 'in need'? Should we expect them to take full responsibility for the consequences of their actions or should we view them as being less capable than adults of understanding and adhering to the rules of society? Should they be dealt with in the same courts as adults and be eligible to the same punishments, or should they be dealt with by specialist courts and personnel who have been trained to understand and remedy their needs? Should there be a wider range of disposals available to judges and magistrates who deal with young offenders than there is for adult offenders? Should we help and guide young people to move away from law-breaking behaviour or should we provide an optimum deterrent in the form of commensurate punishment? Should we punish the young offender's crime or the young offender himself/herself? These are just some of the questions that highlight the dilemmas facing those who structure and work within the youth justice system and form part of what youth justice theorists and practitioners call the 'justice vs welfare' debate that were mentioned earlier in this chapter. These two approaches have dominated youth justice philosophy for a hundred years and though other valid perspectives have been developed (we will examine these in Chapter 2) the justice vs welfare debate still rages in academic, media, governmental and professional practice fields.

The introduction of a distinct system for dealing with young offenders in 1908 represented, in essence, a 'modification' of adult justice – a 'compromise' which resulted in the cross-fertilisation of principles of adult responsibility with notions of welfarism and protectionism. A justice approach, based upon classicist ideas of culpability and responsibility, would involve a strict legal due process system, which sentenced using notions of proportionality and seriousness, providing a sanction that befitted the offence, rather than the offender. A welfare-based approach would involve a less formal and adaptable procedure, one that would conceptualise the offending behaviour, allow for mitigation and a recognition of the possibility of limited responsibility (part of neo-classicism), and allow for non-legal experts to enter the decision-making process and produce a disposal that would fit the offender, rather than the offence. The Children Act 1908 effectively opened up the possibility of these two styles being blended (or possibly muddled) in the context of dealing with young offenders.

This early discovery of the potential of conflict between the polemic welfare vs justice dichotomy was to produce various forms of compromise solutions over the course of the century. We examine in detail these philosophies, legislative developments and features of systems based on principles of justice and those based on principles of welfare in Chapter 2.

As a youth justice practitioner, you will become familiar with the dilemmas between justice and welfare approaches. Primarily, your social work training will have taught you to regard the best interests and welfare of the young person you are working with as paramount considerations. You will soon be aware that in youth justice, while the law sometimes protects and supports those interests (such as in relation to international and human rights protections outlined above), often the application of law conflicts with your guiding social work ethics. For example, you might view a young offender as primarily a child in need and feel that community intervention and offence counselling might be the best way to deal with a troubled young person who is 'acting out' through offending behaviour. Judges, magistrates and the police might have a different opinion and decide that the offence is serious and/or that the only way to protect the public is to put your client behind bars.

The conflict between social work ethics and legal principles is arguably more tangible in the practice of youth justice than in any other area of social work.

Part two: Guiding codes and principles of youth justice social work

Paul Dugmore

Values and ethics within social work

Common to the caring profession, the values traditionally allied to social work include self-determination, choice, empowerment and non-judgementalism. Banks (2001) suggests that such values offer only a partial characterisation of social work as they fail to account for the full remit of social work which also has a controlling role, guided by legal, governmental and agency procedures where ethical issues around justice and fairness are prominent, as in the case of youth justice (Banks, 2001, p2). The value base of social work is laid out in various sets of statements that outline how practice should be according to a range of ethical rules and requirements. These include the International Federation of Social Work (IFSW) and the International Association of Schools of Social Work (IASSW) whose joint statement of principles sees ethical awareness as a fundamental part of the professional practice of social workers whose ability and commitment to act ethically is an essential aspect of the quality of the service offered to those who use social work services. These principles are subsumed under the broad areas of human rights and dignity, social justice and professional conduct (IFSW and IASSW, 2004). The British Association of Social Work (BASW, 2002) Code of Ethics states that:

Social work practice should both promote respect for human dignity and pursue social justice, through service to humanity, integrity and competence.

It contains six principles:

1. Respect basic human rights as expressed in the United Nations Universal Declaration of Human Rights and other international conventions derived from that Declaration.

2. Show respect for all persons, and respect service users' beliefs, values, culture, goals, needs, preferences, relationships and affiliations.

3. Safeguard and promote service users' dignity, individuality, rights, responsibilities and identity.

4. Foster individual well-being and autonomy, subject to due respect for the rights of others.

5. Respect service users' rights to make informed decisions, and ensure that service users and carers participate in decision-making processes.

6. Ensure the protection of service users, which may include setting appropriate limits and exercising authority, with the objective of safeguarding them and others.

In addition to values and ethics being integral to social work practice, they are also a significant feature of social work education and training as outlined within the regulatory framework for social work. Currently, the social care workforce in England, which includes youth justice, is required to act in accordance with the General Social Care Council (GSCC).

The GSCC, established in 2001 under the Care Standards Act 2000 is, at present, the regulator and guardian of standards for the social care workforce in England. It is responsible for social work education and training and maintaining the social care register, although this function will transfer to the renamed Health Care Professions Council following the proposed abolition of the GSCC as part of the government's Health and Social Care Bill (2011) going through parliament at the time of writing.

GSCC Code of Practice

In 2003 the GSCC published a Code of Practice for both employers and employees in order to help raise standards in social care services. The Code of Practice for social care workers consists of a list of statements that define the standards of professional conduct required of all social care workers. These are to:

- Protect the rights and promote the interests of service users and carers.

- Strive to establish and maintain trust and confidence of service users and carers.

- Promote the independence of service users while protecting as far as possible from danger or harm.

- Respect the rights of service users, while seeking to ensure that their behaviour does not harm themselves or other people.

- Uphold public trust and confidence in social care services.

- Be accountable for the quality of your work and take responsibility for maintaining and improving your knowledge and skills.

Thus, the expectation that social work practitioners work with service users in a way that is based upon the values underpinning the profession is clearly outlined in government guidance. Banks (2001) is critical of such codes of practice/ethics, as they assume professional autonomy, when, in practice, social workers are subject to the procedures of their employing agency. She also suggests that ethical practice comes not from a set of codes, but from an individual's own values and ability to exercise compassion and respect and that the codes assume consensus on values within the profession when other values may be seen as important by users of services, other professionals and the media for instance (Banks, 2001).

National Occupational Standards for social workers

Currently, social work qualifying students are assessed against a competence-based framework that was implemented with the degree. These standards were drawn up by the Training Organisation for the Personal Social Services (TOPSS) and are designed to provide a 'benchmark of best practice' in social work competence via a set of six key roles that lay down what a qualifying social worker should be able to do. These standards are subject to review and will be replaced following the work of the Social Work Taskforce (2009) and Social Work Reform Board (2011) which has proposed a new *Professional Capabilities Framework* that is likely to be implemented in the near future. However, at present, the standards include a set of values and ethics that are central to, and underpin, the six key roles that make up the National Occupational Standards. Social work students must be able to critically analyse and evaluate their practice in relation to the six core values and ethics listed below:

- Awareness of your own values, prejudices, ethical dilemmas and conflicts of interest and their implications on your practice.

- Respect for, and the promotion of:

  - each person as an individual;

  - independence and quality of life for individuals, while protecting them from harm;

  - dignity and privacy of individuals, families, carers, groups and communities.

- Recognise and facilitate each person's use of the language and form of communication of their choice.

- Value, recognise and respect the diversity, expertise and experience of individuals, families, carers, groups and communities.

- Maintain the trust and confidence of individuals, families, carers, groups and communities by communicating in an open, accurate and understandable way.

- Understand, and make use of, strategies to challenge discrimination, disadvantage and other forms of inequality and injustice.

So you can see that your ability to practise in a way that is grounded in a strong, ethical value based framework will be crucial to your development as a good social worker.

QAA benchmark statement

In addition to the GSCC, social work qualifying education and training is monitored by the Quality Assurance Agency for Higher Education (QAA) which sets out academic standards for social work. The social work benchmark refers to social work as a *moral activity* that requires students to potentially make and implement decisions that may be difficult and which may *involve the potential for benefit or harm* (QAA, 2001, 2.4). The QAA states that programmes offering the social work degree should include the study of the *application of and reflection upon ethical principles* (2.4). In terms of subject knowledge in relation to values and ethics, the QAA states that during their degree studies in social work, students should *critically evaluate, apply and integrate knowledge and understanding* to:

- The nature, historical evolution and application of social work values.

- The moral concepts of rights, responsibility, freedom, authority and power inherent in the practice of social workers as moral and statutory agents.

- The complex relationships between justice, care and control in social welfare and the practical and ethical implications of these, including roles as statutory agents and in upholding the law in respect of discrimination.

- Aspects of philosophical ethics relevant to the understanding and resolution of value dilemmas and conflicts in both interpersonal and professional contexts.

- The conceptual link between codes defining ethical practice, the regulation of professional conduct and the management of potential conflicts generated by the codes held by different professional groups. (3.1.3).

A social worker within a youth justice setting is presented with, and subject to, a multitude of standards and principles which may, at times, appear to conflict with each other. In addition to the IFSW/IASSW statement of ethics the BASW Code of Ethics and the GSCC Code of Practice, such social workers are also required to work to National Standards for Youth Justice Services (2010).

National Standards for Youth Justice

The National Standards for Youth Justice Services (2010) are published jointly by the Ministry of Justice, Department for Children, Schools and Families, and the YJB. They set out the minimum requirements for relevant organisations providing youth justice services, providing a benchmark against which the effectiveness of work can be measured. The ten National Standards cover all areas of youth justice practice and aim to prevent offending by children and young people by ensuring that:

- There is effective governance, planning and performance management within YOTs to support the delivery of youth justice services.

- All children and young people entering the youth justice system benefit from a structured needs assessment to identify risk and protective factors associated with offending behaviour to inform effective intervention.

- Court orders are managed in such a way that they support the primary aim of the youth justice system, which is to prevent offending, and that they have regard to the welfare of the child or young person.

- Reports prepared by the YOT for courts and youth offender panels are effective and of a high quality.

- The needs and risks of young people sentenced to custodial orders (including long-term custodial orders) are addressed effectively to enable effective resettlement and management of risk.

- Services provided to courts are of a high quality and that magistrates and the judiciary have confidence in the supervision by YOTs of children or young people who offend.

- Those receiving youth justice services are treated fairly regardless of race, language, gender, religion, sexual orientation, disability or any other factor, and actions are put in place to address unfairness where it is identified.

- Strategies and services are in place locally to prevent children and young people from becoming involved in crime or anti-social behaviour.

- Out-of-court disposals deliver targeted interventions for those at risk of further offending.

- Comprehensive bail and remand management services are in place locally.

- Restorative justice approaches are used, where appropriate, with victims of crime and that restorative justice is central to work undertaken with young people who offend.

- All relevant information is captured and recorded accurately on the YOT case management information system.

    (YJB, 2010d, pp5–6)

ACTIVITY 1.3

Take a look at the Code of Practice for Social Care Workers and the National Standards for Youth Justice and consider the differences as well as the similarities between the two.

COMMENT

It is clear to see that while the above statements include guidance that holds similarities with the key values of social work such as treating people fairly, they are also largely concerned with the effective administration of the youth justice system. While important, such a managerialist approach to social work or youth justice practice has been criticised by, among others, Munro (2011) who in her recent review of child protection states that this approach has fed into a view that a good enough picture of practice can be gained from procedural manuals and that the more important part of social work can be carried out on a computer (Munro, 2011). She suggests that as well as knowing what data to collect it is also important how to collect them and analyse them. We will return to this area in later chapters.

Within a youth justice setting, social workers need to develop the ability to practice in a way that is grounded in a strong, ethical value-based framework that is able to reconcile competing and sometimes conflicting values and perspectives.

As individuals we have our own set of values, which are informed by our own beliefs, our upbringing and our culture and these will affect our ability and willingness to practice ethically, in line with the frameworks outlined previously, the point made by Banks (2001) in her criticism of such codes of ethics. Additionally, working in a YOT involves working alongside other professionals who may hold a different value base. The values of a police officer, for instance, may be very different to a social worker. Such diversity of values was identified in the evaluation of the pilot YOTs where it was found that youth justice staff had difficulty in transferring *philosophically and practically* to the newly formed youth offending teams (Holdaway et al., 2001, p6). Research by Souhami (2007) identified how youth justice social workers contrasted the welfarist approach to their work with the punitive approach of other criminal justice agencies. The emergence of YOTs however, blurred boundaries between agencies, led to new, multi-agency practice and often led to youth justice social workers being separated from Social Services Departments as the new stand-alone YOTs were established. Thus the identity of social workers became diluted. This will be discussed further in Chapter 5.

Using values and ethics in your practice

With such a vast array of standards, codes and legal frameworks to consider, it can appear overwhelming for practitioners. How can you ensure your practice takes account of values and ethical issues in accordance with these? When working within youth justice it is important to consider how society views young people generally and young people who offend specifically. We all have personal views about young people and of what expectations are seen as the 'norm'. These may be based on our own experiences of adolescence, drawn from young people with whom we are in contact or from wider society.

ACTIVITY **1.4**

Think about how you view young people. What assumptions do you make about them? What expectations do you have about young people? Are these different from the views, assumptions and expectations you have about young people who offend? Where do your views come from? Look for newspaper headlines about young people. What do they say? How are young people/offenders described? Are these views representative?

COMMENT

Your answers to the questions in this activity will be determined by a range of factors; they may be partly as a result of your age, your experience of adolescence, how you feel about your own children or those of others in your family or network of friends. Your own experience of adolescence may be very different from young people in contemporary society and you may find it hard to empathise. You may have been positive in thinking about young people, describing them as lively, inquiring, exciting and fun. Your responses may have been neutral, such as innocent, naive and impressionable; or negative, such as rebellious, troublesome, argumentative and difficult.

Your responses will more than likely also be shaped by external factors such as the television, newspapers and social policy. Young people are often presented in negative ways by the media, particularly those involved in offending. More recently in the UK much attention has been paid by the government and the press to the rise of anti-social behaviour, particularly among young people. The portrayal within the media of young people in gangs, often synonymous with the term 'hoodie' led to a raft of policy measures by the Labour government, introduced to combat problem behaviour. It could be argued that another 'moral panic' is being created similar to that in the 1970s when the term 'mugging' was designed to describe street robberies, leading to the use of stop and search powers by the police. These powers effectively discriminated against black and minority ethnic people, who were stopped disproportionately by the police (Hall et al., 1978). The term 'moral panic' was coined by Cohen (1973) as a way of emphasising the media's role in amplifying crime and deviance, particularly in relation to youths. It seems ironic that youth crime is so high on the political agenda when recent Home Office figures and the British Crime Survey both show a decline in youth crime over the last few years (Home Office, 2005b). However, public opinion polls suggest that there is an erroneous belief that youth crime is increasing at an alarming rate (Bateman, 2005).

When working with young people who offend it is important to be aware of the attitudes and feelings you have about and towards them. It may be that you have pre-conceived ideas about how young people behave based on what you have learned from the news. Your views may be stereotypical and unfair representations of young people who offend who are, in reality, as diverse a group of people as any other. Young people are often discriminated against because of their age and referred to in negative terms. Haines and Drakeford (1998) suggest that British society does not like young people and the pervasive negativity that informs how young people are treated is amplified for the minority involved in offending who act as the *legitimised target for all the harshest and most destructive impulses directed against their contemporaries as a whole* (Haines and Drakeford, 1998, p1). Pearson (1983) points to the fact that successive generations constantly pertain to the view that the behaviour of younger generations has deteriorated suggesting that young people now are less well behaved and respectful than they were when they were young. Confirmation of this is provided by Hough and Roberts (2004) who found in a survey of adults, over four out of five thought young people today are less respectful than they were a generation ago.

ACTIVITY *1.5*

How might a young offender feel if the overriding picture that is painted of them by society is negative? What impact could this have on the offender and their behaviour?

COMMENT

Young people may internalise what they hear said about them and begin to think that society or adults only see or acknowledge 'bad' behaviour. This might lead them to think that anything else is not recognised. It may also create a divide between young people and adults that could exacerbate the problem. Many adults may feel uncomfortable walking past a group of young people on the streets but how does this make law-abiding young people feel?

Many young people involved in offending behaviour are likely to have issues of low self-esteem and the effects of labelling (as discussed in Chapter 3), only seek to exacerbate this. It is essential that young people are considered within life-course perspectives on adolescence, which take into account psychological, social and physical factors. As Crawford and Walker (2010, p84) suggest: *the challenges of adolescence may result in choices, which lead to a number of problems, some of which peak at this time*. Social workers need to be aware of what kind of behaviour might be expected from a young person going through adolescence, taking into account the developmental stage they are at. Briggs (2008) writing from a psychodynamic perspective suggests that it is essential, when working with young people, to be aware of the emotional impact of internal and external change on a young person's sense of stability, the propensity for this to stimulate fear of fragmentation and the importance of containment amidst such turbulence.

It is important as a social worker to be aware of the reasons that underpin your decision to become a social worker and 'help' people. Bower (2005) suggests it is often based on conscious and unconscious feelings of guilt about how society treats the most vulnerable but it is also often related to our own life experiences and relationships that have damaged us in some way that we are seeking to heal.

It is also worth exploring why you want to work with a particular service user group and what qualities and values are important in being able to work with that group. It may be useful to identify what you see as the opportunities of working within a youth justice setting as well as what some of the difficulties may be. Social work practice in this area can be extremely varied and could involve working with young people at risk of offending, those in trouble with the police for the very first time, right through to young people with significant criminal records who may have been convicted of extremely serious offences.

ACTIVITY 1.6

Read the following cases. How would you feel working with each young person? What might some of the moral/ethical issues be for you personally and professionally?

Imran, aged 16, has been charged with indecently assaulting his three-year old brother. He is not allowed to return home while the police investigation is undertaken. You have to liaise with the children and families team and work in partnership with his family to identify an appropriate placement for him.

Sarah, aged 15, is in a local authority children's home as her mother has left the country and her father is in prison. She has committed numerous offences of burglary and you are writing the pre-sentence report for the court. The judge has indicated that Sarah is likely to receive a custodial sentence. When you discuss this with Sarah she breaks down in tears saying that if she goes into custody she will kill herself.

Andrew, aged 17, is serving a three-year custodial sentence. He is to be released in three months' time. He has nowhere to live on release and he does not want to engage in college, training or employment. He is content to sit around with his friends all day smoking cannabis.

COMMENT

Each of the cases requires quite different responses. You may find it difficult working with Imran as the abuse of children is always likely to provoke an emotional response. You have to remember that at this stage Imran has not been convicted and therefore it is only an allegation. However you may feel about an offence, it is your role to work with the young person and to see him or her as an individual who may have carried out an offence, rather than as an offender. Imran may be very scared about what is going to happen to him, about being separated from his family and being placed somewhere else. You will have to work with his family too, who will undoubtedly be finding the situation very difficult to deal with. The case may raise unresolved issues for you as an individual. You have to ensure that your practice is professional at all times despite the feelings this raises for you. Having a safe space in which to discuss your feelings is vitally important as ignoring them will not eradicate them. This is why supervision that enables you to reflect on your feelings and think about them in relation to theoretical frameworks is essential in order that you are able to acknowledge and work through your feelings so that you are able to prevent them from impacting on your relationship with individuals.

COMMENT *continued*

In cases such as Sarah's, you may feel helpless to stop young people like her having their liberty removed. You can only do what is within your power, and this would probably involve ensuring that your report for the court addresses all the difficulties that she has encountered as well as assessing her needs in order to make a proposal that will deal with the issues that caused her to offend, thereby reducing the risk she poses. It may be that the judge will still sentence Sarah to a period of detention and your role then would be to work with the secure establishment she is sent to so that she is closely monitored and any risk of harm is minimised. The relationship you have developed with Sarah, however short, will be crucial in containing her anxieties and emotional pain and if she perceives this encounter as positive, it will keep her open to developing relationships with other professionals in the future.

Andrews' case illustrates the care and control aspect of social work practice in this area. You may think that at 17 Andrew is almost an adult and therefore capable of making decisions about how he wishes to live his life. However, as your role is to prevent him from re-offending and to look after his welfare, you need to work with his motivation levels and self-esteem as well as provide practical support around accommodation and education or employment. There may be reasons why he does not want to do anything related to how he feels let down by his family or because he does not have a stake in society. Building up a relationship, enabling him to talk about his anxieties so that you can gain an understanding of his internal and external worlds, how he feels about his experiences, his relationships with others as well as with you, will lay the foundations for him to feel valued and respected so that change can be achieved.

Working with young people in the criminal justice system will evoke many different feelings in you and challenge your ethical and moral code of practice. It is important to be aware of how you feel about a particular case in order to know if it is impacting upon your practice. This is where reflective practice (Schon, 1983) is essential so that you can examine the decisions you have made and the actions you have taken in order to analyse the effect of these upon a case. Being able to relate theory to your practice is also an important part of reflective practice. Supervision is one forum where these sorts of issues can be explored with a manager, or you may choose to discuss cases with your colleagues. Ensuring you are undertaking continual professional development, in line with registration requirements, will assist you in developing your skill and knowledge base, as will helping ensure you are informed by evidenced-based practice and able to consider new perspectives. These fundamental issues of good social work practice will be revisited throughout this book.

Discrimination

It is clear that young people as a group may be discriminated against based on the stereotypes that are held by individuals and society. Discrimination and oppression are often complex issues, with some young people facing multiple oppressions, based on their culture and sex for instance. Having an awareness of how oppression and discrimination manifest themselves is especially important in the youth justice system.

According to Home Office statistical data produced in response to Section 95 of the Criminal Justice Act 1991, young people from minority ethnic backgrounds are over-represented within the criminal justice system (Home Office, 2005d). Section 95 of the Criminal Justice Act 1991 requires the Home Secretary to publish statistical data on race and gender with a view to helping the criminal justice system avoid discriminating on the grounds of race, gender or any other improper ground.

RESEARCH SUMMARY

The Youth Justice Board, the organisation that oversees youth justice services in England and Wales, commissioned research to look at whether young people from minority ethnic backgrounds are differentially treated within the criminal justice system. The research examined how young people from minority ethnic backgrounds were dealt with compared to their white counterparts at each stage of the youth justice process. Eight YOTs were selected for the study and information was obtained on 17,054 cases involving males and females aged 12–17 over 15 months in 2001–02. The study, Differences or Discrimination?, *found that there were considerable variations in the extent of over- or under-representation of particular ethnic groups in relation to the proportions served by the YOTs included in the study.*

The research found at various stages of the youth justice process differences in outcome in the treatment of people from different ethnic backgrounds as well as between males and females. Sometimes this was due to relevant variations in the cases; however, there were also differences consistent with 'discriminatory treatment'. These included:

- *A higher rate of prosecution and conviction of mixed-parentage young males.*

- *A higher proportion of prosecutions involving black young males.*

- *A higher probability that a black male would, if convicted in a Crown Court, receive a sentence of 12 months or more.*

- *A greater proportion of black and Asian males remanded in custody prior to sentence.*

- *A much greater proportion of mixed-parentage females who were prosecuted.*

The researchers concluded by stating that 'young black people were substantially over-represented in the caseloads of the police, prosecutors, YOTs and the courts in relation to their numbers in the local population'. *They voice* 'considerable concern about whether there is always fair treatment of minority ethnic young people'. *Moreover, they believe the evidence of the research to be consistent with* 'a more complex phenomenon of justice by race and geography'.

(YJB, 2004a)

The *Differences or Discrimination*? study did not look at why such differences had occurred but this is clearly an area that needs to be explored. The researchers felt that there needed to be a concerted effort to understand the phenomenon of differential patterns within the youth justice system which could only be achieved by a detailed analysis of local sentencing practices, based on a careful analysis of case records and local crime rates, and on close observations of practices at all stages of the system.

Other research offers similar findings (Goldson, 2002; Wilson and Moore, 2004); however, the general view is that studies into discrimination levels within the youth justice system are few and far between. Kalunta-Crumpton (2005) suggests that given the increased incarceration of black and some other ethnic minority young people, there is a need for comprehensive ethnic monitoring of the use made by courts of the more punitive sanctions available, custody in particular. Youth Offending Teams are now required to undertake a race audit and develop an action plan to address discrimination as a specific area on which their performance is measured, in accordance with the Race Relations (Amendment) Act 2000.

The other significant area of research into differential treatment within the youth justice system is in relation to sex. While offending rates by girls are swamped by those of their male counterparts, there is evidence to suggest they are rising, particularly in relation to the use of custody where the increase over the period 1992–2002 was as high as 600 per cent (NACRO cited in Bateman and Pitts, 2005). The Home Office established a working party looking at the discrimination of women by the criminal justice system. Historically girls and young women have been treated differently by a system that has struggled to see them as anything other than mad or bad and in need of welfare services. Hudson (2002) suggests that the difficulties faced by girls in trouble are that they are perceived as emotional and more difficult to work with. She suggests that social workers need to view the girl's behaviour as a response to their oppression and a way of surviving, and that emotionality should be seen as a positive resource. Hudson suggests that the recent drive towards the justice model has meant that girls are being treated less along welfare lines; this could be pushing them up the sentencing framework quicker than boys. A common problem for YOTs is the inability to offer suitable programmes for girls because of the lower number of girls in the criminal justice system. This needs to be addressed if girls are to receive a fair service and one that meets their needs effectively. This issue is exacerbated in the case of black and ethnic minority girls.

There are other groups discriminated by, and within, the youth justice system such as asylum seekers, travellers and 'looked after' children. The Prison Reform Trust (Jacobson et al., 2010) found that in 2008, 56 per cent of young people in custody were known to have experienced at least one period of time in local authority care, had been on the child protection register or had other contact with social services. Data from the YJB (2007) showed that over 70 per cent of young people who offend had a history of being in care or social services involvement. A study by Walker et al. (2006), cited in Whyte (2009), followed 53 young people aged 12 to 16 years for two years from admission in to secure accommodation. Over half were known to social services before the age 10 and all had been looked after and accommodated with 83 per cent being admitted from either a residential unit or school. Two years later over 45 per cent were still in an institutional setting compared to a control group, (who did not get secure accommodation) of whom all were living 'reasonably stable' lives in the community one year later. Thus, not only is the likelihood of entering the youth justice system much higher for young people who have experience of being in public care, research demonstrates their life opportunities may be adversely impeded should they be incarcerated. NACRO (2005) has produced a *Handbook on reducing offending by looked after children* that identifies the ways in which professionals working with looked after children can support them in order to reduce risk factors and improve outcomes.

Research published by the Prison Reform Trust and the Association of Youth Offending Team Managers (Jacobson et al., 2010) found that children with learning disabilities and other impairments are more likely to go to prison than other young people because the youth justice system is failing to recognise their needs and is not fulfilling its legal duty to prevent discrimination. It found that 23 per cent of young offenders have very low IQs of less than 70, and 25 per cent have special educational needs which is a much higher proportion than in the general population.

Social work practitioners need to be aware of the issues facing marginalised minority groups in assessing their needs and providing services, as well as signalling their discrimination to the other agencies within the youth justice system. Social workers also need to listen to the experiences of individuals from such oppressed groups in order to be able to empower them, work in partnership, seek feedback from them and evaluate their interventions to ensure their practice *aims to redress, rather than reproduce, the inequalities and barriers to opportunity which are structured into the lives of the children and families with whom they are in contact* (Haines and Drakeford, 1998, p2).

ACTIVITY 1.7

Read the following case studies and identify the significant issues.

Gemma is 15 years old and from a traveller family. She has been sentenced by the court for shoplifting offences. Her parents have not attended appointments with you and Gemma tells you that they will not be attending even though the court has ordered them to. Gemma does not attend school as her family want her at home looking after her younger siblings with her mother.

Andrei is 17 and from Eastern Europe. He has appeared in court having been arrested for attempted theft from a cashpoint. The court is considering whether to grant him bail and you are assessing his suitability. He tells you that he is homeless, has no family and came to the UK six months ago to seek asylum. When you ask him where he has been staying he is very evasive and will not disclose any information.

John is 16 and lives in local authority accomodation. He is placed in a children's home in the local area on a temporary basis while a long-term placement is found. You are working with him while he is in the area. John has had six placements in the 18 months that he has been 'looked after'. While he attends his appointments with you, he is feeling very low and is not really engaging with you.

In Gemma's case you may have approached the issues from a legal perspective: her parents have been ordered to attend court, and in accordance with the Education Act 1988 Gemma has to be in education at the age of 15. Both issues carry consequences. However, you are working with Gemma who cannot be held responsible for her parents' behaviour. Alternatively you may have looked at the case from the perspective of assessing why Gemma is offending, and found that her non-school attendance and family may be seen to be contributing factors. In either approach it is essential that you meet her parents and explain the situation and try to gain an understanding of their situation. It may be that their previous contact with authorities has been negative and they are reluctant to engage as a result of this. Your local area may have specific services for travellers, including education provision, that you can put them in touch with for support.

Andrei's case might be best approached in a similar way, in that you do not know what he has experienced in his home country. His previous contact with authorities may also have been negative and he may well have experienced trauma of some kind. He could be in the UK as an unaccompanied minor with no adult care and supervision, he could be connected to a larger criminal group, or he could be an illegal immigrant. Whatever his situation, he is probably scared and confused about what will happen to him in a strange country. An interpreter will be needed to communicate with him if his English is not fluent, in order that he is made to feel at ease, his situation explained fully and as much information as possible obtained to ensure he is placed appropriately and given support.

John is probably feeling rejected as he has been moved about so often. You are probably one of many social workers and other professionals that he has had to speak to in that time. You need to acknowledge how he is feeling and let him talk about that. You can offer him support in your sessions and advocate on his behalf to the accommodating local authority so that permanent plans can be made as soon as possible. In any event, you need to have some idea about how long he is likely to be in his current placement as this will affect what provision you can put into place around his education, leisure, etc. It may be that John is offending as a result of being in care and this is something you could work with him on.

In this chapter we have looked at trends and perspectives in youth justice as well as ethical dilemmas facing those who work within a youth justice setting. We have also identified the relevant frameworks setting out the expected conduct of workers within a youth justice setting and observed how values and ethics underpin social work education and practice. We have also considered the implications of the Human Rights Act and international guidelines in relation to working with young people who offend. You have explored your attitudes towards youth and young offenders and you have looked at your own prejudices as well of those of society at large. You have thought about what some of the ethical dilemmas may be in working with young people. The impact of the media and the affect that labelling may have on young people has been considered, as has the importance of being able to place young people according to their stage of life-course development. The issue of discrimination of young people within the youth justice system has been examined and the need for anti-discriminatory practice identified. It is essential that future practice is enhanced by the integration of psychosocial theories of working with young people and young people in trouble as well as evidence-based best practice. Ensuring that this is done within the context of recognising and valuing difference and the impact that such differences have on young people is vital in becoming a fully reflective practitioner.

FURTHER READING

Youth Justice Board (2004) *Differences or discrimination?* London: Youth Justice Board.

Provides a full account of the research highlighted in this chapter.

Youth Justice Board/Ministry of Justice (2011) *Youth justice statistics 2009/10 England and Wales.* Statistical Bulletin January. London: Youth Justice Board/Ministry of Justice.

This contains statistics about youth criminality up to the time of the publication of this book. The latest figures can be obtained from the Ministry of Justice website.

Monaghan, G (2005) Children's human rights and youth justice. In Bateman, T and Pitts, J (eds) *The RHP companion to youth justice.* Lyme Regis: Russell House Publishing.

NACRO (2008) *Children's human rights and the youth justice system.* Youth Crime Briefing. London: NACRO.

This paper contains a comprehensive analysis of to what extent our youth justice system complies with the human rights requirements.

NACRO (2010) *The use of custody for children and young people.* Policy position paper. London: NACRO.

This paper critically assesses the extent of incarceration of children and young people in England and Wales.

WEBSITE

www.justice.gov.uk

For up-to-date information on the youth justice system from the Ministry of Justice.

www.homeoffice.gov.uk

For information on crime and policing.

www.homeoffice.gov.uk/rds/section951.html

For more information on statistical information in relation to ethnicity, gender and crime.

www.nacro.org.uk

Refer to their youth crime section for up-to-date research on youth justice issues.

www.yjb.gov.uk

For information produced by the Youth Justice Board up until 31 March 2011.

www.un.org

For information about the United Nations Convention on the rights of the child and monitoring reports.

www.thenayj.org.uk

The website of the National Association for Youth Justice.

Chapter 2

The development of youth justice philosophies, laws and policies

Jane Pickford

ACHIEVING A SOCIAL WORK DEGREE

This chapter will help you begin to meet the following National Occupational Standards.
Key Role 6: Demonstrate professional competence in social work practice
- Review and update your own knowledge of legal, policy and procedural frameworks.
- Identify and assess issues, dilemmas and conflicts that might affect your practice.
- Assess needs, risks and options, taking into account legal and other requirements.

It will also introduce you to the following academic standards as set out in the social work subject benchmark statement:
5.1.1 Social work services, service users and carers.
5.1.2 The service delivery context.
5.1.3 Values and ethics.
5.1.4 Social work theory.
5.1.5 The nature of social work practice.

Introduction

In this chapter we examine the development of youth justice theory, policy and practice. In order to understand the rationales underpinning any area of social work practice, it is always vital to have an insight into the way your area of practice has been shaped by its history. It is arguable that the study of youth justice, more than any other area of social work practice, is a creature of its historical development. Though new perspectives have emerged over the recent history of juvenile justice policy, the whole structure of the youth justice industry has been imbued by dominant philosophies that have seeped into the roots of the foundations of youth justice practice and thus still monopolise and govern contemporary practice. It is necessary, therefore, to review the bedrock of youth justice theory and practice and trace the evolution of our unique youth justice system over the last century. Only when we understand the origins and maturation processes of a system can we understand the logic behind contemporary practice.

In Chapter 1, we referred to the two (arguably polemic) philosophies that appear to have dominated youth justice theory over more than a hundred years, namely the justice and welfare perspectives. We also noted that, as these standpoints seem to be directly opposi- tional to each other, the historical development of youth justice has been peppered with manifestations of conflicts between these approaches, conflicts that have, perhaps, hin- dered any cohesive advancement in youth justice practice. I have argued elsewhere that the divergent natures of these two leading philosophies of youth justice perhaps render futile any attempt at fusion at the level of practice (Pickford, 2000).

This chapter is split into three parts: in Part 1 I examine the historically dominant approaches of justice and welfare; Part 2 analyses other philosophies that have emerged and have arguably to some extent superseded the justice and welfare perspectives; and in Part 3 I chronicle the historical development of youth justice legislation.

Part one: The two historically dominant philosophies – justice and welfare

In this section I examine the two perspectives of youth justice that dominated policy developments over most of the twentieth century, before going on to examine further perspectives (in Part 2) that have evolved since the latter part of the last century. In order to understand justice and welfare approaches, it is useful to analyse how features of each become manifest in practice. As I have posited that they are polemical positions, the fea- tures of each in terms of contrasting characteristics are outlined below.

Justice vs welfare

- *Due process vs adaptable procedures*. In the justice approach, adherence to a fixed procedure is paramount in order to ensure that all accused persons are treated in the same manner; whereas in a practice based upon the welfare approach there is no fixed procedure – processes are adaptable to the case/issues being discussed (e.g. the court system versus the referral order youth offender panel (see Chapter 4)).

- *Legalisic vs holistic*. The justice perspective emphasises 'formal justice' where legal procedures and legal representation by lawyers are used to ensure that all young people who come before the court are treated equally and fairly; whereas using the welfare perspective, lawyers will generally not be required – other professionals may take part in the hearing (e.g. social worker, teacher, youth worker, health worker) in order to discuss possible solutions to the young person's problematic behaviour.

- *Adversarial vs inquisitorial*. The justice philosophy requires a traditional focus on legal battles between the defence and prosecution lawyers in an effort to find the truth; whereas the welfare philosophy adopts a minimalist approach to fact-finding, avoiding conflictual confrontations.

- *Formalism vs informality*. The justice standpoint requires a sombre procedure in a courtroom, which purportedly reinforces the serious nature of matters being raised – in a Crown Court, lawyers wear gowns, in all courts complex legal language is used; whereas using the welfare standpoint, hearings will take place in an informal atmosphere and there may, for example, be a discussion of the alleged offending event and possible solutions where all parties, including the young person and parent(s) are encouraged to speak.

- *Proportionate vs tailor-made sentence*. To ensure fairness and consistency, using the justice approach the defendant should be sentenced in proportion to the seriousness of the offence; whereas the welfare approach requires that the sentence should be bespoke and should primarily fit the needs of the offender rather than reflect the seriousness of the offence – emphasis is placed upon what kind of intervention is needed to help the young person desist from negative behaviour patterns, and disposals should be aimed at the need to reform. It is noteworthy that the youth rehabilitation order introduced at the end of 2009 under the Criminal Justice and Immigration Act 2008 encourages sentencers to select content options that both (i) reflect proportianality in terms of the seriousness of the offense(s) and (ii) are tailored in a bespoke manner fo 'fit' the needs of the young person.

- *Responsibility and blame vs explanation and causation*. Using the justice perspective, any person aged ten or above (in England and Wales) is presumed capable of forming the level of culpability (*mens rea*) required for the crime and so logically should be made to face up to the full consequences of their behaviour; whereas under the welfare perspective, the reasons behind the offending behaviour are investigated in order to provide suitable interventions and the young person's capacity to form the required level of culpability is considered.

- *Act orientation vs actor orientation*. In the justice paradigm, the emphasis is on the crime – on the action performed rather than on the person who performed it, and appropriate disposals will be decided upon with regard to the act rather than the actor; whereas during welfare-based proceedings, the emphasis is upon the actor rather than the act.

ACTIVITY **2.1**

Now that you have some idea of the different dominant approaches of justice and welfare, let's examine a case study where dilemmas might arise due to the divergences of the dominant philosophies:

Darren, aged 12, has been arrested for writing graffiti on the walls of his local police station. This is his first offence but the police believe that, given the extent of the damage and the cost of repair, the matter should be referred to Youth Court. Darren is sentenced to a six-month referral order and you, as a youth offending social worker, have been asked by your manager to write the referral report and arrange a youth Offender Panel. While interviewing Darren he discloses to you that he and his sister, aged nine, have been physically and sexually abused by their father over a number of years and that their father regularly 'beats up' their mother. You believe that this offence was effectively a 'cry for help'. This is the first time this abuse has come to the attention of any authority.

Continued

ACTIVITY **2.1** *continued*

- *What ethical dilemmas are you faced with by this case?*

- *How do the justice and welfare approaches relate to this case?*

- *Is the youth justice system the proper place for such a case?*

- *Should Darren be punished for his criminal act?*

- *What recommendations regarding the content of the referral order would you propose? (see Chapter 4).*

COMMENT

This seems like an extreme example of youth offending being symptomatic of a dysfunctional family life, but is based upon an actual example from a few years ago. The ethical dilemmas in this case relate to the dual roles you will have to fulfil: first as an officer of the Court in terms of writing the report and focusing on the criminal justice matter and secondly, as a social worker your training will prompt you to be primarily concerned with protecting Darren and his siblings and prioritising their welfare.

You may feel that the fact that Darren has committed an offence pales into insignificance when it is contextualised into the wider family crisis and that its commission was totally justified in such circumstances. However, you will have to deal with the criminal matter and make a referral to the child protection team of your local authority. In essence, you will be wearing two professional 'hats' in this case, and though the roles overlap, they relate to two different systems of dealing with Darren's case.

These twin track approaches will run alongside each other: the criminal case will be processed via the youth court and the youth offending panel (whether you believe it is appropriate or not) and a child protection investigation will be undertaken and you will probably have to attend meetings in relation to this process. This example clearly illustrates the overlap and conflicts between justice and welfare approaches and procedures.

In terms of the report – you would probably recommend mainly welfare measures within the order requirements (see Chapter 4 for the possible content of referral orders).

Incompatibility of dominant philosophies?

There have been many attempts by successive governments to fuse the justice and welfare approaches, in the belief that these contrasting philosophies could melt together to form a seamless, merged practice. This has arguably never succeeded. When one examines the history of youth justice legislation (below) one realises that each government has failed dismally in its attempt to fuse these principles, and on every occasion both approaches have been unhappily forced together by the growing weight of ill-conceived legislation, resulting in a piecemeal mish-mash of justice and welfare measures lying uneasily together at different points of youth justice practice. Should we be surprised that a happy alliance has never been forged? If we put oil into water or squeeze lemon into milk do they mix? The oil floats on top of the water and the milk curdles. It is impossible to fuse two divergent substances that are composed of completely different elements. Similarly, the enforced union of two oppositional philosophies will not result in a joined practice. The problem with this attempted merger is that they are inimical approaches. They cancel each other out. Any attempted merger is, therefore, inevitably doomed to failure. (Even the most cursory critical analysis of the history of youth justice policy and legislation exposes this failure – see Part 3 of this chapter.)

Prior to Labour's election success in 1997 the incompatibility of the two paradigms had been recognised. The then Shadow Home Secretary Jack Straw stated that at the root of the problem with the youth justice system was a fundamental confusion over philosophy:

> *At the heart of the crisis in youth justice is confusion and conflict between welfare and punishment. Too many people involved with the system are unclear whether the purpose is to punish and to signify society's disapproval of offending or whether the welfare of the young offender is paramount.*

> (Home Office, 1997g, p9)

The solution proposed was a reworking of philosophy: *This confusion cannot continue. A new balance has to be struck between the sometimes conflicting interests of welfare and punishment*, which would involve *resolving some of the confusion between the relationship of welfare and punishment in dealing with young offenders* (Home Office, 1997g, pp9,18).

However, as noted by Fionda (2005) by 1997, in order to justify their proposals to mix justice and welfare initiatives in the Crime and Disorder Act, the government appeared to have changed their mind and denied any incompatibility between *protecting the welfare of the young offender and preventing that individual from offending again* (Home Office, 1997d, para 2.2). In Chapter 4 we look at whether this confusion has been resolved by sweeping reforms that have taken place since 1997.

In addition to New Labour's brief recognition of the contradictory nature of justice and welfare approaches, various prominent academics in the area of youth justice have also clearly noted the antagonism between the dominant paradigms.

> *The history of youth justice is a history of conflict, contradictions, ambiguity and compromise. Conflict is inevitable in a system that has traditionally pursued the twin goals of welfare and justice . . . As a result it continually seeks the compromise between youth as a special deserving case and youth as fully responsible for their own actions.*

> (Muncie and Hughes, 2002, p1)

Muncie and Hughes further argue that the conflict has given rise to an expansion of the remit of the youth justice industry while in pursuit of a compromise.

Perhaps as a result of these irresolvable philosophical tensions, theoreticians (but not yet practitioners) seem to have abandoned the justice vs welfare debate, contending that it is 'moribund' and arguing that attempted legislative solutions to this dilemma have resulted in broadening levels of state control of young people, as witnessed in youth justice legislation in the last few decades (Muncie, 2009). The creation and expansion of civil orders against children and young people in the form of anti-social behaviour contracts, orders and curfew orders are key examples of the widening of social control measures.

Fionda also refers to *internal conflicts within policy* producing *ambiguous legislation* that can *badly misfire* due to *an inability to choose one approach over the other* (2005, pp40, 43). Rutherford (1992) and Pratt (1989) have also discussed the incompatibility of these two ideologies.

By the end of 2009, the government appeared to have forgotten their early appreciation of the tensions between welfare and justice and fully abandoned any hopes of reconciliation. In November 2009, to correspond with the introduction of the new youth rehabilitation order (see Chapter 4) the Sentencing Guidelines Council published *Overarching principles – Sentencing youths*. This new 'definitive guideline' for sentencers of 10–17 year olds broke with tradition, as the Council had never previously produced any general directions for the sentencing of youths (apart from some earlier advice in relation to sexual offences and robbery). Interestingly, the document effectively air-brushed out any reference to conflicts between principles of justice and welfare that policy makers had referred to a decade or so earlier. However, the document juxtaposed the two approaches in a seemingly non-prob-lematic fashion, effectively vaporising the issue of incompatibility for the foreseeable future. The following passages illustrate the then Labour Government's amnesia about their pre-vious acknowledgement of justice's and welfare's incongruous natures, by the manner in which it proximates the two approaches throughout the document. For example:

> . . . a court sentencing a young offender must be aware of obligations under a range of international conventions which emphasise the importance of avoiding 'criminalisation' of young people whilst ensuring that they are held responsible for their actions.

Sentencing Guidelines Council 2009, para 1.3

Also, while

> . . . the approach to sentence will be individualistic, and the youth of the offender is widely recognised as requiring a different approach from that which would be adopted in relation to an adult, however the sentence must remain proportionate to the seriousness of the present offence.

Sentencing Guidelines Council 2009, paras 2.1, 2.2 and 2.3

Additionally,

> Whilst a court is required to aggravate the seriousness of an offence where there are previous convictions . . . a sentence that follows re-offending does not need to be more severe than the previous sentence solely because there had been a previous conviction.

Sentencing Guidelines Council 2009, para 2.4

Moreover, the document cites the justice principle that sentencing decisions should bear in mind the principal aim of the youth justice system as stated in section 37 of the Crime and Disorder Act 1998, namely the prevention of offending by children and young people, stating that this aim:

*incorporates the need to demonstrate that such conduct is not acceptable in a way that
makes an impact on the offender . . . and . . . incorporates the need to demonstrate
that the law is being effectively enforced and to sustain confidence in the rule of law.*

(Sentencing Guidelines Council 2009, para 2.6).

However, on the other hand, the document re-states the welfare principle enshrined in
section 44 of the Children and Young Persons Act 1933 and further states that courts
should be aware of the *high incidence* of mental health problems, abuse, self-harming,
vulnerability and learning difficulties amongst young people who come into contact with
the criminal justice system. (Sentencing Guidelines Council 2009, para 2.9)

As is apparent from the above extracts, that the guidance is littered with numerous examples of juxtapositioning contradictory justice and welfare approaches, leading us to the
conclusion that the government has finally and conveniently ignored the incompatibility
issue. Perhaps their neglect to properly tackle this conundrum is evidence of their tacit
acknowledgement that they were tying to resolve the irresolvable.

In an attempt to evidence the contradictory nature of justice and welfare approaches, I
have noted elsewhere (Pickford, 2000) examples of the various strategies that have been
adopted by successive governments in an attempt to fuse justice and welfare approaches.
Each has failed and each arguably represents evidential proof of the impossibility of
merger at both levels of theory and practice. The failed strategies include:

- *Bifurcation strategy*. Distinguishing between different types of children and young
  people who come before the justice system. This involves differentiating those who
  need help from those who deserve punishment; serious offenders from non-serious
  offenders; persistent offenders from those whose behaviour, it is believed, can be
  'nipped in the bud'.

- *Sequencing strategy*. Creating different types of procedures/processes that utilise
  divergent approaches, e.g. a justice approach in relation to trial and conviction – a welfare
  approach in relation to mitigation and sentencing; pre-trial/court diversionary schemes.

- *Institutional strategy*. Developing practices whereby different institutions/organisations
  will deal with different types of young offenders, e.g. Youth Offender Panels or courts;
  social services or the formal youth justice system.

- *Double-edged strategy*. The introduction of measures that have both a welfare and
  a justice function, e.g. the criminal care order introduced by the Children and Young
  Persons Act 1969 (now abolished) and the various requirement options available to
  sentencers making a youth rehabilitation order, some of which are justice oriented,
  others welfare oriented.

- *Career criminal strategy*. A young offender may experience a more welfare-oriented
  approach at the start of their offending career, e.g. by the use of reprimands and final
  warnings or other diversionary measures. If they continue to offend, more justice-
  oriented procedures and sanctions will be implemented.

All the above forms of compromise amount to techniques or splitting strategies which attempt to distribute incompatible elements across the system in different ways (Pickford, 2000, pxxxiv).

When we examine the history of youth justice legislation (in Part 3, below) you should be able not only to assess the legislations in terms of justice and/or welfare measures, but also to identify any of the 'splitting strategies' that might have occurred in order to facilitate implementation.

Given the tendency of academics to deal with these inevitable and unsolvable tensions by moving away from an incessant focus on justice and welfare paradigm (see below) is it not time for government too to overhaul youth justice theory and provide some consistency?

ACTIVITY 2.2

In groups, discuss whether (1) you favour a justice or a welfare focused system and (2) whether justice and welfare approaches can work together and succeed under the same system. Can you think of any other strategies/approaches that might assist a seamless merging of these approaches?

COMMENT

It is useful to think about your personal views about these polemic approaches to youthful offending before you examine more modern approaches later in this chapter. Do you favour a justice or welfare approach? Why? Do you prefer an approach that combines the two approaches and if so how could they be combined in practice? Do you think there should be a justice approach for some kinds of offences or offenders? Do you think there should be a welfare approach for some kinds of offences or offenders? Do you believe that both approaches can operate together – if so do you favour a system that is mainly justice or mainly welfare orientated – and to what extent (e.g. 25 per cent welfare with 75 per cent justice!)? Strategies that have been used in the past to try to fuse the two approaches are listed above.

Part two: Other perspectives of youth justice

In addition to the traditional dominating dual perspectives of justice and welfare, academics over recent history have developed/defined a veritable smorgasbord of approaches to youth justice. Their analyses cover recognition of a number of youth justice styles.

Preventionism

It could be suggested that a further principle of youth justice was born (in embryonic form) at the end of the 1960s: the prevention principle, which has arguably always been a nascent feature of welfarism, emerged in the Children and Young Persons Act 1969 and, in a distinctly overt form, in preventative measures introduced by the Crime and Disorder Act 1998, such as anti-social behaviour, curfew and child safety orders (ASBOs, COs and CSOs).

Its rationale is that pre-emptive early intervention should prevent potential future offending behaviour. This approach was given further momentum by the Anti-Social Behaviour Act 2003, which entrenched and expanded police and local authorities' powers to obtain civil orders against young people, whether or not they had committed a criminal offence, and further extended powers relating to parenting orders (POs) introduced by the Crime and Disorder Act 1998. Broader measures, in the form of acceptable behaviour contracts (ABCs) as an interim measure issued prior to a full ASBO, coupled with the introduction of individual support orders (ISOs) targeted at young people subject to ASBOs (from May 2004), are evidence of a government willing to stretch out the tentacles of state control and draw non-offenders into the youth justice net. Additionally, anti-social behaviour injunctions ('gangbos') were introduced under the Crime and Security Act 2010 for 14 to 17 year olds (introduced in 2009 for adults). These civil injunctions include bans on meeting other gang members, wearing gang colours, going to certain locations or having a violent dog in a public area. Breach can result in the imposition of a supervision order for up to 6 months (with activity and/or curfew conditions) or a detention order for up to 3 months.

We noted in Chapter 1 the legal implications of these measures, and the issues in terms of human rights legislation of civil orders issued by a government which, if breached, result in criminal sanctions. We also referred to some challenges that had been mounted by lawyers, in particular regarding ASBOs and human rights breaches. As social work practitioners, this is an area where you should be constantly vigilant in order to ensure that state bodies do not issue controls on your clients in breach of their human rights. Although purportedly welfare-based, it is arguable that preventionism produces labelling and net-widening effects (see Chapter 3) pulling young people who may not yet have committed any criminal offences into the ambit of the criminal justice system; it is, therefore, essentially a latent form of social control.

Such measures are part of what Ashworth (1994) has called a 'pincer movement' in youth justice, which has been in evidence since the 1970s; this movement gained momentum following the death of toddler James Bulger in 1993 at the hands of two 10 year olds and the ensuing media moral panic that led to what various criminologists have called the 'demonisation' of youth (Jenks, 1996). Hendrick (2002 and 2006) asserts that this case was transformative in that it led to the abandonment of the 'romantic' model of childhood innocence that had been dominant for many decades and caused a resurgence of the 'evangelical child' model – the notion that children are born evil and that we should be wary of them. Fionda states that youth justice law *ensures that more devils are drawn into a wider net with a thinner mesh* from which it is harder to escape (Fionda, 2005, p58). Thane (2009) argues that notions of childhood are not fixed but change over time and differ between legal cultures. Conceptions of childhood are constructed in order to circumscribe the role of children and young people within a particular society and to facilitate social control.

The growth of the youth justice industry over the last decade, produced by a focus on preventionism, was vast, with prevention teams performing major roles in most Youth Offending Teams across the country. In addition to this, the introduction of a range of preventative orders (noted above and in Chapter 4) since 1998 and the expansion of the preventionism rationale led to the setting up of various organisations and initiatives under new Labour. For example:

- Youth Crime Action Plan: Focused on crime prevention via assessment, early intervention, targetted support and sharing information between local services, e.g. schools, police, youth, social and health services.

- Youth Intervention Programmes (YIPs), aimed at 13–16 year olds in a community who are deemed most at risk of offending.

- Safer Schools Partnerships.

- Youth Intervention and Support Panels (YISPs), consisting of 13 schemes across the country aimed at 8–13 year olds who are deemed most at risk of offending.

- Youth Taskforce, which evolved from the Respect Taskforce and aimed to meet the Children's Plan committment to improve outcomes for the most at risk children.

- Youth Taskforce Action Plan, which provided funding and support for positive activities.

- On Track Scheme.

- Sure Start.

- Challenge and Support Projects were set up in 52 areas where anti-social behaviour is a problem.

- Locally based prevention projects run by local authorities and/or local police authorities, including summer activity schemes.

- Locating Youth Priority Areas, involving targetted youth support initiatives especially directed at disruptive young people and young people not in education, employment or training.

- Positive Futures Programmes.

- Association of Chief Police Officer's Neighberhood Policing Youth Toolkit.

- Safer Schools Partnerships.

- Neighberhood Action Plans, developed by neighberhood police teams.

- Anti-social behaviour action teams attached to local authorities.

- Family Intervention Projects.

- Youth Alcohol Action Plan.

- National Award Scheme, aimed at young people who turn their life around or make a contribution to the community.

Although we have noted some of the dangers of a focus on prevention in terms of expansionism, the Labour government was certainly pro-active in targeting preventative strategies. It is likely that the Coalition government will scale back this approach as part of its cost cutting exercise. The government's austerity package has already led to cutbacks in some of the above initiatives, especially those funded by local councils who are having to make drastic savings. Many youth offending teams across the country are similarly facing budgets restraints and redundancies.

Corporatism/managerialism/partnerships/systems management

This approach to youth justice practice has been differently named by various academics, hence the broad heading. However, in essence, following negative feedback from the Audit Commission's report (1996) into the old Youth Justice Teams (Misspent Youth, 1996) in relation to the disparate and often lax management processes, systematic and corporate-style management techniques that had already begun to emerge in some quarters were pushed to the foreground in an effort to improve and standardise the practice of youth justice. This was formalised in the Crime and Disorder Act 1998 by the setting-up of multi-disciplinary Youth Offending Teams across England and Wales from April 2000 and the creation of the Youth Justice Board to standardise best practice and monitor the youth justice profession. Furthermore, local areas were required to establish multi-agency panels of key managers in police, probation, youth justice, education, youth services and social services, in order to address issues of crime and disorder and construct local crime strategies. Local authorities were given a statutory obligation to prevent youth crime. In addition, the fast-tracking of young offenders through the criminal justice system was prioritised as a key aim that contributed to better cost-effectiveness. The development of the Youth Crime Action Plan and the Youth Taskforce Action Plan from 2008 onwards continued the partnership approach to tackling crime and anti-social behaviour among young people.

Muncie (2009) alleges that by the late 1980s, principles of welfare and/or justice had somewhat dissolved into a *developing corporatist strategy which removed itself from the wider philosophical arguments of welfare and punishment . . . The aim was not necessarily to deliver 'welfare' or 'justice' but rather to develop the most cost-effective and efficient way of managing the delinquent problem*. Causational issues are largely ignored when applying this approach and traditional youth justice was *redefined as a problem that needed to be managed rather than necessarily resolved* (Muncie, 2009, pp296–97). This new model fitted well with the bifurcated strategy adopted by the Thatcher government in the 1980s (see Part 3, below), whereby serious and persistent offenders were dealt with harshly (with custody) whereas other offenders were diverted from custody by the development of a range of community sentence packages for use as alternatives to an expensive custodial disposal.

The move towards managerialism and multi-agency strategies in youth justice in the 1990s followed a pattern being adopted generally over the whole of the public sector. This posited the notion that social issues such as health, poverty, crime and delinquency were problems that needed to be properly managed using corporate techniques (Clarke and Newburn, 1997). Adopting the perspective of managerialism in relation to social problems such as youth crime arguably by implication suggests a pessimistic recognition that such problems simply exist in our society and are probably irresolvable. Therefore learning to manage these problems more effectively is the only way forward. This method appears to mirror developments in theoretical criminology over the latter part of the twentieth century. Following Martinson's (1974) nihilistic claim that 'nothing works', theoretical criminology seemed to reach a crisis in theory development, which arguably led to an era of philosophical stagnation. This resulted in both essentialism – a focus on empiricism (largely funded by the Home Office and later the Ministry of Justice) – and implosion in the form of the development of postmodern criminologies which either attempted to rework old theories or simply dismantle and criticise earlier paradigms as being fundamentally flawed.

Authoritarianism/correctionalism/popular punitiveness

Linked partially to the justice rationale is a classicist notion (see Chapter 3) that crime is chosen rather than caused, that young people are capable of wickedness and that they deserve to be punished for their sins. The post-Bulger media moral panic, which led to the rise of what has been called 'popular punitiveness', reveals that it would be electoral suicide for any political party to appear to be 'soft' on serious and persistent young offenders. Hence, despite the reduction in youth crime figures over the ten years to 2004 (NACRO, 2009) the figures for receptions into custody in terms of both remanded and sentenced youths rose. The Youth Justice Board's figures for 2008 indicated that, in contrast to 1993 when approximately 1300 young people were detained, by 2008 that figure had risen to just under 3,000. The numbers for 2010 indicate a decline to around 2,300 – perhaps as a result of the changes introduced by the Criminal Justice and Immigration Act 2008 (see Chapter 4). This 'law and order' approach that is reflected (created?) in newspapers such as the *Daily Mail* and the *Sun*, has ensured that any proposals that involve a radical element in terms of diversion or de-incarceration, are subject to a popular (and sometimes judicial/magisterial) backlash. The conclusion reached by politicians and policymakers is that custodial sentencing options must be preserved and used robustly where considered necessary.

The justification for incarcerative disposals is further assisted by the historically developed notion that custodial establishments for young people are educative and reforming in nature. As Muncie and Hughes (2002) note, reformatories were viewed as reformative in nature, borstals as places that fostered rehabilitation through training, while detention centres are viewed as 'softer' than adult custodial organisations, secure training centres (12–14 year olds) as places of education, and the detention and training order introduced by the Crime and Disorder Act 1998 emphasises training and community support upon release. All these examples have created the impression that depriving a young person of their liberty is not as severe as depriving an adult, as the regime they will face is not as bad as in an adult prison and has their reformation and education as a central focus. This attitude has perhaps helped to justify rises in youth incarceration, despite the harsh reality of the severely detrimental impact of custody upon young people, both in terms of potential reformation and recidivism, clearly documented in research (NACRO, 2003c and 2009; Goldson 2006 and 2009; Youth Justice Board 2009a) in addition to the tragic cases of deaths in youth custody that have happened over the last few years. Given the recent focus on the actuarially based risk management or the 'what works' agenda (via the introduction of the scaled approach risk assessment (see Chapter 4)) it is, perhaps, astounding that clear evidence is repeatedly ignored by policy-makers with regard to custodial effectiveness. Their selectivity in this regard is pure political pragmatism. The transparency of their motives is clear, but their failure to follow evidence-based results in this area reveals an unjustifiable inconsistency of approach that panders to neo-conservative authoritarian rhetoric.

Authoritarianism is further in evidence through other measures introduced by the Crime and Disorder Act and subsequent legislation, such as tagging from the age of ten, the introduction of civil orders such as ASBOs, ABCs, anti-social behaviour injunctions, individual support orders, curfew orders and parenting orders, etc, and the removal of state benefits for those who fail to comply with community orders.

Responsibilisation

David Garland (1996) developed the notion of the responsibilisation perspective as a description of government policies that seek to tackle the problem of crime by subtly encouraging the transfer of some responsibility for crime control away from formal agencies (e.g. the police, community support officers) to informal controls and mechanisms (e.g. private security, Neighbourhood Watch, local crime reduction schemes). Under these initiatives, the message to individuals, businesses and communities is clear: the chance of becoming a victim of crime is not something that official agencies can alter, rather it is a matter of personal risk management – each person is responsible for the management of their risks of becoming a victim of crime. All citizens must practise practical avoidance methods in order to reduce the opportunity for crimes to be perpetrated against them, including target-hardening measures (burglar alarms, steering locks) and increased private surveillance (security lighting, CCTV). Muncie and Hughes (2002) describe this as a 'neo-liberal' method of government, which diverts the responsibility for crime away from the state. It is somewhat ironic that, in tandem with the growth of victim rights in this country, we have witnessed the concomitant rise of victim blaming: the latter is a logical result of the upsurge in the responsibilisation strategy.

In the area of youth justice, responsibilisation has further meant a devolution of control of crime to local authorities who have been made responsible for crime control strategies in terms of multi-agency panels of various managers within authorities (police, probation, social services, education) devising local youth justice plans. Consequently, local agencies are accountable for the 'crime problem' in their locality.

Furthermore, as Muncie and Hughes (2002) note, the responsibilisation strategy is arguably also in evidence in two other areas of youth justice reform following the Crime and Disorder Act 1998. It is noticeable first in terms of the growth of focus on restorative justice (Youth Justice Board, 2010) part of the purpose of which is to make the young person face up to the reality of their action and take full responsibility for their law-breaking behaviour. Second, the abolition of the principle of *doli incapax* ('incapable of evil') – whereby it had to be shown that young people aged 10 to 13 possessed the ability to form the required level of culpability necessary for the offence for which they were accused – abandoned a 'buffer zone' of protection for the youngest people who come before our courts. Now these young people are automatically considered able to form the required level of *mens rea* ('guilty mind'). This now forsaken principle of *doli incapax* had been in evidence in our criminal justice system since the Middle Ages (Allen, 1996; Stokes, 2000).

Paternalism

From the advent of the Welfare State after the Second World War onwards, it is arguable that the state has acted as guardian of its citizens. Even prior to this era, Section 44 of the Children and Young Persons Act 1933 enshrined what became known as 'the welfare principle' in relation to young offenders. This provided recognition of the young offender as a vulnerable, developing character and stated that all courts dealing with young people must primarily have regard to their welfare. This ethos of the state as the protective guardian continued to be in evidence in youth justice legislation and practice up to the

1980s, having its heyday in the 1960s and 1970s (see below). When the Thatcher government promoted principles of individualism and autonomy evidenced in Mrs Thatcher's famous statement, *There is no such thing as society, there are individual men and women and there are families*, (published in *Woman's Own* magazine, 31 October 1987) this led to a return to a classicist analysis of crime causation (see Chapter 3) and a belief that crime was simply an activity *chosen* by individuals. Alongside the resurgence in this notion came the belief that individuals were, therefore, responsible for their law-breaking behaviour – they could no longer blame deprivation, poverty or other social causes.

This attitude was part and parcel of the responsibilisation strategy, noted above. However, as Muncie and Hughes (2002) assert, aspects of youth justice legislation have still clung on to the notion of paternalism, despite a general move towards individualism and responsibility. This is witnessed not only by the British government being a signatory of international treaties in relation to the treatment of young suspects (see Chapter 1) but also in measures such as parenting, individual support and curfew orders, which are couched in the language of assisting and supplementing parental guidance (though their true purpose might be seen by some as merely an extension of state control into family and private life).

Remoralisation

Muncie refers to a further perspective which he labels the *neo-conservative remoralisation discourse* (2009, p347). As hinted in the previous section, an alternative analysis of the changes that have taken place in youth justice could argue that rather than the government moving away from being responsible for the crime problem by responsibilising its citizens and stepping back from micro-management of communities, in fact the opposite has happened. The advent of additional civil orders such as ASBOs, parenting orders, curfew orders, individual support orders and anti-social behaviour injunctions (in 2010 for 14–17 year olds) is testimony to a desire on the part of government to supplement and amend child-rearing practices as part of a control via re-education by force strategy. This re-education is, in reality, a form of remoralisation of a targeted community – the 'underclass'.

The fear of the underclass is the catalyst that has prompted this move towards remoralisation. Ken Auletta, the journalist who coined the phrase 'underclass' in 1982, referred to them as representing the 'peril and shame' of governments. The reason the remoralisation approach is dubbed 'neo-conservative' is that the movement gained academic credence through the theories of underclass, crime and anti-social behaviour developed by right-wing ('right-realist') criminologists in both the USA and the UK (Murray, 1984, 1988, 1990; Dennis, 1993). It has a moral agenda, as its proponents allege that a great deal of crime and social disorder is caused by feckless young male members of the underclass and that their behaviour is linked to a decline in moral standards, a rise in single parenthood (the youths have no positive male role models) and teenage pregnancies, a lack of application to education/employment, the use of drugs, etc. (see Chapter 3). Behind this notion of dysfunctional and anti-social families is a moralistic notion of how a 'proper/normal' family should behave. However, state control of these populations is *clouded in a rhetoric of 'child protection' or 'family support'* (Muncie and Hughes, 2002, p9). Thus, the targeting of surveillance and social control strategies not only at the criminal population but at families and communities who are deemed to be disorderly or 'at risk' of offending is justified by this approach: *By proclaiming that the principle aim of the youth justice system is to prevent offending, action against legal and moral/social transgressions is legitimised* (Muncie and Hughes, 2002, p9).

Restorative justice

In practical terms, principles of restorative justice underpinned the introduction of the referral order by the Youth Justice and Criminal Evidence Act 1999 (the referral order came into effect in England and Wales in April 2002). The rationale behind this order was that the young offender would have the opportunity in a Youth Offending Panel meeting to face up to the full consequences of their actions and that a practical package could be put into place whereby the young person would make amends for the wrong committed. Ideally, it was envisaged that the victim would attend panel meetings and that an individual agreement of restoration could be forged through the young person apologising or making amends in some practical or financial way. Unfortunately, the participation of victims in panel meetings has been low (Earle, 2005). The referral order is examined in more depth in Chapter 4.

Although notions of general redress appear initially to be related to the justice approach, it can be argued that at the heart of the principle of reparation is the belief that, having been forced to confront the full impact of their offending, the young person will experience self-reproach and desist from offending behaviour in the future. In essence, therefore, restorative justice prompts rehabilitation and as a consequence falls within a positivistic criminological analysis, believing in the reformation of the subject. As such its natural home is, perhaps, within a welfare-oriented perspective.

Prior to the introduction of the referral order, other sentences were available (and still are) that fell within the restorative ethos. Reparation is surely three-pronged: it relates to reparation to the victim, to the community, and of the offender. Thus any sentence aimed at restoration in any of these three senses falls within this category. Specifically though, disposals such as compensation orders, reparation orders and any reparation apology, mediation or community work undertaken as part of a youth rehabilitation order are directly aimed at making amends. The principles of restoration are arguably linked to civil law ideals about restitution and compensation and as such represent a departure from ideas of punitiveness. Alternatively however, some academics assert that there is a conceptual relationship between restorative justice and punishment – and point to affinitives between principles of restorative justice and 'law and order' conservatism (Mantle, Fox and Dhami, 2005).

The theoretical grounding and rationale for restorative justice is perhaps most famously attributed to John Braithwaite. Braithwaite (1989) examined the concept of 're-integrative shaming' as an ideal in any justice system. This involved practices such as those used in Japan and New Zealand Maori culture whereby the focus of justice procedures was on the wrongness of the act rather than on the actor, and that once an offender had confessed to the crime, they would be welcomed back into the community after making amends for the wrong. He contrasted these practices with our criminal justice system, arguing that the focus on the offender being bad (rather than the offence) amounted to 'dis-integrative shaming', whereby court procedures led to stigmatisation and the offender being treated as what Becker referred to as 'an outsider' (Becker, 1963). Braithwaite (and other criminologists) examined restorative justice models as they operate in Aboriginal, Native American and Maori cultures – more particularly family group conferencing and other community mediation practices – and concluded that it leads to a more satisfactory form of community-based justice and a sense of justice being done (Braithwaite, 2003).

In this country, the Labour government adopted principles of restorative justice when it stated in its White Paper *No more excuses* (Home Office, 1997d) that the three principles underpinning their reform of the youth justice system were 'restoration', 're-integration' and 'responsibility' (the three Rs). The pursuit of the first and second of these aims can be seen in the introduction of the reparation order and the referral order. It is arguable that the growth of and continuing focus on restorative justice is a concomitant part of the recognition and expansion of victims' rights within our criminal justice system generally over the last 20 years, culminating in the *Code of Practice for Victims of Crime* (Home Office, 2005a) which came into force in April 2006.

The principle of restorative justice continued to have an impact on youth justice legislation and practice, as evidenced by the Youth Justice Board's review of current restorative justice initiatives in 2010. Further, the Coalition government's green paper on sentencing reforms published in December 2010 specifically promotes the idea of making young offenders 'pay back' to their victims and communities.

Treatment model

Fionda (2005) refers to the treatment model of youth justice. She states that this model is very similar to the welfare approach; indeed, it developed in tandem with welfarism. The treatment ethos however, is specifically linked to the positivist school of criminology (see Chapter 3) which posited that crime is 'caused' by forces beyond the offender's control (early positivists examined biological/genetic causes, then psychological causes, and finally social and environmental causes of crime and delinquency). Nevertheless, whatever the causational triggers for crime, under the treatment approach the young person is assumed to be not fully responsible for their actions, but instead is reacting to social, psychological and/or biological prompts.

The treatment approach became weakened in the 1980s with a return to the classicist notion of crime as choice and a focus on individual responsibility. The treatment model had always had more credence when applied to juveniles who have been generally regarded as less responsible for their actions than adults due to developing capacities. Although this approach was largely abandoned by the government post-Bulger – by the mid-1990s, it was arguably kept alive by researchers and practitioners within the youth justice industry, particularly youth offending team officers, many of whom were trained social workers. By the turn of the century, policy makers were again becoming interested in the psycho-social and environmental triggers of delinquency. Research into 'risk factors' that might precipitate anti-social and offending behaviour was undertaken by the Department of Children, Families and Schools (especially via the Youth Taskforce and the Youth Crime Action Plan), the Home Office, the Ministry of Justice, the Youth Justice Board and NACRO. As noted in Chapter 1, risk factors in relation to youth offending were identified as fourfold:

- *the family* e.g. inadequate, harsh or inconsistent parenting;
- *the school* e.g. low achievement, disaffection, truancy or exclusion;
- *the community* e.g. low community cohesion, crime hotspots or easy access to drugs;
- *personal factors* e.g. being male, mixing with offending peers, poor physical or mental health or misuse of drugs or alcohol.

(NACRO, 2009)

These elements are at the centre of assessments undertaken by youth offending teams, who use the Youth Justice Board's assessment tool (Asset) in order to 'score' a young person's risk factors by using 'the scaled approach' introduced in November 2009 by the Criminal Justice and Immigration Act 2008 (see 'the scaled approach' in Chapter 4 and Asset in Chapter 6). The aggregated score will determine the level of risk, which in turn will dictate the intensity of intervention. Interventions should be specifically targeted at the risk factors identified for each young offender. The resurgence of the treatment model is arguably visible in the growth of this type of tailor-made disposal – which is made possible at the community sentence level by the vast array of options (18 of them) available to sentencers who recommend a youth rehabilitation order (see Chapter 4).

Developmental model

Though the popular notion in relation to the Thatcher years is that of a tough stance on criminality across the board, in fact the Conservative government of the 1980s adopted a bifurcated strategy towards youth justice: a twin-track method that separated serious and persistent offenders from low-level offenders who were largely diverted away from the full rigours of the criminal justice system. This is evidenced by the sharp rise in the use of cautions and the officially sanctioned practice of multiple cautioning for non-serious offenders (Home Office, 1985). This practice was boosted in many local areas by the existence of diversion panels, run by youth justice teams (see Rutherford, 2002 for further details of this model). Such panels would regularly issue a 'caution plus', the equivalent of the final warning, whereby a young person would receive a caution from the local youth liaison police officer and be required to attend for voluntary support sessions at the youth justice team (re-introduced by the Criminal Justice and Immigration Act 2008 in the form of the youth conditional caution).

However, at the opposite end of the spectrum, despite the rhetoric, numbers entering custody fell over this period due to the development of robust alternatives to custody by the government, in the form of restricted criteria for youth custody (Criminal Justice Act 1982 and 1991) alongside the introduction of funded Intermediate Treatment schemes and the Specified Activities disposal. This reduction in the use of the custodial sanction was further assisted by youth justice team practitioners being largely opposed to custody (some teams even operated 'no custody' policies) and being proactive in devising high-tariff alternatives to custody, regarded as acceptable by some local magistrates. Rutherford argues that additionally some magistrates at that time had become sceptical about the usefulness of custody as reformatories for young offenders.

Fionda argues that the developmental model grew as a result of the above factors and that this model regards the adolescent as a developing subject.

> *The key feature of this model is that crime is viewed as part of the adolescent or traumatic 'storm and stress' phase in a teenager's life. Therefore most . . . young offenders are likely, . . . to grow out of their offending behaviour . . . The response to youth crime therefore needs to . . . not hinder the child's growth.*

(Fionda, 2005, p39)

Under this approach, where intervention is necessary it should be kept to a minimum in order to avoid stigmatisation. Furthermore, custody should be reserved for only a few of the most serious offenders.

Communitarianism

It is possible to link communitarianism to the responsibilisation approach as it involves placing the responsibility for and the solution to crime firmly within designated communities or areas. Local crime strategies and local initiatives under the Youth Crime Action Plan are formed from within the community for that community (by local multi-agency experts) in order to directly address the particular crime issues or 'hotspots' within that community. According to Hester (2000), the acceptance of the concept of 'community safety' as a key factor of the communitarian approach can lead to tensions, in that on the one hand it implies the ability to reach a consensus within local areas but on the other it seems to have sanctioned the adoption of exclusionary tactics such as those that inevitably stem from, for example, an acceptance of 'zero tolerance' strategies or from the proactive targeting of ASBOs against certain communities/families. In this vein, the communitarianism approach can be viewed as negatively linked to the remoralisation strategy and thus can be regarded as feeding into an agenda that stigmatises and represses certain target (underclass) communities. As Hester states, *the fact remains that in times and places where there is fractured consensus, attempts to create a spirit of community might involve the exclusion of those unable or unwilling to 'belong'* (2000, p162). In some localities intolerance to youth delinquency has led to the publication of posters or news paper photographs of young people subject to ASBOs or police intervention, promoting local stigmatisation and isolation rather than encouraging integration.

Actuarialism/risk management/'what works' approach

The crime risk management model is partly related to the preventionist approach in that its aim is to reduce youth offending within a community. Prior to the Crime and Disorder Act 1998, the Morgan Report on crime prevention (Home Office, 1991) had been influential in stressing the need for a community-based multi-agency approach.

Such strategies should be based on effective empirical research that will produce accurate crime-mapping of localities so that problem areas and issues can be specifically targeted. This evidence-based practice is part of the 'what works' agenda, favoured by the Audit Commission's *Misspent youth* report (1996) and reviewed by the Home Office (Goldblatt and Lewis, 1998) which posits that action needs to be targeted as a result of constantly reviewed data about effectiveness and that alternative inefficient approaches should be abandoned.

This ideology follows what has been called 'actuarial justice' principles or the 'new penology' (Feeley and Simon, 1992). It is linked to positivistic techniques of identification and management of individual offenders on the basis of levels of 'dangerousness' – an assessment requirement that has gained statutory force since the Criminal Justice Act 2003 in relation to both adult and young offenders (see Chapter 4). In addition, Youth Offending Teams (YOTs) are required to evaluate the risks to the public in relation to all the young people they deal with by means of the completion of the Asset assessment (see Chapter 6).

Muncie alleges that when compared with the old justice vs welfare approaches, the whole risk management ethos amounts to a *less philosophically defensible aim of preventing offending by any pragmatic means possible. In place of the pessimistic 'nothing works' paradigm evidence-based research and fiscal audit were turned to reveal interventions that might 'work'* . . . *in the search for 'value for money' and cost-effective, measurable outputs* (Muncie, 2004, pp271–2).

The actuarial, risk calculation approach to youth justice has gained much momentum over the last few years, culminating in the wholesale adoption of the belief that an accurate mathematical enumeration of collective risk factors is possible – in the form of the introduction of 'the scaled approach' risk assessment method introduced alongside the youth rehabilitation order on 30 November 2009 (see Chapter 4). This approach appears to negate any recognition that choice, chance and opportunity might have an impact on youthful offending, effectively vaporising the ideas of the classicist school of crime causation (see Chapter 3).

However, despite the Youth Justice Board hailing the scaled approach as 'groundbreaking', youth offending team practitioners (see www.communitycare.co.uk 30/11/09) and leading academics have criticised the method (see Chapter 4 for a broader description and critique). Bateman (2009) said that the scaled approach was 'patently unfair'. The aggregate score (in number form) of multiple risk factors determines the level of risk and in turn the intensity of intervention, potentially 'up-tariffing' a young person on the basis of welfare rather than offending factors.

Additionally Case (2007) and Case and Haines (2009) have presented robust research to suggest that the technique is reductionist, generalist, ambiguous and fundamentally flawed. The strategies used for the scaled approach gained impetus under New Labour's research based 'what works' approach to social problems, an approach that wholeheartedly embraces positivist notions of determinism, i.e. that the presence of particular factors will almost certainly lead to predicted outcomes.

The Labour government's naive acceptance of this uber-positivist methodology as being flawless (despite much academic scepticism about the validity of scientific methodology in relation to social science, arguably stretching back over many decades since Durkheim (1895) posited the questionable idea that social phenomena were calculable – using the same methods adopted by natural/pure science) is quite astonishing. Case and Haines (2009) refer to the young people who are being assessed in youth offending teams using the fixed scaled approach as 'crash test dummies'.

It is also noteworthy that the actuarial measurements adopted focus on individual rather than structural factors relating to offending, such as government policy, unemployment, poverty, discrimination, marginalisation, etc. (Smith, 2007).

The perceived managerial benefits of actuarialism are clearly expounded by Case and Haines (2009, p4) as follows:

> *the exponential prioritisation of risk-centred,* evidence-based practice, *within the youth justice system of England and Wales not only reflects a response to the uncertainties of the risk society and the increasingly pervasive and invasive audit based mentality of modern public sector managerialism, but also concerns within the government and the Youth Justice Board about 'undue' youth justice practitioner discretion, perceptions of poor practice and a perceived ineffectiveness in the system in controlling young people and crime.*

A meze of theoretical approaches, or a maze?

In relation to the practice of youth justice, Ashworth (2000) has referred to the growth of youth sentencing options as creating a 'cafeteria' style justice (which Fionda, 2005 describes as 'à la carte' sentencing). This 'smorgasboard' approach has continued in the form of the eighteen different content requirements that sentencers can choose from when issuing a youth rehabilitation order (introduced at the end of 2009). Similarly, it could be argued that in terms of youth justice theory we have a meze of approaches (though for some students it might appear to be a maze). Indeed, Fionda alleges that youth justice *policy attempts to try all approaches at the same time, . . . in the hope that within the melting pot we will discover that 'something works'* (2005, p58).

In addition to the list of philosophical approaches listed above, Muncie and Hughes (2002, p13) further discuss 'hybrid agendas', saying that it is difficult to state that one approach is prioritised above another or to assert that while one particular strategy is in the ascendant another is necessarily falling out of favour. Indeed they refer to

> *a diverse array of strategies that is available to achieve the governance of young people. It is an array that is capable of drawing in the criminal and the non-criminal, the deprived and the depraved, the neglected and the dangerous. This broad ambit is secured because the discourse . . . is sufficiently imprecise to be all-encompassing.*

Reviewing philosophical bases in 2009, Muncie concludes that *youth justice has evolved in a state of constant flux . . . it is an accretion of numerous levels of discourse* (p346).

ACTIVITY **2.3**

ACTIVITY **2.3**

Having examined all the models/approaches in relation to youth justice, discuss which one(s) you prefer and why.

COMMENT

This is your opportunity to examine how you would manage youth justice in England and Wales if you were in charge and had a blank sheet with which to design a new management strategy for youth offending! Which of the many approaches discussed above do you believe would provide the most appropriate method of managing the youth crime problem? Would you adopt a combination of approaches or settle for one defined philosophy/management strategy? Justify your choice(s).

Part three: A brief legislative history

The development of youth justice practice since 1997 is discussed in Chapter 4; this section briefly describes the historical development of youth justice policy prior to 1997. I refer to my previous analyses of this period (Pickford, 2000 and 2008).

ACTIVITY **2.4**

As we trace the legislative history of youth justice (below) see if you can spot which of the theoretical approaches outlined above apply to each legislative enactment. Can you spot any incompatibility of approaches and if so (how) has this tension been resolved?

COMMENT

Using the information you have studied above relating to different theoretical approaches to youth justice, examine each of the major historical periods of legislative reform described below and try to identify which approaches have informed or been the basis for these legislative changes.

For example, when we analyse the provisions of the Children and Young Persons Act 1969 a number of approaches are arguably evident – largely due to the political battles that raged in the consultation period prior to its enactment. Consequently, in addition to there being a mixture of justice and welfare provisions, we can see elements of prevention-ism (identifying common triggers of youthful offending) paternalism (supplementing and even supplanting the role of parents by state intervention where deemed necessary) and treatment (a belief that criminality was caused by social factors beyond the young person's control and that a tailor-made 'cure' could be provided by social work professionals).

Prior to 1908 there existed no separate system for dealing with young offenders. The Children Act 1908 created juvenile courts and although these were presided over by the same magistrates who sat in the adult courts their establishment indicated a vague under-standing that the reasons why children and young people commit crime, and the needs of children and young people who come before the courts, might be different from those of adults. However, it can be argued that some confusion arose at this inception stage between the quite different approaches required for those children in need of care, and those who had committed criminal offences, as the Act gave the juvenile court jurisdiction over both criminal and care issues. The unfortunate coupling of these dual roles of care and control had the practical effect of the same judicial body being called upon to deal with both the so-called 'depraved' and 'deprived'.

A recognition of the differences between adults and young people in terms of responsibility and blameworthiness, embodied in the 1908 Act by the creation of a distinct system of youth justice, gave birth to a latent and perhaps concomitant acknowledgement of a process of distinguishing between the different types of young people who came before the juvenile justice system – those who deserved punishment and those who needed help to overcome their difficulties. The tacit appreciation of this difference is arguably a tenuous but early manifestation of a bifurcated approach to dealing with different kinds of young people who came before the juvenile courts which was to develop over the course of the twentieth century.

The next significant piece of legislation was the Children and Young Persons Act 1933. The Act was passed as a result of the report of the Moloney Committee (Home Office, 1927) which contained a blend of classicist and positivist explanations of criminality in children and young people (the classicist and positivist approaches are outlined in Chapter 3). The Committee regarded law-breaking as a deliberate act of defiance, which had to be dealt with by formal court procedures and sanctions, while recognising that delinquent behaviour may be caused by psychological or environmental factors that were beyond the young person's control. Morris and Giller (1987, p71) contend that the report thus presented:

> dual images of the delinquent [which] were placed not side by side but in sequence. In the first instance . . . the offence was used as a conscious act of wickedness. Once the act was proved or admitted, however, it was viewed as a product of personal or external forces.

The 1933 Act was instrumental in establishing what became known by professionals as 'the welfare principle', which is still of paramount importance for the court when dealing with young offenders. Under Section 44 of the Act, a court must: *have regard to the welfare of the child or young person and shall in a proper case take steps for removing him from undesirable surroundings or for securing that proper provision is made for his education or training.*

An early recognition of the inappropriateness of young people in social need being dealt with by the same institutions that dealt with juvenile offenders, can be seen in the report of the Care of Children Committee in 1946, which accepted that it was undesirable for approved schools to provide identical services and regimes for non-offenders and offenders. The report also precipitated the formation of the local government children's authorities, effectively a social service department established by the Children Act 1948, to deal with both deprived children and children subject to criminal court orders.

The Children and Young Persons (Amendment) Act 1952 allowed courts to remand young offenders to local authority accommodation and created an approved school licence release whereby those released from approved schools were to be supervised within the community by local child-care officers. This Act in effect created two provisions whereby the systems of control (the criminal justice system) and of care (the welfare system) became intertwined when dealing with young people made subject to such orders.

In the 1960s, as a result of the Ingleby Report (Home Office, 1960), a more liberal under-standing of youth criminality than had been seen previously began to be evident, perhaps reflecting a recognition of the influence of criminological debates of the time which focused upon social and environmental rather than individualistic causes of crime. There was also an acknowledgement of the labelling perspective that flourished in criminological circles at that time. This promoted recognition of the probable negative results of stig-matising young people and the impact of this stigma on their life chances. The report recommended a reduction in the criminal jurisdiction of the juvenile court via the diver-sion of non-serious offenders away from the formal criminal justice system and a focus upon welfare provision for those who came before it. This warming towards welfarist models, coupled with professional doubts about the effectiveness of punishment for young offenders among social work personnel, continued throughout the 1960s and was reflected in the policy debates concerning youth criminality over that period.

An appreciation of deprivation and social inequality as causal factors in juvenile delin-quency, together with a recognition of the stigmatising effects of early criminalisation, was also clearly visible in a radical white paper (Home Office, 1965). It proposed that young offenders should be completely removed from the court system and dealt with exclusively by social service departments. This radicalism of the mid-1960s met with vociferous opposition, mainly from lawyers within the Conservative party, and led to a jus-tice-oriented backlash that resulted in an uneasy compromise in the form of the Children and Young Persons Act 1969 introduced by the then Labour government. Some of the more welfare-oriented provisions of that Act, such as the raising of the age of criminal responsibility to 14 and the proposal to allow local authorities to deal with most juve-nile delinquents by means of supervision and care arrangements, never came into force due to the incoming Conservative government's refusal to implement them. However, in the same period in Scotland there was little opposition to a welfare model of youth jus-tice as proposed by the Kilbrandon Report in Scotland (Home Office, 1964). A treatment approach was implemented north of the border at the same time as a justice backlash was occurring in England and Wales (see Pickford, 2000, Chapters 8 and 9).

The Act also granted the criminal court the power to pass a criminal sanction on a young person that in effect amounted to a welfare provision – the criminal care order (abolished in 1989). In that sentence, the 'deprived' and the 'depraved' became as one; the welfare measure became a criminal sanction.

The battlefield of the debates surrounding the passing and implementation of the 1969 Act resulted in a youth justice landscape that produced in the 1970s *a widening of the net of control as elements of the new system brought into being by the 1969 Act were absorbed into a larger system which retained its traditional commitment to imprisonment* (McLaughlin and Muncie, 1996, p267).

In effect, the 1969 Act created greater powers of discretion for social workers and did nothing to stem a rising tide of custodial disposals. Social workers were given wider

professional discretion, which enabled them to expand their client group – a kind of professional entrepreneurialism – and this resulted in many non-serious delinquents being drawn
into the social control net of the youth justice system under the guise of preventionism.

The Conservative victory in the 1979 general election saw the start of the Thatcher era and a
move towards individualism and consumerism. The 'rule of law' and 'law and order' rhetoric, which dominated the Conservative's election campaign, began to be made flesh by the
introduction of the (soon abandoned) 'short, sharp shock' militaristic custodial sentence.
The Criminal Justice Act 1982 restricted the criteria for custodial disposals and transformed
borstals into youth training centres, aimed at giving young offenders an experience more
akin to an adult prison. A policy of bifurcation was pursued in the succeeding years of
the Conservative government, and arguably continued until the post-Bulger panic in the
1990s. This practice involved 'getting tough' on those deemed serious and persistent young
offenders, while endeavouring to divert first-time and non-serious juvenile offenders away
from the more stigmatising effects of the criminal justice system. Indeed, a general trend
away from incarceration can be seen as early as the 1982 Act, which created the specified
activities order as a high-tariff community disposal that was later to become a direct alternative to custody under the Criminal Justice Act 1988.

It is arguable that the Criminal Justice Act 1982 contributed towards a trend of lowering
numbers of young offenders who were sent into custody, which is clearly in evidence by
the mid 1980s (Rutherford, 2002). Over the period of the mid 1980s the number of custodial disposals fell significantly. Additionally, Section 1 (4) of the Criminal Justice Act 1982
(as amended by section 123 (3) of the Criminal Justice Act 1988) stated that a custodial
sentence should not be imposed unless:

> (i) the young person has a history of failure to respond to non custodial penalties
> and is unwilling or unable to respond to them; or (ii) only a custodial sentence would
> be adequate to protect the public from serious harm from him; or (iii) the offence
> of which he has been convicted or found guilty was so serious that a non custodial
> sentence for it cannot be justified.

The Home Office circulars during the 1980s officially encouraged the use of cautions for
young offenders (Home Office, 1985) and in many areas this resulted in the practice of
multiple cautioning of some young people. This arguably allowed flexibility for professionals in dealing with young offenders whom they regarded as non-serious and who
were likely to 'grow out' of their delinquency. This discretion has largely been lost by
the creation of the more rigid final warning system in the Crime and Disorder Act 1998.
Additionally, the Conservative government of the 1980s provided local authorities with
funds to set up intermediate treatment centres and programmes for young offenders (there were approximately 100 at the peak of this initiative) as custodial alternatives
(unfortunately, funding for these was reduced by the end of that decade).

The Criminal Justice Act 1988 further restricted the criteria for the use of custodial disposals for young offenders (beyond those listed in the earlier Criminal Justice Act of 1982).
Under the 1988 Act custody was to be given as a last resort for the most serious and dangerous young offenders. The Act also re-named custodial facilities for young law breakers
to 'young offender institutions'. This Act thus further consolidated a trend towards

non-custodial disposals that started earlier in the 1980s. Fionda (2005) argues that this tendency was given further impetus firstly by youth justice practitioner's pro-active creation of diversionary schemes (including the development in some local teams an early form the current youth conditional caution under the title of 'caution-plus' interventions for repeat non-serious offenders) and secondly by a growing acceptance among magistrates at that time of the damaging impact upon the young person of an incarcerative disposal.

The Children Act 1989 placed a duty upon local authorities to establish diversionary schemes; attendance at these schemes could be ordered as part of a court sentence. The Act also required social service departments to provide alternatives to secure accommodation remands for young people awaiting trial.

The Criminal Justice Act 1991 represented an unusual fusing of various approaches. In terms of sentencing policy generally (adults and juveniles) the Act can be regarded as a move towards justice ideas of proportionality in sentencing (including fines). However, welfare-oriented provisions for young offenders are in evidence by a number of measures introduced by that Act (Gibson, 1994). This Act established a statutory model for sentencing youths and adults based on the notion of *proportionality*. The Act also introduced reforms that were specific to young law breakers that amounted to a consolidation of a trend away from custodial disposals for all but the most serious and/or persistent young offenders. New arrangements were proposed for young people relating to remand and additionally community disposals were strengthened. Significantly, there was an expansion of the upper age limit in the 'youth court' (re-named from 'juvenile court') to include 17 year olds. In addition, the Act stressed parental responsibilities in relation to young people who come before the courts. Further, more robust pre-sentence reports replaced the old social inquiry reports and a report became a statutory requirement where a youth faced a custodial or high-tariff community disposal. Restrictions were placed upon considering the whole of a defendant's sentencing history: when sentencing a strict calculation system was imposed in the form of 'unit fines'. Lastly, section 95 of the Act introduced statistical monitoring of the criminal justice system with a view to identifying any areas of disproportional of treatment in relation to sex and/or racial background.

The Criminal Justice Act 1991 was the culmination of several years of discussion led by the then Home Secretary, Douglas Hurd. A twin-track or bifurcated approach to all offenders (both youth and adult) was mooted in a consultation paper published in 1988 entitled *Punishment, Custody and the Community*. Fionda (2005) alleges that this paper clearly favoured the extended use of community disposals and a minimal approach to custodial disposals. Twin approaches were discussed: Track A – custody – should only be used for serious and dangerous offenders, while Track B – strengthened non custodial disposals – should be used where incarceration was not regarded as necessary for retribution and/or incapacitation. Non-incarcerative responses were regarded as particularly suitable for young offenders who, when compared to adult criminals the consultation paper alleged, were more 'likely to grow out of crime' (Home Office, 1988: 15). It is arguable that part of the motivation behind this dual-pronged approach was linked to concerns about the escalating cost of the criminal justice system and in particular the cost of incarcerative disposals. A hint of the birth of the *managerial* approach to youth crime management is evident in the rationale behind this bifurcated agenda as outlined in the consultation paper.

The doctrine of proportionality, introduced in statutory form by this Act, was viewed as a pivotal principle and was arguably based on the philosophy of *just deserts*, as outlined in the white paper, published a year before the Act was passed. A duty was placed on sentencers to undertake an assessment of the severity of the offence(s) to be dealt with and to pass a sentence that was 'directly related to the seriousness of the offence' (Home Office, 1990). Fionda asserts that previous legislations had led to confusion among sentencers as to which of the conventional principles of sentencing (rehabilitation, retribution, incapacitation or deterrence) they should prioritise. The Criminal Justice Act 1991 moved away from this pick and mix style of justice, from an *'à la carte' cafeteria to a 'prix fixe' system . . . where proportionality is the leading determinant for sentencing* (Fionda, 2005, p142).

The Criminal Justice Act 1991 introduced measures directly targeted at young offenders. Significantly these included: reducing the maximum custodial sentence in a Young Offender Institution to 12 months (excluding very serious offences that were covered by section 53 of the Children and Young Persons Act 1933 – now covered by the 'grave crimes' procedures sections 90 and 91 of Powers of the Criminal Courts (Sentencing) Act 2000); raising the minimum age that a young person could be sentenced to a custodial punishment to 15; expanding community sentences for 16 and 17 year olds (probation, community service and combination orders available as high-level community disposals for this age group); and creating a duty on local authorities to develop new remand arrangements (including remand fostering) for 15 and 16 year olds. Despite the latter requirement, alternatives to secure and custodial remands are still infrequently used due to a lack of alternatives available. This is arguably in direct contravention of the United Nations Convention on the Rights of the Child 1989 and our Human Rights Act 1998.

With regards to parental responsibilities, in essence the Act placed statutory duties on parents and carers which were obligatory on parents/carers of under 16s and at the discretion of the court for parents/carers of 16 and 17 year olds. Specifically, section 56 required parents/carers to attend court, section 57 placed a duty on parents/carers to pay any financial penalties imposed on the young person (under the newly introduced 'unit fine' system that imposed strict criteria for calculation) and section 58 created a parental bindover (up to a value of £1000) whereby a parent/carer would be obliged to surrender a set amount to the court should they fail to exercise proper care and control over their youngster. Section 58 was expanded by the Criminal Justice and Public Order Act 1994 that further extended the bindover provision to include imposing a parental bindover to ensure their child's compliance with a community order.

Ironically, perhaps, certain more general provisions of the Criminal Justice Act 1991 regarding proportionality of sentencing were not received well by the more conservative magistrates who seemed to believe in a type of 'welfarism' that was expressed in individualised disposals and who felt that their discretionary powers to sentence the offender (rather than the offence) had been severely curtailed. As a result of these criticisms, the Criminal Justice Act 1993 removed the classicist tariff-based restrictions placed by the 1991 Act on those sentencing, in both adult and youth courts, and allowed the full offending history of the defendant to be taken into account when deciding an appropriate disposal. Also, offences committed on bail were to be regarded as an aggravating factor, and the unit fine system was abolished.

A justice oriented backlash was developing and various academics (Fionda, 2005, Hendrick, 2002 and 2006, Jenks, 1996) have accepted that one case in 1993 changed the direction of youth justice policy and public opinion in relation to young offenders. The case involved the killing of a toddler, James Bulger by two 10-year-old boys. The public outcry (largely media fuelled) that followed this case led to a 'moral panic' (Cohen, 1973) about the law breaking behaviour of children and young people. Indeed Jenks (1996) argued that the case led to the 'death' of childhood innocence and the subsequent 'demonisation' of youth. The popular press reflected this discontent and the Conservative government at that time was being accused of being 'soft' on crime.

From that point onwards the tide of youth justice turned. Children were no longer pure and incorrupt; they were capable of the greatest evils. Hendrick (2002) argued that images of childhood became readjusted: we abandoned the 'romantic' model of childhood (that children were born innocent and so needed protection from a corrupt society) and adopted the 'evangelical' model – they were born capable of evil and so needed to be firmly controlled. Media stories about young offenders who were allegedly being treated 'softly' by the juvenile justice system swayed public and political opinion towards an era of 'getting tough' on youth criminality.

The Bulger case eventually led to the abolition of the presumption of innocence for 10–13 year olds in the Crime and Disorder Act 1998. As a result, the Criminal Justice and Public Order Act 1994 arguably represented a politically motivated lurch towards a more punitive response in relation to children and young offenders. The use of police detention and secure remand was introduced for those as young as 12 years old; secure training centres were to be established as a custodial sentence for persistent offenders aged 12 and over; the maximum young offender institution sentence was increased to two years; and the 'grave crimes' procedure became operational from the age of 10.

This statute was followed up by a Home Office circular (Home Office, 1994), which officially restricted the use of more than one caution for young offenders and later by the Crime (Sentences) Act 1997 which continued the tidal flow of pro-justice measures. This Act extended electronic tagging to those under 16 as part of a curfew order; allowed judges and magistrates to lift reporting restrictions in cases concerning young defendants; permitted the application of a community sentence for offences that would not otherwise reach the community disposal threshold in cases where a young person had committed a series of previous petty offences and/or not paid fines; and allowed convictions incurred while 17 or under to be taken into account when imposing the criteria for the application of new mandatory sentences for 18 year olds and over.

This was the last major piece of youth justice law-making under the then Conservative government. I will examine the policy debates of the mid-1990s and the 'New Labour' transformation of youth justice practice and more recent initiatives in Chapter 4. In Chapter 8 I will analyse recent proposals for reforming youth justice initiated by the Coalition government from 2010 to publication.

CHAPTER SUMMARY

In this chapter we have examined the various theoretical perspectives of youth justice that have developed over the last one hundred years. We analysed, first, the traditional philosophies of justice and welfare and noted both the contrasting nature of these approaches and their historical dominance of youth justice theory. We then went on to trace the emergence of other philosophies that have been developed (or recognised) by various academics over the more recent history of youth justice policy. There now seems to be a myriad of approaches and analyses of the juvenile justice system, each one backed by evidence from examination of policy by various academics. Though this may appear to be a theoretical maze through which students and practitioners of youth justice are left to wander, the variety of approaches has certainly enriched contemporary debates about ways of addressing youth criminality. Last, we took a short historical tour through the development of youth justice legislation. There we saw no evidence of a consistent approach to tackling juvenile criminality being adopted by successive governments. However, friction between the dominant philosophies of justice and welfare was notable in policy debates and legislative content over the course of the last century.

FURTHER READING

Case, S and Haines, K (2009) *Understanding youth justice: Risk-focused research, policy and practice.* Cullompton: Willan.

This book provides a comprehensive critique of risk assessment in the field of youth justice.

Fionda, J (2005) *Devils and angels: Youth policy and crime.* Oxford: Hart.

This book provides a comprehensive analysis of the history of youth justice policy.

Muncie, J (2009) *Youth and crime*, 3rd edition. London: Sage.

This text provides a critical analysis of a wide range of issues surrounding young people, disorder and crime.

Smith, R (2007) *Youth justice: Ideas, policy, practice*, 2nd edition. Cullompton: Willan.

This book analyses changes in youth justice theory and policy, as well as examining various government initiatives relating to youth criminality.

Chapter 3

Criminological theories in relation to young people who offend

Jane Pickford

ACHIEVING A SOCIAL WORK DEGREE

This chapter will help you begin to meet the following National Occupational Standards.
Key Role 1: Prepare for and work with individuals, families, carers, groups and communities to assess their needs and circumstances
- Review case notes and other relevant literature.
- Evaluate all information to identify the best form of initial involvement.

It will also introduce you to the following academic standards as set out in the social work subject benchmark statement:
5.1.1 Social work services, service users and carers.
5.1.4 Social work theory.
5.5.3 Analysis and synthesis.

Introduction

Having examined theories in relation to perspectives of youth justice in the previous chapter, here I analyse other hypotheses that are useful in youth justice practice. These theories relate to understanding why young people commit crimes and take part in anti-social or delinquent behaviour. The ideas have been developed by criminologists and study of them requires us to undertake a basic theoretical tour of some of the mainstream criminological theories. Due to constraints of space and considering that you are being trained to be reflective in your studies, the mainstream theories are outlined in their basic form without critiques. You can assess their usefulness yourself in terms of how they might assist your future practice as you go through them.

Major theories of criminology

Mainstream theories of criminology will inform your analysis of the causal factors of youth offending when preparing pre-sentence reports for courts. The perspectives will be traced in chronological order relating to historical development.

Classicism

In tracing the genealogy of criminology, it is generally accepted that modern criminological thoughts can be tracked to writings of the eighteenth century. Mannheim (1960) cites Cesare Beccaria and his classical school of criminology (as outlined in *On Crimes and Punishments*, first published in 1764), as the pioneer of criminological thought. However, it could be said to be misleading to describe classical and neo-classical schools of thought as criminology, as classicism does not concern itself with aetiological (causational) questions in an empirical way (Garland, 2002). The classicist theories can be described as 'pre-criminology', in that they were concerned with philosophical questions about the nature of society and the nature of human behaviour, and were based on speculation as to both.

Relating the justice and welfare perspectives examined in Chapter 2 to theoretical criminology, it can be argued that the philosophy of the classical school of thought supports the justice approach to youth justice, as it views offending behaviour as basically a matter of choice. Further, notions of proportionality of crime and sanction are central to the justice model of youth justice, as are beliefs in the rationality of the offender and the deterrent value of sentences, and all these ideas are to be found in the classicist paradigm. Splitting the classical approach into principles, Beccaria asserted that:

- All people are free but are by nature self-seeking – they will seek out pleasure and try to avoid pain – and so all people are capable of committing a crime if they think that crime would benefit them and that the benefits would outweigh the costs.

- However, there exists a consensus in society regarding the need to protect personal welfare and property.

- To prevent anti-social behaviour, all people freely enter into the 'social contract' whereby they abandon some of their freedoms in return for protection from the state.

- Education (via the Enlightenment) helps to prevent crime. Crime is essentially irrational behaviour. Beccaria advocated that laws should be made more understandable. He thought that education of young minds would be more effective in decreasing crime rather than mere coercion: *leading them towards virtue . . . and directing them away from evil* (1963, p62).

- Punishment must be used in order to deter people from violating the rights of others and to demonstrate the irrationality of law-breaking behaviour. The state has been given the right to punish via the 'social contract' and punishment must be prompt, certain and public in order to act as a deterrent.

- Punishment must be proportionate to the interests violated (i.e. the harm done) not for reformation or retribution.

- Laws and legal procedures should be few and simple and legal procedures should adhere to a strict process so that everyone is treated equally. Discretion in sentencing should be avoided.

- All people are responsible for their actions; people are rational actors, choice-makers. There should, therefore, be no excuses or mitigations for criminal behaviour. (However, under neo-classicist revisionism, lack of criminal capacity of young children was acknowledged and mitigation was allowed, but only as explanation, not as an excuse for criminal behaviour.)

The classical school of criminology has had a major impact on the way our criminal justice system operates, particularly adult justice, but also upon the justice oriented features of our juvenile justice system. See Figure 1.1 in Chapter 1 for an analysis of the overlaps between classicism and youth justice theory and practice.

The positivist approach

The positivist school of thought, in contrast to the classicist paradigm, can be regarded as a critique of the legal system, viewing it as an inept means of dealing with crime as a social problem because of its focus on the morality of acts rather than the dangerousness or reformability of the offender. The focus for positivism is upon the person of the criminal. The studies undertaken by positivist researchers have represented an attempt to present empirical facts in order to confirm their ideas that crime was determined, rather than an act of individual choice that was the exercise of free will. The early positivists believed that they could scientifically prove that certain identifiable factors caused a person's criminality. Using this approach, the offender is destined to become a criminal due to:

- Biological or genetic factors (biological positivism); or/and

- Psychological factors (psychological positivism); or/and

- Social or environmental factors (sociological positivism).

A positivist believes that crime is not chosen but caused largely by factors beyond the offender's control. In essence, the belief is that offenders simply can't help themselves. Certain genetic, psychological or environmental factors have influenced their behaviour and the existence of these factors means that offenders are almost pre-programmed to become criminals. With this in mind, one of the great contradictions of the positivist approach to crime is its focus on reformation and rehabilitation. Taylor et al. (1973) refer to this as the 'therapeutic paradox': if the criminal is totally determined, how is reform possible? While this has sometimes been seen as a confusion, the argument has been advanced that what is necessary is an alteration of the determining factors.

It could be argued that the classical and the positivist approach are oppositional. Further, the classicist theory seems to support the justice approach to youth offending (crime is chosen, the offender should take full responsibility for his or her actions and punishments should be proportionate) while the positivist paradigm seems to support the welfare approach (crime is caused by a variety of possible factors, these factors should be taken into account regarding culpability and individualised treatment packages are required to address these causational factors).

A positivistic system of justice requires a broad range of possible sentences/treatments so that professional discretion can be used to choose the disposal most likely to produce reformation. It is arguable that the Crime and Disorder Act 1998 and the Youth Justice and

Criminal Evidence Act 1999 and the Criminal Justice and Immigration Act 2008 created a vast range of possible disposals for young people who come before the penal system. The youth rehabilitation order alone has 18 possible content combinations (see Chapter 4). This, coupled with a focus on preventionism, indicates positivist oriented approach within the youth justice system.

Matza (1964) has argued that there are three identifiable major assumptions within the positivistic framework. These are:

- *Determinism*. This is the idea that criminal behaviour is caused by factors outside the individual's control. As noted earlier these could be biological, psychological, or socio-logical causes of behaviour.

- *Differentiation*. Criminals are viewed as different from non-criminals due to their biological constitution, psychological traits or socialisation process/environmental influences.

- *Pathology*. Criminals are viewed as different from non-criminals because something has gone 'wrong' biologically, psychologically or sociologically.

In summary, therefore, the positivist school promised to utilise science in order to objectively discover the causes of criminality and provide a cure. While a thorough examination of bio-logical and psychological positivism would be very interesting, it is beyond the scope of this book. Some of the other theories of criminology below (ecology, anomie and subcultures) fall within the third category of sociological positivism. See Figure 1.1 in Chapter 1 for an analysis of the overlaps between positivism and youth justice theory and practice.

ACTIVITY **3.1**

Discuss the crime control measures that might be used in a youth justice system based purely on (a) classicist principles, and (b) positivist principles.

COMMENT

Crime control measures based on an acceptance of classicist explanations of youth criminality would include practical crime control measures that are aimed at reducing the chances of /opportunities for a crime taking place (called 'target hardening') and/ or increasing the chances of the perpetrator being apprehended and, therefore, the deterrent factor (e.g. CCTV). Students should list and discuss possible crime control measures for crimes such as domestic burglary, street robbery and internet crime. Addressing crime using a positivist perspective would involve analysing the offender in order to locate crime triggers within the offender or his/her environment and tailoring a package of interventions to specifically target those triggers.

Ecology or crime and the environment

Ecological theory is basically concerned with the geography of criminality. The original theory has been developed extensively by various criminologists and is utilised practically within the youth justice industry in terms of crime mapping, local crime plans, target-ing youth crime action plans and identification of crime 'hotspots'. The theory tries to explain why crime and disorder often seem to be concentrated in particular locations – frequently inner-city areas. It examines what it might be about the nature and characteristics of that area (and the people who inhabit it) that appears to precipitate criminal and anti-social behaviour.

The zonal hypothesis

Park (1936, Park and Burgess, 1925) Thrasher (1927), Wirth (1928) and Shaw (1931, Shaw and McKay, 1942) developed a theory about the ecology of crime. They studied the geographical development of different groups in relation to their evolution in the context of the city of Chicago. They used the metaphor of the city as a living organism and examined ecology from the biological perspective of habitat. They asserted that people displayed the aggregation characteristics of animals in their habitat. The theory of ecology was a segmental view of the problem of crime and incivilities in the context of the city. Park contended that the growth of a city is natural rather than planned and that its differential development merely reflects the different tasks each area is called upon to perform. Using the metaphor of plant ecology, he contended that areas of the city experience changes much like a process of balancing in nature, where a new species may move into an area and then come to characterise that area in a process of invasion, domination and succession.

In devising the 'zonal hypothesis' the Chicago sociologists were responding to their interest in how cities tended to become 'internally differentiated'. They claimed that cities tend to evolve in a series of concentric zones of activity and life (see Figure 3.1).

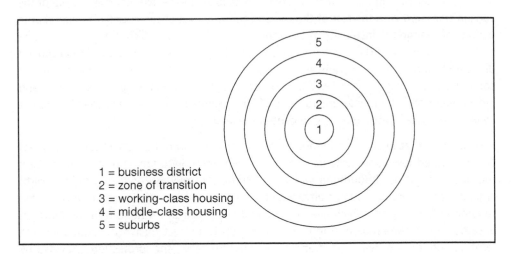

1 = business district
2 = zone of transition
3 = working-class housing
4 = middle-class housing
5 = suburbs

Figure 3.1 Burgess's 'zonal hypothesis'

The sociologists asserted that each of the areas had distinctive characteristics that differentiated them one from another. The areas represented unplanned groupings of similar people, and as such mirror the natural world, where there is a division of species in terms of habitat. The effect of this is to transform a geographical area into a 'neighbourhood', which Park described as a *locality with sentiments, traditions and a history of its own* (1925, p6).

The Chicago sociologists began to fix their attention on the zone in transition. In this area the population was fluid; people would move out as soon as they bettered themselves. Further, the area seemed to have a concentration of what was called 'pathological behaviour', including mental disorder, prostitution, suicide, alcoholism, juvenile mortality, disease, poverty, juvenile delinquency and crime. In examining the characteristics of the zone in transition they discovered that it tended to be an area of cheap rents and poor housing and was home to the most recent groups of immigrants; a succession of ethnic groups tended to live there, and each of these groups seemed in turn to produce similar patterns of behaviour. The area was also characterised by its lack of settled institutions and poor provision of local resources and facilities. The zone was distinguished by what was described as its 'unruly' nature and it tended to house people who were unaccustomed to city life, to America and to one another.

Park found that many of the inhabitants of this area had left very different cultures in order to establish a new lifestyle in a strange and unfamiliar environment. This lack of cohesion was described as 'disorganisation' and 'moral dissensus'. The latter term was later elucidated by Wirth as *the degree to which the members of a society lose their common understanding*, and argued that *the degree to which consensus is undermined, is the measure of a society's state of disorganisation* (1964, p46). This disorganisation was characterised by the fragmented, fluid and anonymous features of urban life.

In examining the internal relationships within the zone in transition, it was noted that inadequate social and economic conditions had led to mistrust and heterogeneity. As populations moved in and out of the area, change became normal: life became unpredictable leading to instability in terms of social cohesion. A focus of the external relationship of the zone in transition with the rest of the city and the wider American society revealed that in periods of change the instability of the zone was exaggerated, which in turn may precipitate a breakdown in social order. This may further lead to the zone in transition becoming dislocated from the larger society and taking on a characteristic of its own (e.g. the Italian community in Chicago in the 1930s). If this occurs, the community becomes isolated and independent and the master institutions of social control (such as law, the church, the courts, the police), become unable to control the area.

Park asserted that in such a community moral habits could not be effectively implanted. People formed few commitments outside of their immediate family or community and thus ideas of any neighbourhood initiative of crime control was doomed to failure. Wirth argued that the proliferation of different ethnic communities in the zone in transition led to 'amoral familiarism', which eventually could transform the zone in transition into an unsettled and unsafe region. Gangs may spring up to protect their own community and territory and impose their own brand of security. However, the 'protection' provided by the gangs only resulted in exacerbating the insecurity of the region.

People who moved to the USA were faced with the problems of both cultural discontinuities and coping with instability in the area in which they lived. Park argued that this was a particular problem for second-generation immigrants; language, custom and tradition could fall into disuse or change its significance or importance. Young second-generation males in particular, he argued, often saw themselves as marginalised from the culture they had left behind, from their family and from America. These boys often created their own social order that would correspond neither to the culture of their parents nor to the wider culture of the USA, but amounted to an order that moved unstably between both. A resort to crime by these young men was seen as a solution to the problems of their exclusion from wider society due to prejudice, lack of opportunity and economic and political impotence. In effect, rebellion was a structural response to deprivation, to growing up in an insecure city environment, deprived of economic control and resources.

The theory of ecology and its zonal hypothesis has been applied by criminologists to cities in the UK (e.g. the Islington crime surveys in the 1980s) and its basic premise is evidenced today in modern crime prevention strategies that utilise the British Crime Survey and crime mapping techniques to directly target criminogenic and anti-social areas. Situational crime prevention strategies aimed at target hardening and increased surveillance are all practical methods of targetting the location of criminality – and they arguably stem from the original ideas of the Chicago school sociologists.

ACTIVITY **3.2**

Apply the 'zonal hypothesis' to a city you are familiar with. Does the 'zone in transition' correspond with known crime hotspots? Are local crime and disorder control mechanisms targeted at that area?

COMMENT

You should examine a map of the city you have chosen (from the internet – you can get a crime map of your area from www.police.uk) and then draw the zonal chart over it to see if the crime hotspots fit with this original hypothesis developed in Chicago.

Anomie

In order to examine the question of what factors cause some people to become criminals and others to be law abiding, Merton utilised Durkheim's (1893, 1897) conception of anomie as a state of normlessness and used it as a springboard for developing a general theory of crime. He borrowed Durkheim's notion of infinite aspiration and linked this to dissymmetry between social culture in the USA and social structure in developing his theory of anomie. The basis of his work can be seen in his 1938 article, 'Social structure and anomie'. However, one crucial difference between the ideas of Durkheim and Merton is that Durkheim asserted that human aspirations are not socially learned, as Merton contended, but are innate and natural. Merton was concerned with *how some social structures exert a definite pressure upon certain persons in the society to engage in non-conformist rather than conformist conduct* (1938, p672).

Goals and means

In examining American society, Merton noticed the social pressure (which he called 'strain') people experienced in terms of their desire to achieve financial success and status. He asserted that the capitalist nature of the USA, coupled with the all-pervading notion of meritocracy, produced an image of America as the land of opportunities where anyone, no matter how lowly their background, could achieve success with hard work and enterprise. He called this the 'American Dream'. Merton used two concepts as the basis of his theorising:

- 'Cultural goals' he described as people's aspirations and desire to succeed. He asserted that such goals are socially learned. In America the emphasis was on monetary success.

- 'Institutional means' he defined as the availability and distribution of legitimate structural opportunities to achieve the cultural goals (e.g. a good education, employment, career progression, equality of opportunity, social and economic inclusion).

In a society where there is an emphasis on goals without sufficient provision of equal opportunities to the means of achieving those goals, people may develop a willingness to use any means to achieve the goals. Merton said that the *most feasible procedure, whether legitimate or not, is preferred to the institutionally prescribed conduct. As this process continues, the integration of society becomes tenuous and anomie ensues* (1938, p674).

It is possible for societies to overemphasise either the cultural goals or the institutional means. Merton alleged that in the USA there is an over-emphasis on achieving the cultural goals, without sufficient attention to the institutional means. He asserted that there is an overwhelming desire for financial prosperity and material gain but that the institutional means of fulfilling those goals are not always available or are denied to a substantial proportion of the population. Merton's so-called ideal situation, where there is an equilibrium within society between the goals and the means, implies that either an equality of opportunity is provided by the government in order to enable people to achieve their desires, or that the learned cultural goals are constricted, so that people's aspirations do not fix upon the unobtainable. The problem with the first position is that as in a capitalist society greed is endemic and addictive, there will always be winners and losers (we can't all be multi-millionaires). In relation to the second proposition, that people would have to be socialised to fix their cultural goals or aspirations upon the achievable, implies notions of Victorian principles of everyone knowing their proper place and of a structured hierarchical society.

Reaction types

According to Merton, deviant behaviour results when cultural goals are accepted (people would like to be financially successful and to have status), but access to these goals is structurally limited (e.g. a well-paid job and career structure is unavailable). It is this 'strain' that Merton described as a state of anomie. He went on to outline possible reactions or adaptations or types of people who may be socially produced due to this strain, which may occur when the goals that have been internalised cannot be legitimately attained. These possible adaptations will occur when the means of a society are not distributed fairly due to the political structure of a society.

- *The conformist* – someone who has accepted the goals of society and is able to achieve them by legitimate means.

- *The innovator* – a person who has accepted the goals but is unable to achieve them by legitimate means and so resorts to illegitimate means in order to achieve them (i.e. the criminal).

- *The ritualist* – an individual who has not accepted societal goals but adopts only legitimate ways of behaviour.

- *The retreatist* – This is the person who neither accepts the cultural goals of society nor has the means of achieving them. Using the language of his day, Merton described these people as 'drop-outs' or 'tramps' and also included within this category alcoholics and addicts.

- *The rebel* – an individual who has rejected the goals and the legitimate means of achieving these goals and seeks to replace them by a different system (the political activist).

Merton's prime concern was with the innovator, the person who uses illegitimate means to achieve their goals: (e.g. a person who, for instance, achieves financial success by theft and robbery rather than obtaining a well-paid job, investing in a savings account, etc). He asserted that inequalities in the social structure encourage criminality as people are indoctrinated to strive for financial and material success but are denied the means of achieving it. It is the lack of co-ordination of the goals and means that in Merton's view leads to a state of anomie. Merton stated that the dream of financial success encourages everyone to have *exaggerated anxieties, hostilities, neurosis and anti-social behaviour* (1938, p680).

ACTIVITY **3.3**

Discuss whether there is a 'British Dream'. If so, is it the same as the 'American Dream'? Can strain theory/anomie explain criminality among young people in Britain?

Subcultural theory

The research of the subcultural theorists essentially amounted to extensions of Merton's approach to explaining deviance – an extension that involved the investigation of youth gangs in urban areas. In order to attempt to make sense of even the most hedonistic non-utilitarian youth delinquency, sociologists began to develop the notion that, far from these actions being disorganised and senseless, they did indeed make sense in that the behaviour was a result of some sort of adherence to an alternative cultural pattern.

I will briefly examine a few of the ideas of the 'founding fathers' of the subcultural explanation of delinquency.

Albert Cohen

In accepting the basic tenets of Merton's strain theory as a basis of his theorising about the development of gangs, Albert Cohen in *Delinquent Boys* (1955) attempted to examine the features of the dominant mainstream culture that might lead young men into committing delinquent acts. Cohen also concured with Merton's basic notion that delinquency could be related to impediments to success in conventional terms, which lower-class males in particular may experience.

Cohen examined delinquent subcultures in lower-class life and concluded that the patterns of behaviour he observed within these groups were very different from the larger dominant culture. He proposed that gang delinquency was a group solution to status frustrations that may be experienced by lower-class males. These boys, who were denied status in middle-class terms, would be led to seek status through alternative means, in this case via the gang. Essentially, Cohen proposed that boys who experience similar problems in relation to their lack of success in conventional terms would group together in order to resolve their somewhat masculine problems of failing to achieve status in normatively accepted ways. They would develop a subculture in which they could achieve status by creating their own alternative social order. He argued that criminal behaviour, like any other behaviour, is learned behaviour transmitted by interaction and communication with others largely within interpersonal groups.

In relation to those juveniles belonging to subcultural groups, Cohen asserted that they displayed six prevalent features. They were

- *Non-utilitarian*. The boys might undertake activities that seem nonsensical as they would lead to no particular gains, e.g. breaking a window, or stealing goods and disposing of the items.

- *Malicious*. The boys felt excitement in observing rules being broken, taboos being challenged and viewing other people being disconcerted by their activities and destructiveness.

- *Negativistic*. This was a general trend to invert the values of the wider culture, e.g. whereas studying and doing well at school would be viewed as 'good' by mainstream society, this might be viewed as 'bad' by the boys in the gang.

- *Versatile*. The boys showed an ability to become involved in a variety of delinquent activities and anti-social behaviour, including committing criminal offences.

- *Short-run hedonism*. This included the need for instant gratification without any assessment of the long-term effects of their activities.

- *Group autonomy*. The group viewed itself as being separate from the wider society and there was an acknowledgement among the boys that the gang was to be their first priority.

Cohen asserted that the gang was made up of like individuals *with similar problems of adjustment* to society (1955, p59). Working-class boys become dependent upon their peer groups when they encounter status problems through not being able to adhere to predominant middle-class norms or values. They turn to the gang for status when they encounter middle-class values that would classify them as failures. In effect, Cohen alleged that boys who form into subcultures do so as a means of hitting back at a society that has branded them as worthless; this is what Downes and Rock call *the D Stream's Revenge* (2003, p146). According to Cohen, *the hallmark of the delinquent subculture is the explicit and wholesale repudiation of middle class standards and the adoptions of their very antithesis* (1955, p129).

The gang is created due to 'reaction formation' against middle-class values: the gang not only violates middle-class norms, it *expresses contempt for a way of life by making its opposite a criterion of status* (1955, p134).

Cloward and Ohlin
In *Delinquency and Opportunity* (1960) Cloward and Ohlin suggested that class was a primary element in the formation of delinquent gangs, while criticising Cohen's emphasis on the negativistic nature of delinquent gang activity. They examined subcultural formation and subcultural group types and argued that the type of gang that will develop in

a particular area will be dictated by the opportunities available, the pressures suffered and the situation in which the young men find themselves. They asserted that all subcultures are not alike and that there will be different forms of adaptation to strain, which will result in different outcomes.

They focused specifically on urban gangs, asserting that the particular strains caused by urbanality lead to a greater prevalence of gangs in city areas. They contended that there were three types of delinquent subcultures:

- *Criminal*. This type of gang may take part in property-related offences as a means of gaining success and prestige. They tend to form where delinquents and criminal adults are closely connected. The adult criminal will provide a role model for the juvenile and help develop their criminal skills. Stable patterns of relationship are present and often networks may develop to facilitate law-breaking behaviour. In such a gang, there appears to be an acceptance of a level of criminal behaviour, which usually focuses upon theft and other property offences.

- *Conflict*. This type of subculture displays violent behaviour as an expression of frustration due to the absence of conventional opportunities and stable relationships, either criminal or non-criminal. Violence is a symbol of discontent, which is used to gain status and to exhibit courage. The frustration experienced by the boys leads to chaotic displays of intermittent violence.

- *Retreatist*. This grouping is made up of young people who are unable to achieve success in either legitimate or illegitimate ways and who resort to alcohol or drugs instead of violence as a way of 'leaving' mainstream society in which they have not had much success. This group is reminiscent of Merton's category of the retreatist; of the 'double failure' who rejects both the goals and means of society.

Cloward and Ohlin asserted that the lower-class gang is formed as a response to the problems faced by lower-class males due to the acceptance of culturally induced goals and access to limited means in order to achieving those goals. Moreover, lower-class males do not, they alleged, accede to middle-class values (as Cohen asserted); instead, they refuse to accept the legitimacy of middle-class norms. The gang is essentially a 'collective adaptation' to strain and is formed due to 'solidarity' of situation among lower-class males.

Walter Miller

In his article 'Lower class culture as a generating milieu of gang delinquency', Miller (1958) presented a different picture of subcultural formation. He challenged Cohen's assumptions that boys from the lower classes form gangs due to frustrations they feel about not being able to achieve success in middle-class terms. On the contrary, Miller alleged that these subcultures form as an attempt to conform to lower-class traditions, not as a reaction to middle-class traditions. The subculture does not amount to a response to middle-class norms, but in fact is a positive attempt to achieve status in lower-class terms. Thus the gang is normal, not oppositional: Miller argued that life among the lower-classes displayed certain key features or 'focal concerns' – issues that receive a high level of commitment among the lower-class communities. He contended that these 'focal concerns' can be used to characterise lower-class life, but that they are particularly noticeable among lower-class delinquent gangs. These can be outlined as follows:

- *Trouble*. The tendency to conflict with institutions of authority as a way of generating status also involves the use of physical confrontation, sexual activity and the use of drugs.

- *Toughness*. The display of manliness, prowess, physical ability and courage is used when young men feel the necessity to assert their masculinity.

- *Smartness*. The ability to outwit others without being tricked oneself is a skill that can lead to more status than displays of toughness.

- *Excitement*. This is a concern with generating excitement by drinking, drug-taking, gambling, sex, etc., and is used as a means of escape from the boredom that may otherwise dominate their lives.

- *Fate, fortune and luck*. This relates to feelings that they are not able to change their lifestyle and that their lives are often subject to forces beyond their control.

- *Autonomy*. There is a resentment of the restrictions that may be put on their behaviour by institutions of authority and a desire to be liberated from any external controls.

Miller argued that, by adhering to these lower-class focal concerns and cultural patterns, legal norms might be violated. Also, law-breaking may produce more immediate results with less effort – it might be easier to steal than to get a highly paid job. Essentially, Miller asserted that illegal behaviour is the expected response to certain situations of lower-class life.

Matza and Sykes

Perhaps the most influential work of Matza and Sykes is *Techniques of Neutralisation* (1957). They asserted that delinquents often rationalise their criminal behaviour in advance; they present justifications for committing infractions of the law that function as defences or valid excuses for the law-breaking act using their own personal assessment. Thus, Matza and Sykes proposed that delinquency is not in opposition to mainstream society but in fact amounts to an 'apologetic failure'.

These justifications, called 'techniques of neutralisation', can be outlined as follows:

- *Denial of responsibility*. The young person contends that their behaviour is beyond their control – that it is the result of a deprived background, poor parenting, etc.

- *Denial of injury*. The young person argues that no one has really been hurt – for example, in the case of a burglary, the person can claim the money back from an insurance company.

- *Denial of victim*. This is the idea that the victim somehow deserved what happened to them, or that the criminal actions were in some way justified – for example, the victim was foolish to be walking home late at night on their own with their handbag open and their purse visible, or that the victim will quickly get over the incident.

- *Condemnation of the condemners*. The young person criticises those who condemn him/her as hypocrites, as spiteful, or as corrupt.

- *Appeal to higher loyalties*. This is the notion that the young person must support the group or gang, even if this necessitates breaking the law.

Sykes and Matza also discussed the view that delinquency is made attractive by the exaggeration of what they call 'subterranean values'. These include three factors: the seeking out of excitement; the disdain for routine work; and the interlinked values of toughness and masculinity. They argued that these 'subterranean values' are visible throughout society and are in fact leisure ideas, but that the young delinquent will exaggerate these. The combination of these three elements, they argue, encourage lower-class males in the 'limbo' of adolescence to manufacture excitement by rule-breaking.

As noted earlier, the subcultural theories above represent the founding ideas about gang activity were regarded as seminal works and provided a springboard for many studies that followed over the last 50 to 60 years. Numerous studies of subcultural activity were undertaken over that period. The 1960s was viewed as a period where youths became politicised (and criminalised). Young people across America and Europe were taking part in political protests and demonstrations against the old oppressive systems that their parents experienced – challenging class, race, gender and sexual oppression as well as government decisions to go to war. Ideas of youth counterculture and fears about drug use by youngsters (Young, 1971) were gaining popular momentum in the press. In the UK, the first 'moral panic' about youth criminality and subcultural activity was created. Stan Cohen (1973), provided a study of Bank Holiday events in Clacton, Margate and Hastings in 1964 (where groups of young people converged on seaside towns) and produced a theory of deviancy amplification in relation to the handling of the event by the authorities. His comprehensive account examines the initial event; the over-reaction of control agencies; the primary deviations of some of the attendees at the seaside towns; the heavy surveillance and heavy-handed responses of the police; the subsequent moral panic fuelled by obsessive media reporting on the events; the creation of two sub-cultures as distinct grouping (the 'mods' and 'rockers'); and the consequential adjustment of self-definitions in order to accommodate the result of the institutional over-reaction.

Some of the most influential contributions in this country from the 1970s include the work undertaken in this area by the Birmingham Centre for Contemporary Cultural Studies (see especially Hall and Jefferson, 1976). Studies of youth subcultures identified groups of stylised formations rather than distinctly criminal cultures (Hebdige 1979). By the 1980s it became apparent that much subcultural work had failed to take account of gender disparities (women and girls had been neglected by criminologists) or diversity issues in gang formation. From the early 1990s the rave and acid house movements again led to a revival by the press of ideas relating to presumed links between youth partying and drugs (Redhead, 1993). Late-modernity has witnessed a growth of polycultural styles and subjective expressions of identity and lifestyles that transcend/elude the traditional deterministic analyses of the founding fathers examined at the start of this section. Cultural criminology has, therefore, supplanted subcultural criminology (see Ferrell et al., 2004) and focuses on transgression and criminality in the context of cultures and life experiences.

> ### ACTIVITY 3.4
>
> 1. *To what extent do subcultural theories help us to understand some types of youth criminality?; and*
>
> 2. *Discuss whether we can use subcultural perspectives to explain crime perpetrated by girl gangs.*
>
> #### COMMENT
>
> *It has been argued by Leonard (1982) and others that the traditional research on gangs that were undertaken by the American theorists cannot be applied to an examination of girl gangs at all. Though not explicit, in reality all the research focused on male gang members. This 'gender blindness' in theoretical criminology was typical of mainstream theorists and results in much of conventional criminology being inapplicable when we examine questions of criminality in relation to women and girls. Do you agree?*

The labelling perspective

In Chapter 2 we noted that youth justice services grew rapidly from the 1960s onwards and that more young people have been drawn into the net of youth justice services. Over the last decade we have witnessed a massive increase in the numbers of workers within the youth justice industry (though numbers of staff might diminish under recent coalition cutbacks). This professional entrepreneurialism is resulting in an extension of the labelling process to ever increasing numbers of young people. Why as a society are we producing ever more young people who are coming into contact with the broad sweep of youth justice and anti-social agencies? How will this impact upon their lives: upon their image of themselves, how others perceive them and upon their life chances? Let's examine the ideas of two of criminology's most prominent labelling theorists in an attempt to answer these questions.

Lemert's primary and secondary deviations

Lemert, in Social Pathology (1951), examined the meaning of action upon the actor and others within the subject's interpersonal and social groups. He noted that while some types of interaction may lead to the actor normalising their behaviour and therefore regarding the behaviour as insignificant in the context of their personality, some interactions may lead the actor to fully take on board the self-perception of being labelled as deviant. Such a process, which Lemert argued promotes secondary deviation, is a kind of realignment or adjustment of self-identity based upon symbolic reactions. As a result of this a secondary deviation may be sparked off; the person now labelled as deviant will realign themselves within this definition and this may provoke the development of defensive or antagonistic feelings due to the isolating effects of the social stigma.

Lemert asserted that primary deviance has many causes but secondary deviance results from being labelled until one accepts the deviant role. This is an eight-stage process:

- The commission of the act of primary deviance.

- Social penalties that follow from this act.

- Possible further primary deviations.

- This results in stronger social penalties and possibly isolation and rejection.

- Further deviation may take place, which may lead to the formation of resentment, anger and hostility focused upon those who are administering sanctions.

- A crisis may then ensue in relation to the 'tolerance quotient' of society which may be expressed in terms of taking formal action against the deviant and stigmatising them.

- The deviant behaviour may be strengthened as a reaction to the stigmatisation and the application of sanctions.

- The person may eventually accept the label of 'deviant' and their self-image may be adjusted in order to accommodate this new social status.

Lemert argued that primary deviation refers to the initial acts of (usually) a juvenile that may provoke societal reaction; he contended that such primary acts of deviation may occur at random or have been precipitated by a diversity of factors. It is important to note that Lemert stressed that the initial act of deviance will have little effect upon the person's self-concept. However, secondary deviation has a direct causational link with the societal reaction and flows directly from it. Thus Lemert proposed that secondary deviations result as a realignment or reconsideration of self-concept. His thesis involved an acceptance that secondary deviation may lead to the creation of a new self-image, which is often overtly recognisable: *Objective evidences of this change will be found in the symbolic appurtenances of the new role, in clothes, speech, posture and mannerisms, which in some cases heightened social visibility* (1951, p76).

Becker's outsiders

In his book *Outsiders: Studies in the sociology of deviance* (1963) Becker suggested that societies create deviance by generating and applying rules that cast certain people out of mainstream or normal society. These 'outsiders' are then left to wander beyond the limits of conventionality, suffering the sanctions that are meted out by respectable society and often being forced to adopt an alternative lifestyle as a result of this rejection. Becker did not just focus upon the creation of criminality but specifically investigated the creation of concepts of deviance and concluded that all deviants become the cast-outs of society; these include not only criminals but also those who are mentally ill or have mental disabilities, the homeless, political activists and homosexuals. The labelling theory essentially tackles the processes involved in creating 'difference' as a justification for the use of social and penal sanctions. He said:

> Social rules define situations and the kinds of behaviour appropriate to them, specifying some actions as 'right' and forbidding others as 'wrong'. When a rule is enforced, the person who is supposed to have broken it may be seen as a special kind of person, one who cannot be trusted to live by the rules agreed by the group. He is regarded as an outsider. (p1)

Becker argued that there is no inherent quality to deviance, but that it is purely relative. He stressed that definitions of deviance are variable and asserted that society creates deviance by the application of rules that provide the facility to label and stigmatise those who breach the rules. Thus deviant behaviour is not related to the quality of the behaviour; there is no inherent definition of behaviours that are deviant within all societies. Deviance is a relative concept and is identified solely by the actions that follow the behaviour – the social sanction.

This process of manufacturing a deviant may depend upon societal perceptions of the person who has committed certain acts. Becker notes that boys from the lower classes are more likely to be perceived as delinquent than boys from middle-class backgrounds. Similarly, he alleged that the stigmatisation processes are also more likely to be applied to people from black and minority ethnic groups. Lastly, he noted that crimes committed by companies are not perceived as being as threatening as those committed by individuals, and thus white-collar 'criminals' may avoid social and criminal sanctions. As Becker suggested:

> deviance is not a simple quality, present in some kinds of behaviour and absent in others. Rather, it is the product of a process which involves responses of other people to the behaviour. The same behaviour may be an infraction of the rules at one time and not at another; may be an infraction when committed by one person, but not when committed by another; some rules are broken with impunity, others are not. In short, whether a given act is deviant or not depends in part on the nature of the act . . . and in part on what other people do about it. (1963, p14)

Additionally, Becker maintained that we cannot know whether or not an act is deviant until we have waited to see the reaction to it:

> we must recognise that we cannot know whether a given act will be categorised as deviant until the response of others has occurred. Deviance is not a quality that lies in behaviour itself, but in the interaction between the person who commits an act and those who respond to it. (1963, p14)

Becker conjectured that there is no consensus within society and an absence of homogeneity leads to differing opinions about the acceptability of behaviours. He noted that society is highly differentiated on class, occupational, cultural and ethnic grounds.

Becker, like Lemert, was also interested in examining the effect upon individuals of the application of labels, and of how this may create a deviant career. In relation to this he commented that *one of the most crucial steps in the process of building a stable pattern of deviant behaviour is likely to be the experience of being caught and publicly labelled as deviant* (1963, p31).

In this assertion, Becker echoes Lemert's ideas about the process of 'secondary deviation', whereby the person labelled eventually readjusts their self-concept and views themselves as criminal/deviant. In effect, he/she becomes what the label implies; this process amounts to an adaptation of the popular 'give a dog a bad name' argument. So Becker asserted that the process of labelling is a process which creates a self-fulfilling prophecy and that the formal and informal vehicles of stigmatisation that spring into action following the discovery of certain behaviour is, in effect, a course of action that seeks to *conspire to shape the person in the image people have of him* (1963, p34).

ACTIVITY 3.5

Discuss the following question: To what extent is contact with the youth justice system counter-productive for children and young people who encounter it?

COMMENT

If we accept the ideas of the labelling theorists you have just examined, it could be argued that the youth justice system is indeed counter-productive. Given that (as noted in Chapter 1) almost a third of males come into contact with the criminal justice system during their youth (and those are just the ones who are caught!) we could put forward the proposition that youthful offending is normal for a substantial minority of the male population – so why make so much official fuss about it! Making a fuss leads to these young men getting labelled, getting a criminal record and having their life-chances hampered by the negative stereotyping that follows. Wouldn't a less stigmatising alternative system be preferable?

Radical/Marxist perspective

Becker's insistence that criminality and deviance were essentially social constructs, and that certain groups of people, who just happened to be the least powerful in society, had been singled out for special categorisation and stigmatisation, opened the flood-gates for further critical appraisals that were to challenge the very nature of social order and lead to the politicalisation of crime, deviance and difference. The developments in the late 1960s and early 1970s within the field of sociology of deviance cannot be examined without a brief reference to the political climate in both Europe and the USA at the time. Anti-establishment demonstrations were taking place across Europe and the USA. Students were occupying their universities; Sartre and Foucault were challenging the very foundation of knowledge and power; civil rights marches demonstrated out-rage at the arrogance of the USA in relation to Vietnam; Malcom X represented black indignation and exhaustion at the barbarism of racism and social apartheid; women were angrily marching out of their kitchens; and the Stonewall riots encouraged les-bians and gay men to march out of their closets. All this, together with flower power, Woodstock and free love, challenged the very fabric of the status quo. Things would never be quite the same again.

It was the age of politicalisation, demonstration and rebellion. There was a re-examina-tion of Marxist ideology by sociologists, and they liked what they saw. Demonstrations signalled a rebellion against traditional lifestyles and morality; they amounted to celebration of diversity. Politics were radicalised and resistance was not viewed as coun-terproductive, but as meaningful and political. Deviance itself became politicalised: it was not only criminals who were pushed under the umbrella of deviance – they were now in the company of nuts, sluts and queers. All 'difference' began to be seen as good, as political, positive, as a challenge to the system. The labels themselves, which had once been the most powerful objects of oppression, were claimed and seen for what they really were – the instruments those in authority utilised to socially control those to whom they were directed. The deviant was not a passive actor (as the labelling theorists had implied) but a political rebel.

Radical theory viewed the deviant as active, as a rebel whose actions were in essence political. Personal deviance amounted to public challenge; breaking the law was a way of confronting the pervasive power of the state. As Sumner says, *any sign of resistance was to be welcomed as political and meaningful . . . Deviance was politicised . . . it was politicised completely* (1994, p253).

The social and resistance movements that were emerging resulted in the growth of a unique perspective within the field of criminology/sociology of deviance. These contributions generally had a Marxist framework and have been called, variously, 'new criminology', 'radical criminology' and 'conflict criminology' (Quinney 1970; Young 1971; Taylor et al., 1973). The concerns of the theorists within this perspective were generally what they perceived had been seen as lacking from other theories (especially labelling), including: first, a full structural analysis; second, a focus on the unequal distribution of wealth and power within society; and last, a radical social and political analysis. Criminal law, it was argued, does not reflect the views of the majority but in fact serves the interest of the ruling class. Law corresponds with the economic conditions within society and will, therefore, inevitably support those conditions. The focus of the new movement in criminology was to provide an analysis of the nature of law. Crime, it was alleged, is a result of contradictions and inequalities inherent within a capitalist society. Crime is inevitable in an unequal society. The unequal distribution of wealth and power will foster rebellion and criminality. The solution to crime, therefore, does not lie in individual treatment or punishment, but in the creation of a new type of society, which is egalitarian in nature. Using this perspective, the young law breaker is not viewed as criminal but as criminalised by an unequal society that has created social conditions that precipitated their behaviour. By breaking the law they are actively challenging an oppressive system that has probably provided them with few opportunities and branded them as worthless.

Realist criminologies

In the 1980s the Home Office began to fund research programmes that would consider cost-effective methods of crime control, based on neo-classicist notions that crime control interventions should focus upon the cost-benefit analysis of criminality: the idea that crimes are committed due to the availability of opportunities, and that resources should be targeted to decrease those opportunities and increase the risks in taking part in criminal activity. This new wave of criminological research was called 'new administrative criminology' and was posited on the acceptance that rather than sitting around discussing the possible causes of criminality, effective measures were needed to tackle the impact of crime. Two new strands of criminological thought began to develop over this period: the first was based on left-wing pragmatism and the second based in a neo-conservative remoralisation paradigm.

Left realism

Left realism came to criminological attention in 1984 with the publication of Lea and Young's text *What is to be done about law and order?* This work acknowledged that the lived realities of crime are indeed problematic and recognised the need to address victimisation in a practical and constructive manner. Jock Young in 1994 described left realism as follows:

> Left realism, as a critique of existing criminological theory, emerged in the 1980s . . .
> Its central aim is to be faithful to the reality of crime – to the fact that all crimes must,
> of necessity, involve rules and breakers (criminal behaviour and reaction against it) and
> offenders and victims. (p102)

This approach espoused a practical criminology, based on empirical research: an acceptance that crime is inevitable and a recognition that crime is experienced disproportionately by those who are the least powerful within society. The left realists conducted local crime surveys in Islington the early 1980s in and these were later replicated across other metropolitan areas. It is arguable that the left realists are to be credited with providing the momentum for the annual British Crime Survey, a comprehensive survey of victimisation that is widely regarded as criminologically more valid than any other official method of collecting and recording statistics about crime. This movement also contributed to the recognition of the value of local crime statistics, local crime plans and the targeting of crime control strategies on the basis of sound evidence. Left realism can also arguably be credited with the adoption by governments of the benefits of a multi-agency approach to tackling local crime problems.

Young posits ten points of left realism to comprise a co-ordinated, systematic approach to tackling the reality of crime. Of these, we will concentrate on three pivotal facets, namely the square of crime, the theory of relative deprivation and the multi-agency strategy.

The square of crime

Left realism puts forward the idea of the 'square of crime' (see Figure 3.2). Any analysis of a criminal event should take into account factors that might impact upon each of the four corners/points of the square, namely the interaction between (1) the police; (2) other agencies of social control; (3) the offender; and (4) the victim; ((1) and (2) cover the reaction to the crime event and (3) and (4) cover the act itself).

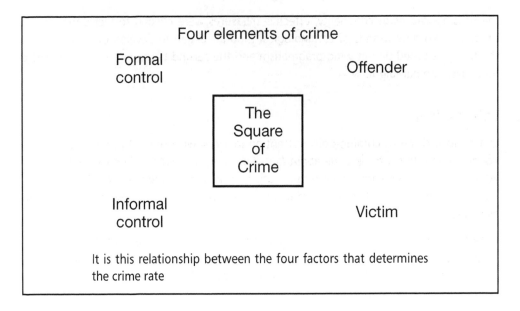

Figure 3.2 The square of crime

Figure 3.2 illustrates the concept of the 'square of crime'. At each point of the square we observe a factor that has contributed to the official measurement of crime in the form of the official crime statistics. In examining the creation of crime statistics we must refer to this four-fold aetiology, namely:

- Causes of offending (the domain of traditional criminology).

- Factors that make victims vulnerable (e.g. lifestyles).

- Social factors that affect public tolerance (e.g. towards smoking cannabis, violence, etc.).

- Police practice and enforcement.

The traditional focus of criminology was to concentrate only upon the factor in the top right-hand corner, namely the offender, and to consider causational aspects of their offending. Within this point on the square of crime we should, according to Young, analyse theories of crime causation which may go some way towards explaining the triggers of deviant behaviour.

Victims, at the bottom right-hand point of the square, are the second factor contributing towards the production of the crime rate. In relation to this factor, it is assumed that the victimised individual may in some way contribute towards their own victim status by their behaviour. For example, in order to avoid becoming a victim of crime a person might change their behaviour: not walking alone late at night, walking purposefully instead of slowly, wearing clothing that does not attract attention. A person's lifestyle might impact upon the chance of them becoming a victim of crime. Further other factors might affect their potential for becoming a victim by, for example, fitting car alarms, window locks, etc. Additionally, the victim's relationship with the offender may have a precipitative effect upon the outcome of their interactions.

Young asserts that most citizens of western societies are becoming more sensitive to and less tolerant of violence. This heightened sensitivity, to violent crimes in particular and all crimes in general, will lead to an increased willingness of the public to report incidences of perceived criminal behaviour to the police, thus contributing towards the increase in officially recorded crime. Indeed, Young says, realist criminology recognises that crime rates are a product not only of changes in behaviour, but also of changes in definitions of what is seriously criminal. A number of 'new crimes' have seemingly been discovered over the last 20 years, such as racial violence, child abuse, internet porn, violence against women and, over the last few years, white collar and corporate crime. He argues that the so-called 'civilising factor' within western societies has led to an increased sensitivity to anti-social behaviour generally.

Having examined the right-hand side of the square, we can see that these two points that contribute to the production of crime, the offender and victim interaction, provide an explanation of the criminal act but not of the societal reaction to it. Moving to the left-hand side of the square, we see that the other two points deal with the official and unofficial reactions to crime; Young calls these the social control elements that contribute towards the production of crime. With regard to the formal control agencies – the police, Police and Community Support Officers (PCSOs), private security – Young asserts that these formal mechanisms contribute towards the production of crime statistics in a number of ways. The health of the relationship between the police and the public within a particular locality will contribute towards the production of crime statistics. A community that trusts its local police to investigate crime properly and fairly will be more willing to report crime than one that has lost faith in police fairness and efficiency. Further, this relationship will be affected by the level of perceived accountability of the police to the locality. Also a police force may decide to target particular types of crime and concentrate resources in certain areas, but this may produce a crime wave in another area. Finally, the numbers of police, PCSOs and security measures (such as CCTV) might be subjected to financial constraints which could impact upon the amount of offences brought to justice.

The fourth point on the square of crime, informal public control, involves those controls the public may initiate, such as surveillance of a neighbour's property. It also includes the issues discussed earlier in relation to examining the victim's contribution towards crime statistics. There is less public tolerance of criminality, particularly specific types of crime (such as violent crime) and this increased sensitivity towards anti-social behaviour will in turn be transmitted via the democratic system into public opinion and media debate. Eventually it may lead to the creation of new crime by the legislature responding to public opinion and pressure groups. In short, as public and media opinion becomes less accepting of some behaviours, those behaviours are increasingly likely to become criminalised.

Young asserts that it is the relationship between these four factors on the square of crime that determines the crime rate.

Relative deprivation

Regarding the offender point on the square of crime, left realists view the theory of relative deprivation as the most forceful explanation of crime, and note that other theories of criminology (e.g. anomie, subcultural theories) utilise the concept of relative deprivation. Young argues that relative deprivation is a potent notion because (a) it is not limited to the lower-class criminal and thus can be used to explain middle-class and corporate crime; (b) it is not concerned only with economic crimes but can be utilised to explain violent offences committed as a response to relative deprivation; and (c) it is not limited to absolute poverty and can explain the paradox of why some crimes of the economically deprived may focus upon obtaining the symbols of material wealth (e.g. designer clothes), rather than obtaining food and basic survival items.

The realists assert that there is no evidence to support a proposition that absolute deprivation leads to crime. They assert that this assumes that the causational flow is non-problematic. The process is not automatic. Not all people who are desperately poor commit crime; only some do. Young cites crime statistics of the 1930s during the Great Depression that indicate that crime rates decreased during this period of severe economic restraint. The realists propose that relative deprivation, coupled with the experience of unfairness with regard to the allocation of resources, leads the individual to seek a solution: this solution may involve law-breaking.

Multi-agency strategy

Young explains this as the co-ordinated response of social institutions to the issues of crime and disorder. He argues that the problem with unco-ordinated interventions based on a variety of policy of initiatives with no overarching rationale is that they will inevitably be doomed to failure. Such interventions are often poorly resourced and may indeed overlap and possibly even conflict with each other.

The system of dealing with crime should not involve a uniform approach as different crimes require different processes. It is not merely the police, the Crown Prosecution Service and the courts who are involved in processing crime; various other agencies may handle a case at particular stages of its process. For example, the action taken to deal with an allegation of burglary will be markedly different from actions taken to deal with an allegation of child abuse. Young contends that any social control interventions in relation to crime reduction should involve all the agencies who may be involved in processing all types of crime. Table 3.1 illustrates the left realist's approach to multi-agency intervention in relation to crime control.

In relation to youth offending, the similarities between the left-realist paradigm and youth justice policy over the last fifteen years are manifest. The Labour government (1997–2010) adopted a multi-agency approach to tackling youth crime from the outset. This was evidenced by the creation of multi-disciplinary Youth Offending Teams in 2000 (see Chapter 5) which brought a holistic methodology to youth justice practice whereby diverse professionals (social workers, teachers, police officers, health and housing workers, counsellors, drugs workers, probation and prevention officers, etc.) were brought together in the same team to develop bespoke packages (involving various agencies) to address offending behaviours. Additionally, youth crime prevention adopted a mutli-agency ethos over this period as seen in initiatives such as the Youth Crime Task Force, SureStart programmes, Children's Plans, the common assessment framework, etc.

Table 3.1 The left realist's approach to multi-agency intervention

Stages in the devlopment of crime	Factors	Agencies
Causes of crime	Unemployment	Local authority
	Housing	Central government
	Leisure time	Businesses
Moral	Peer group values	Schools
Context	Community cohesion	Public
		Family
		Mass media
Situation of	Physical environment	Local authority
commission	Lighting	Public
	Security	Police
Detection of crime	Public reporting	Public
	Detective work	Police
Response to offenders	Punishment	Courts
	Rehabilitation	Police
		Social services
		Probation/NOMS
Response to victims	Insurance	Local authority
	Public support	Victim support
		Local community groups
		Social services

ACTIVITY 3.6

Can you spot any further similarities between left realism and the government's approach to tackling youth crime?

COMMENT

There are many parts of the left realist approach to criminality that the Labour government seemed to adopt during its time in office between 1997–2010. These include: a multi-agency approach to tackling crime including youth crime; localisation of crime prevention plans and youth crime plans; 'joined-up' policies and strategies on tackling youth crime developed by liaison between various departments/professionals nationally and locally; a focus on crime mapping, crime 'hotspots' and targeting of resources; a focus on victimisation, multiple victimhood and links with social exclusion and inequality; the creation of preventionist schemes and projects such as Sure Start and On Track (listed in Chapter 2); a focus on victim rights and strengthening sanctions for some offences ('tough on crime') while examining – and aiming to tackle – the causes of social exclusion ('tough on the causes of crime'); increasing focus on the importance of informal controls in relation to crime prevention and the 'resonsibilisation' of the citizen; etc.

Right realism

In the 1980s there was a growing cynicism about the effectiveness of the criminal justice process and pessimism regarding the perceived failure of criminology to put forward any viable proposals for the reduction of crime. Martinson's (1974) phrase 'nothing works' was adopted to describe a general dissatisfaction with crime control policies. These growing seeds of scepticism found fertile soil in the burgeoning conservatism that characterised the political landscape of both the USA and UK in the 1980s; there was a revitalisation of classicist notions of free will, choice, crime control, proportionality and deterrence. Further, there was a refocusing upon the individualistic theories of crime and a shift away from critical criminologies that had firmly placed the blame for crime on the state due to its failure to alleviate poverty, deprivation and inequalities that allegedly precipitated criminal behaviour.

The new right gurus of the underclass school in Britain were led by Charles Murray (1984, 1990 and 1994), who transported his theory over the Atlantic in the mid-1980s. It was further developed in a UK context by Norman Dennis (1992, 1993 and 1997) who asserted that many inner cities in the UK and other peripheral estates were becoming dominated by a growing 'underclass'. This underclass or 'yob culture' supposedly consists of feckless young men who show disdain for work and of irresponsible single mothers who live on benefits and are unable to instil any traditional moral values into their children, who consequently fall into a life of crime. According to Murray, these people who are supported by welfare, seek pleasure in drugs and try to gain further income from illegal activities. This underclass culture is cyclical: without positive role models, young men who are inadequately socialised will take part in illegal activity to create excitement and to supplement their welfare benefits.

Murray claims that the underclass can be identified by reference to certain behavioural traits that are in evidence among sections of the poorer population. These factors, he alleges, are two-fold: welfare dependency and the tendency to commit petty crime. He stresses that these two behavioural tendencies are not irrational when contextualised in the lifestyles of the underclass and the incentives that are built into the system of welfare provision. He maintains that the behaviour is rational but only in terms of short-term gain. It is destructive in the long term, but the under-educated have no ability to defer gratification.

Murray traces the origins of the resurgence of the idea that there are two categories of poor people, the deserving and the undeserving. It could be argued that this split in the lower classes in the UK was caused by the 'drawbridge effect' of the policies of Thatcherism in the 1980s. The 'yuppyisation' of parts of the UK in the 1980s, which began to slow down by the end of the decade, had created a radical re-evaluation of the traditional class structure in Britain. In relation to the working classes it had caused disjunction – a lack of solidarity between the non-working and the working lower classes.

Murray made several assumptions about the nature of criminal behaviour. He claimed that single parenthood is a predictive factor in criminal behaviour and that habitual criminals are invariably young, male members of this underclass. Single parenthood, he alleged, is encouraged by the provision of welfare and housing benefits. The welfare state produces a dependency culture and the proliferation of a 'culture of poverty'. Referring to young men and fatherhood, Murray argues that the growth of single parenthood among females has led to a loss of fatherhood responsibilities and the consequential 'civilising' effects of having to provide for children. He suggests that the welfare state encourages this situation and also promotes unstable and multiple relationships. Young boys in such an environment have no positive adult role models and the pattern of dependency is then repeated through generations. Murray describes the young male members of the 'underclass' as 'essentially barbarians, civilised by marriage' and argues that the features of the 'underclass' include crime, promiscuous self-indulgence, ungovernability, inability to defer gratification and lack of self-control. Murray concludes that crime is an easy option for these young men because of slim chances of being caught, low clear-up rates, and the tendency of magistrates and judges to give light sentences.

Dennis and Murray's ideas were pivotal to the development of the 'zero tolerance' agenda and the 'broken windows' thesis (Wilson and Kelling, 1982) both of which have had an impact on youth justice policy; particularly, these ideas might have supported the growth of the use of civil orders such as ASBOs to deal with lower level acts of delinquency and civil disobedience.

ACTIVITY 3.7

Bob and Sam are twins aged 18. Both live in the family home on a run-down inner-city council estate and they went to the same school. Their secondary school was average in terms of school league tables but had a high level of exclusions. Their parents are unemployed and in receipt of social benefits. Both boys associated with the same friends until the age of 15. Their mother is a recovering alcoholic and their father is a habitual criminal who has been convicted of burglary and several domestic assaults.

Bob was excluded from school at the age of 15 and has three convictions for possession of heroin, robbery and assault. Sam achieved three A grades in his A levels and is currently studying law at UCL.

Account for the criminality of Bob and the non-criminality of Sam.

COMMENT

This is a very difficult question to answer (!) and illustrates one of the major problems with the social science of criminology. The ideas of criminologists, though often tested via empirical research, can only predict and they might predict wrongly. One would expect both boys to turn out the same – but they don't – the question is why? Sometimes people surprise us and don't turn out as 'experts' might have predicted. A discussion of this problem goes to the heart of the irresolvable tensions between the nature versus nurture debate and illustrates that the methodology of social science is not always to be trusted!

CHAPTER SUMMARY

In this chapter we have examined some of the major theories that have shaped the historical development of criminological theory. An insight into mainstream causational explanations of offending behaviour should help your knowledge of the nature of crime, criminality and criminalisation. It is vital that you develop skills of criminological analysis to assist your understanding of young people who come before the courts who you will deal with in your youth justice practice. Pre-sentence reports produced by youth justice practitioners must analyse the reasons why the young person has committed the crime in question and assess possible risk factors. An ability to apply criminological theory to casework is, therefore, vital in terms of enhancing your professional practice and the quality of your reports.

FURTHER READING

Jones, S (2009) *Criminology.* Oxford: Oxford University Press.

Provides a focus on explanations of criminality which are predominantly based on societal influences. The author also summarises genetic and psychological perspectives of crime causation and thus produces a full summary of major theories.

Tierney, J (2010) *Criminology: Theory and context,* 3rd edition. Harlow: Pearson Education.

A comprehensive coverage of criminological theory.

Walklate, S (2006) *Criminology: The basics.* London: Routledge. Chapter 4, 'The search for criminological explanation', provides an interesting summary of theory.

Chapter 4

The laws and sentencing framework of contemporary youth justice practice

Jane Pickford

Introduction

In Chapter 2 I examined the philosophies and history of our youth justice system. This chapter outlines the legislation that shapes contemporary youth justice sentencing practice. As a social worker within the youth justice industry you will need to be familiar with the law underpinning your practice and the rationales that guide the current legal framework. I examine sentencing options for young offenders, and also analyse non-criminal orders, which have the force of civil law constraints on young people who take part in anti-social and disorderly behaviour. Diversionary disposals (reprimands, final warnings and youth conditional cautions) and the rules relating to bail and remand decisions are covered in Chapter 5.

ACTIVITY **4.1**

As you read about the contemporary legislation discussed in this chapter, try to analyse the law in terms of the theoretical perspectives we examined in Chapter 2. For instance, which philosophical approach(es) are evident in current youth justice laws? Examine whether current legislation is similar to past statutes. Ideologically, does present day practice represent a radically different method from historical approaches, or is it simply a reworking of old ideas?

The shaping of current laws

In order to understand fully the political momentum for the changes to the legal framework that took place from the late 1990s, it is necessary to revisit some of the debates about youth justice that were raging in the mid-1990s. I mentioned earlier (in Chapter 2) that various academics (Fionda, 2005; Hendrick, 2002 and 2006; Jenks, 1996) have agreed that one case in 1993 changed the direction of youth justice policy and public opinion in relation to young offenders. This was the killing of the toddler James Bulger by two 10-year-old boys. The public outcry (largely media fuelled) that followed this case led to a 'moral panic' (Cohen 1973) about the law-breaking behaviour of children and young people. Indeed Jenks (1996) argued that the case led to the 'death' of childhood innocence and the subsequent 'demonisation' of youth. It is interesting to note that a similar case in 2009 – the Edlington case – where two brothers aged 10 and 11 tortured two younger victims (who suffered severe injuries), was described by the judge as 'truly exceptional' and the boys' identities were protected. Though this was arguably the most notorious crime committed by children since the Bulger case, the defendants did not suffer the same level of public reprehension. Indeed, the main target of recriminations seemed to focus upon the alleged failures of Doncaster Social Services in managing the case of the defendants who were in care due to their violent and anti-social behaviour.

Following the Bulger case, the tide of youth justice turned. Children were no longer pure and incorrupt; they were capable of the greatest evils. Hendrick (2002) argued that images of childhood became readjusted: we abandoned the 'romantic' model of childhood (that children are born innocent and so need protection from a corrupt society) and adopted the 'evangelical' model – that children are born capable of evil and so need to be firmly controlled. Media stories about young offenders allegedly being treated 'softly' by the juvenile justice system swayed public and political opinion towards an era of 'getting tough' on youth criminality.

The quasi-hysteria about the 'problem' of youth crime appears to make little sense when we analyse the statistical data for that era. According to published criminal statistics the number of young offenders aged 10 to 17 found guilty or cautioned of an indictable offence fell by 30 per cent between 1987 and 1997. According to NACRO (1999), *since 1987, the number of male juvenile offenders has fallen by 33% and female young offenders by 17%.*

However, the number of young people receiving custodial sentences rose over that period. Whereas the numbers of young offenders detained under sentence fell by approximately 50 per cent between 1980 and 1993, this figure rose by almost 56 per cent in the four years up to and including 1997. In addition to the media frenzy, this rise also corresponded with the development of a definition of the so-called 'persistent offender' over this period and the 'getting tough' policies in relation to those so categorised.

The political debates surrounding the run-up to the 1997 general election promised a 'law and order' agenda from all the major parties. The Labour Party's promise to get 'tough on crime, tough on the causes of crime' extended to youth crime. Once in office, they established a Youth Crime Task Force and the momentum for reform of criminal justice continued, with no less than seven consultation papers being released, five of which were directly related to youth justice:

- Community safety order (Home Office, 1997a)

- Getting to grips with crime (Home Office, 1997b)

- New national and local focus on youth crime (Home Office, 1997c)

- No more excuses: A new approach to tackling youth crime in England and Wales (Home Office, 1997d)

- Preventing children offending (Home Office, 1997e)

- Tackling delays in the youth justice system (Home Office, 1997f)

- Tackling youth crime (Home Office, 1997g)

The government at the time argued that the reason for change stemmed from the negative comments about the organisation of youth justice practice discovered by the Audit Commission and noted in their report *Misspent youth* (1996). The consultation papers of 1997 outlined the Labour Party's stated proposals for youth justice practice, noting that the current system was in disarray:

> *The youth justice system in England and Wales is in disarray. It simply does not work. It can scarcely be called a system at all because it lacks coherent objectives. It satisfies neither those whose principal concern is crime control nor those whose principal priority is the welfare of the young offender.*

> (Home Office, 1997g)

It is noteworthy that at this point in history at least, the problematic nature of youth justice practice was recognised by the then Labour government to be related to the tensions between justice and welfare approaches. This recognition was sadly ignored in the legislation that followed in the next 13 years.

What now follows is an outline of all the key legislations that have formed the current youth justice framework.

The Crime and Disorder Act 1998

Subsequent to these 'consultation' papers (Fionda (2005) points out that the consultation deadline allocated for *No more excuses* ended *after* the Bill had been published!) the Crime and Disorder Act was passed in 1998. The Act promised a 'root and branch' overhaul of the youth justice system to be implemented over a number of years, following the establishment of and feedback from pilot schemes and pathway sites, which tested the ground of the new reforms (one might argue that pilot schemes and viability should be tested prior to passing legislation). Section 37 of the Act emphasises the primary aim of prevention and states: *It shall be the principal aim of the youth justice system to prevent offending by children and young persons.* It also places a duty on all personnel working within the youth justice arena to have regard to this paramount aim while carrying out their duties.

In order to deliver the principal aim, the Home Office Juvenile Offenders Unit set out a number of key objectives for the reformed youth justice system:

- Tackling delays – halving how long it takes for young offenders to be processed from arrest to sentence from an average of 142 days in 1996 to a target of 71 days (this has been achieved).

- Confronting the young offender with the consequences of their offending and encouraging responsibility for actions.

- Intervention into 'risk factors', including family, social, personal and health factors.

- Introduction of a new range of penalties in order to enable sentencers to punish in proportion to the seriousness and persistence of offending.

- Encouragement of reparation.

- Reinforcement of parental responsibilities.

The Act set out six key themes (noted below) that would assist in achieving the above objectives.

Partnership and multi-agency working

Sections 6 and 7 of the Act encourage the development of local partnerships to provide a local framework and strategy for identifying crime and disorder problems within a particular locality. Section 39 required local authorities to establish multi-agency Youth Offending Teams (YOTs) by April 2000, bringing together professionals from social services, police, health, education and probation. Teams must produce an annual youth justice plan for tackling crime within their area of responsibility. (Multi-disciplinary YOTs are discussed in Chapter 5.) Further, the Youth Crime Action Plan targets problem areas of crime and anti-social behaviour with focused multi-agency initiatives using the common assessment framework.

Tackling offending behaviour and providing early intervention

This key theme was actioned by the following measures:

- Child safety orders (Section 11), placed on a child under the age of 10 to prevent him/ her from growing into criminal behaviour. This genre of support measures was supplemented by the introduction of Individual Support Orders for 10–17 year olds by the Criminal Justice Act 2003.

- Local child curfews (Section 14), aimed at preventing anti-social behaviour in local areas by children under the age of 10 (raised to 16 by the Anti-Social Behaviour Act 2003).

- Reprimands and final warnings (Section 65), replacing the cautioning system with a fixed procedure for diversionary disposals. Such diversionary orders were strengthened by the addition of the Youth Conditional Caution under the Criminal Justice and Immigration Act 2008.

- Action plan order (Section 69), a three-month, intensive order that combines elements of reparation, punishment and rehabilitation to help prevent re-offending and include parental involvement (abolished by the Criminal Justice and Immigration Act 2008 and replaced by the generic Youth Rehabilitation Order).

As noted above, the first two of these orders have been subsequently supplemented by the Anti-Social Behaviour and Criminal Justice Acts and the introduction of acceptable behaviour contracts and individual support orders (see Chapter 2 for a discussion of these and a list of agencies that have developed to implement this expansionist agenda). This reflects the government's commitment to tackle both crime and social disorder. These civil measures (many of which have criminal consequences if breached) are part of a focus on preventionism and extend the reach of the youth justice system beyond offenders to those who are deemed anti-social or at risk of offending. (The human rights implications of these orders are discussed in Chapter 1; the dangers of net-widening and stigmatising are covered in Chapter 2.)

The action plan order, which was introduced in 2000, was aimed at young people who are low-level offenders or who find themselves in front of a courtroom for the first time. The order was a short term (three-month) package of YOT intervention aimed at 'nipping offending in the bud'. This order was widely used over the first two years of its availability but was less frequently used since the availability (from April 2002) of the (mainly compulsory) sentence of a referral order for young people appearing in court for the first time. The action plan order was finally abolished and replaced by the youth rehabilitation order in November 2009 (see below under the heading Criminal Justice and Immigration Act 2008).

Focus on reparation

Section 67 established the reparation order, designed to help the young person face up to the consequences of their offending behaviour. The young person may be required to make reparation to the actual victim of their crime or to the local community generally. The theme of responsibilisation is evidenced in this order, which encourages the offender to contemplate the actual impact of their law-breaking in terms of the injury and suffering caused to victims. Anecdotal accounts from practitioners indicate that this order is not widely used, as elements of reparation such as unpaid work can be part of the more comprehensive community sentence of a Youth Rehabilitation Order. Reparation is also a central theme of the referral order, introduced in 2002.

Focus on parenting

Section 8 of the Act reinforces parental responsibility by introducing the parenting order. This is aimed at 'helping' parents, through support and guidance, to control the anti-social behaviour of their children. Such an order may place specific responsibilities on a parent, for example to impose a curfew on their child. In addition to the existing powers to fine and bind-over parents, the order represents a further move to hold parents responsible for the sins of their offspring and provides the government with a way of punishing parents by means of a potentially criminalising sanction for their presumed failure to properly care for or bring up their child. It remains to be seen how much further this country will move down the pathway of parental punishment and also, how far we will continue to usurp and supplant the parental rights of those we consider to be bad parents by the use of anti-social behaviour orders, acceptable behaviour contracts, curfew orders, individual support orders, child safety orders and even remands in local authority accommodation. You may find it useful to monitor the types of parents who become subject to parenting orders and other intrusive orders in your area of practice in terms of their socio-economic backgrounds; for instance, whether it is predominantly single parents or co-parents who are targeted for such interventions. Note that parenting order powers now extend to parents/carers of children or young people who:

- offend; and/or
- have received an ASBO; and/or
- truant; and/or
- are subject to a several offences Protection Order; and/or
- are subject to a child safety order.

The Crime and Security Act 2010 makes it compulsory for a court (except in exceptional circumstances) to impose a parenting order when a young person under 16 breaches an ASBO.

More effective custodial sentences

Section 73 established the detention and training order, implemented from April 2000. This purported to be a constructive and flexible custodial sentence with a clear focus on preventing re-offending behaviour. The order can be used by Youth and Crown Courts in respect of all young offenders under the age of 18 who have been convicted of an offence that if committed by an adult would be an imprisonable offence. If the child is aged 10 or 11, a further order will be required by the Home Secretary to allow such a sentence to be passed. The sentence is supposed to be 'seamless', though half the order is spent in detention and the other half under supervision in the community. The numbers of young people being sentenced to custody has continued to increase. As Bateman has noted (2003) though, the number of children and young people locked up in this country has received 'damning' criticism from the UN Committee on the Rights of the Child. Indeed the Youth Justice Board in 2010 (see Ministry of Justice website for the most recent figures) noted that numbers of young people in secure estate appeared to peak at just under 3,000 in 2008. By February 2010, this figure had decreased to 2,340. However, this is still almost twice as high as the average in 1993 when approx 1,300 were detained in the secure estate.

A national framework

Section 41 set up the framework for the national Youth Justice Board's operation. This is to encourage and monitor nationwide consistency in the implementation of the system of youth justice, to draw up standards for service delivery and to help disseminate good practice. (The role of the YJB is discussed in Chapter 5.) However, the Coalition government in 2010 virtually abolished the YJB and moved its functions (albeit slimmed down) to the Ministry of Justice (see Chapter 8).

ACTIVITY 4.2

In reference to Activity 4.1 above, can you identify which theoretical perspectives underpin the Crime and Disorder Act 1998?

COMMENT

Fionda (2005) has argued that the Crime and Disorder Act 1998 represents a continuation of the mixing of justice and welfare philosophies, despite the assurances of the Labour government when drafting this legislation (see Pickford, 2000).

However, other theoretical approaches can be seen within the provisions of the Act. These include: preventionism (by the introduction of civil orders such as anti-social behaviour orders and parenting orders targeted at 'problem' families); managerialism (by the introduction of the Youth Justice Board to standardise, inspect and manage procedures across all multi-disciplinary youth offending teams, as well as introducing multi-agency partnerships); authoritarianism (by the expansion of state control via civil orders and increasing electronic tagging of juveniles); responsibilisation (of communities, by making local area crime management partnerships accountable for the crime problem in their area); remoralisation (by targeting social control strategies not only towards criminal populations but also (via civil orders) at families deemed to be disorderly or anti-social); and restorative justice (by a focus on making amends, especially in relation to the introduction of the reparation order).

The Youth Justice Criminal Evidence Act 1999

The Youth Justice and Criminal Evidence Act 1999 (as amended by the Powers of the Criminal Courts (Sentencing) Act 2000, the Criminal Justice Act 2003 and the Criminal Justice and Immigration Act 2008) gave effect to further reforms proposed in the 1997 White Paper *No more excuses* (Home Office, 1997d). It created a (largely compulsory) sentence of a referral order for young people convicted for the first time. The young person is referred by the court to a Youth Offender Panel (YOP) drawn from the local community (established by YOTs) and serves the sentence for a period of between three and 12 months. A 'contract' is drawn up with the young offender and their parents, specifying the details of the order; each contract is tailor-made to suit the needs of the young person. The referral order is designed to address offending behaviour, in an attempt to prevent further offending. The order should include reparation and can also involve community work, curfews, mediation, contact with the victim and participation in specified activities or education programmes.

The YOPs resemble the system adopted in 1971 in Scotland to deal with young offenders (see Pickford, 2000, Chapters 8 and 9 and McNeill and Whyte, 2007). The similarities with the Children's Hearings north of the border are clear: parents are to play a crucial role in attending and being asked to help prevent anti-social behaviour; other significant adults, such as social workers or teachers, may also be required to be present; victims are able to attend panel meetings and explain to the young offender the effects of their criminal behaviour and suggest appropriate reparation; the meetings are conducted informally, without the presence of a legal representative; and the young person is encouraged to participate fully in the proceedings. Once the order is completed, the young person's offence is 'spent' for the purposes of the Rehabilitation of Offenders Act 1974.

In its original form, the conditions under which a referral order had to be made were fixed, but later amendments provided more flexability. Basically, a referral order will be made against all young people who are convicted of a first offence, except where:

- the court orders an absolute discharge;
- the sentence for the offence is fixed by law;
- the court decides to make a custodial sentence; or
- the offence is one that is non-imprisonable (2003 amendment).

Since April 2009 a court also has the discretion (under the Criminal Justice and Immigration Act 2008) to make a referral order when:

- the young person has one previous conviction but did not receive a referral order; or
- the young person has been previously bound over to keep the peace; or
- the young person has previously received a conditional discharge.

It should be noted that the offender must have pleaded guilty to the offence (or to one offence, if charged with more than one offence).

Furthermore, a court can:

- exceptionally make a second referral order after a recommendation by the local youth offending team;

- revoke a referral order if the young person is making good progress

- extend a referral order for up to 3 months for poor progress.

The type of requirements that can form part of a 'contract' include:

- Financial or other reparation.

- Attendance at mediation sessions.

- The carrying out of unpaid work in the community.

- Being at home at specified times.

- Attendance at school, training or work.

- Participation in specified activities (e.g. attending drug treatment centre).

- Presenting to named persons or institutions as and when specified.

- Avoiding specified places or persons.

Some problematic issues have arisen despite the 'flagship' status this order was given by the government. These include:

- A low level of attendance of victims at panels – 13 per cent during the pilot period (Earle, 2005).

- The fact that legal representation is prohibited.

- These informal meetings follow no set procedures, due process requirements are not followed and each Panel tends to reflect the character and attitude of the Panel members. Thus 'justice' is meted out in an inconsistent, non-standardised manner (see Crawford and Newburn, 2003).

- A 'contract' implies equality of bargaining power, yet the young person must 'agree' to the 'contract' or be referred back to court for non-compliance (see Pickford, 2000).

- No appeal is allowed.

- As this sentence is largely compulsory, young people who have committed trivial offences, which are technically 'imprisonable', may face a minimum of a three-month order. This may be considered an 'over-reaction' to the original wrongdoing. (The amendments under the Criminal Justice and Immigration Act 2008 have addressed this concern in part only).

- Sentencers are not able to exercise total discretion in sentencing: if the criteria for the referral order sentence are satisfied, sentencers must make a referral order – although they have some discretion, as mentioned above. Earle (2005) remarks that youth magistrates resented the curtailment in their powers following the implementation of the order in April 2002; this led to the government (Home Office, 2003b) extending discretion to issue other sentences where the offence is non-imprisonable. However, this concession only related to a small number of situations, e.g. motoring offences. The 2008 Act partly bestowed discretion to magistrates and judges, but some restrictions still apply.

- In some areas panel volunteers might not reflect the social class, economic, sex, religious or racial background of the community from which they are drawn (Crawford and Newburn, 2002).

- The system relies on volunteers who are unqualified to make decisions about the sentence content of young offenders on court orders. How does this square with the overall move towards professionalisation, standardisation and evidence-based practice of youth justice?

However, as Earle remarks: *Stationed at the gateway of the new system are over 5000 volunteers. Each year they greet approximately 27,000 young people with a novel experience of justice* (2005, p105). The introduction of magisterial/judicial discretion by the 2008 Act has increased the number of referral orders being made and, therefore, expanded the use of this welfare-oriented disposal and involved even more community volunteers in decision making within the youth justice system.

ACTIVITY 4.3

In reference to Activity 4.1 above, can you identify which theoretical perspectives underpin the Youth Justice and Criminal Evidence Act 1999?

COMMENT

It could be argued that the Youth Justice and Criminal Evidence Act 1999 was largely a welfare-based statute in relation to youthful offenders. This is because it basically introduced the referral order for young people who were in court for the first time – an order that, if completed successfully, did not carry with it a criminal record. Further, it introduced an additional community/lay element into the youth justice arena by the introduction of youth offender panels run by volunteers from local communities. These panel members decide upon the contents of the referral order, which can be fashioned in a bespoke manner to address the offending triggers of each young person who comes before them. This welfare based panel seems to reflect the system of children's panels that are the bedrock of the Scottish youth justice system.

Aspects of other perspectives of responsibilisation (making young people face up to the consequences of their offending – the victim is invited to the panel meeting), development (the young person is given a second chance and receives no criminal record if the order is successfully completed) and restorative justice (individual restoration to the victim concerned) are also evident philosophies underpinning the referral order.

Powers of the Criminal Courts (Sentencing) Act 2000

This Act introduced special measures for young people who have committed 'grave crimes' (see Table 4.1). Section 90 deals with young offenders convicted of murder and requires them to be detained 'during Her Majesty's pleasure'. This is an indeterminate sentence and the sanction is equivalent to the mandatory 'life' sentence for adults. The young person must serve a mandatory minimum (tariff) period fixed by the court. They will stay in custody until the end of that period. After that, they can then be released only with the permission of the parole board and will remain on 'licence' for the rest of their life.

Section 91 covers the procedure for other 'grave crimes' – primarily crimes for which an adult can be sentenced to 14 or more years in custody. Generally, the court is given the same maximum sentencing limits for young people charged with these crimes as adults. As Bateman (2005) has noted, since this Act *a succession of legislative changes has brought an ever greater number of offences within the ambit of section 91* leading to a dramatic increase in long-term custodial sentences for young offenders (2005, p160).

The Act also amended and detailed rules relating to referral orders (subsequently amended) and other (mostly now abolished) community orders. It also introduced the exclusion order, a requirement which can now form part of a Youth Rehabilitation Order. Fionda describes the statute as *a very muddled set of provisions* (2005, p155).

Criminal Justice and Court Services Act 2000

This statute removed powers regarding the length of custody to be served by young people who commit serious offences from the Home Secretary to the judiciary. The European Court of Human Rights in *Thompson and Venables [1999]* (re: the killing of the infant James Bulger) ruled that sentencing should be left to judges to decide and recommendations should not be overruled by politicians (the boys were originally sentenced to 8 years by the trial judge, this was raised to 10 years by the Lord Chief Justice and then to 15 years by Michael Howard, the then Home Secretary). Now, the sentencing of juveniles convicted of the gravest crimes will be set by the Lord Chief Justice on a recommendation of the trial judge. The Criminal Justice and Court Services Act 2000 put this ruling on a statutory footing.

Further, the Act also re-named certain sentences applicable to 16 and 17 year olds and re-stated their purposes: probation became community rehabilitation, community service became community punishment and a combination order became a community punishment and rehabilitation order (these sentences have now been abolished by the Criminal Justice and Immigration Act 2008 with the creation of the generic community sentence – the youth rehabilitation order).

The Act also gave the courts further powers over parents of truants – to be fined or imprisoned for up to three months for failing to 'cause' a young person to attend school.

Criminal Justice and Police Act 2001

Section 23 allowed electronic tagging as a condition of bail, including those on remand to local authority accommodation (from the age of twelve). Prior to this Act a court could only deprive a young person of their liberty while on remand if this was the only measure that could protect the public from serious harm. However, Section 130 allows a remand to custody (or secure accommodation) of a young offender whose offending is deemed problematic (including offending while on bail). A young suspect can be refused bail if the court decides that certain criteria are satisfied (it is noteworthy that section 130 does not use the phrase 'persistent' offender, a concept favoured by previous legal provisions). Factors to weigh in the balance encompass: firstly, asking whether there is any evidence (including the new alleged matter) of 'repeatedly' offending while on bail; and then secondly, deciding whether the young person presents a risk of commission of imprisonable offences or whether there is a need for a custodial/secure remand in order to protect the public from serious harm. Prior to this Act, a court could only deprive a young person of their liberty while on remand if this was the only measure that could protect the public from serious harm. So this legislation increases the courts' powers to deprive a young person of their liberty while they are being processed by the courts, prior to any finding of guilt. Indeed, Goldson accuses the Act of *penological irrationality and indifference to the welfare of child remand prisoners* (2006, p144).

Additionally, this Act extended the age limit for local child curfews (civil order) to under 16s and allows such orders to be imposed on an area as well as an individual. Lastly, it introduced 'on the spot' penalties for designated street/public offences applicable any perpetrators aged ten or over.

Justice for All

This white paper (Home Office, 2002) proposed that trials for serious offences, now held in the Crown Court, should be heard in the Youth Court by a judge sitting with youth magistrates. This has not been implemented.

Criminal Justice Act 2003

This statute introduced new provisions for custody regarding young people (and adults) convicted of certain violent or sexual offences who are judged by the court to be 'dangerous'. New orders were introduced in December 2005 giving additional sentencing powers; these include (1) extended sentencing and (2) indeterminate sentence for public protection. The philosophical approach to these provisions is preventionism (see Chapter 2) and custodial orders are made on the basis of protection of the public rather than on the basis of proportionality. Under the new provisions the maximum sentence for such crimes committed by young people who fall within these categories can be increased.

Under category (1) if the young person has committed a sexual or violent offence ('specified' under section 15) for which an adult could receive two years or more and the court deems that there is a significant risk of serious harm to the public, they could receive extended detention which involves a licence extension of up to eight years for a sexual offence and five years for a violent offence. Young offenders who fall within the latter category (2) have committed a violent or sexual offence carrying a maximum penalty of ten years or above for an adult, and thus become eligible for an indeterminate sentence. Practitioners should monitor the use of these provisions, which could potentially further increase the use of long custodial disposals for young offenders. Significantly, robbery is listed as a 'specified' offence and so an assessment of dangerousness of all robbery cases is necessary even if the violence (or threat thereof) was minimal.

Other provisions of the CJA that impact upon youth justice include:

- Individual support orders were introduced for young people aged 10–17 who were subject to an ASBO.

- Parenting orders could run alongside referral orders (previously prohibited).

- Parents must attend referral order panel meetings and can be referred to court for non-compliance.

- The general admissibility of 'bad character' introduced in criminal proceedings.

- Minimum of 3 years custodial sentence for 16/17 year olds found in possession of firearms.

- YOTs must comply with risk assessments under Multi-Agency Public Protection Arrangements (MAPPA).

- Police allowed to detain after charge to test for class A drugs from the age of 14.

- Privacy issues regarding the hitherto protective restrictions imposed on courts: courts can now release the names of those convicted of a crime and those against whom a post-conviction ASBO has been made.

It is noteworthy that the statutory purposes of sentencing set out in section 142 of the Act apply to adults and not juveniles. However, parts of the sentencing framework and threshold do. For example section 148 cities the criteria of the offending behaviour being 'serious enough' to warrant a community disposal or 'so serious' that no alternative to custody can be justified. In 2009 the Sentencing Guidelines Council published definitive guidelines for sentencing young people (see below).

Anti-Social Behaviour Order Act 2003

Following a white paper *Respect and Responsibility: Taking a stand against anti-social behaviour* (Home Office 2003d) this Act extended the powers of public bodies in relation to civil orders associated with anti-social behaviour (as noted in Table 4.6). Human rights implications are discussed in Chapter 1. Significant extra measures, in addition to powers already granted, included:

- Expansion of the range of authorities/bodies that can seek ASBOs.

- Introduction of a presumption in favour of making a parenting order where an ASBO is made against a young person under 16.

- Introduction of a presumption against reporting restrictions.

- Allowing hearsay evidence to be used.

- Introduction of individual support orders (ISOs) which could be ordered to run alongside ASBOs.

- Introduction of penalty notices for disorderly behaviour by young people (largely proved to be unworkable).

- Introduction of group dispersal orders.

- The anti-social behaviour strategy was further consolidated by the development of the *Respect Task Force and Action Plan* in 2006 (Home Office 2006b).

- Later amendments include the Criminal Justice and Immigration Act 2008 which requires a youth ASBO to be reviewed after 12 months and the Crime and Security Act 2010 which requires a parenting order to be made if there is a breach of an ASBO imposed on an under 16 year old.

- The Coalition government announced plans in 2011 to reform ASBOs and re-brand them as 'criminal behaviour orders' (see Chapter 8).

Youth justice – *The next steps* and *Every child matters*

The green paper *Every child matters* (Home Office, 2003a) outlined proposals for reforming children's services generally and led to the Children Act 2004 (below). Alongside this paper the government published a companion document, *Youth justice – The next steps* (Home Office, 2003c), a separate consultation document covering proposed reforms to the youth justice system.

The paper made reference to nine key areas (see NACRO, 2003a):

- *The basic approach.* Though England and Wales has the lowest age of criminal responsibility, at 10 years, compared to other European countries, the government does not propose to change this. This failure to increase the age of criminal responsibility is in direct opposition to the recommendations of the UN Committee on the Rights of the Child, the Committee on Human Rights and the stated view of many children's charities.

- *Pre-court diversion.* The government wished to increase the use of diversionary schemes, and though there are no proposals to change the current reprimand and final warning system, there are calls for views about the possible expansion of referral order type measures, which ensure the greater participation of victims and the local community.

- *Sentencing structure and rationale.* The sentencing of young people was dominated by three principles: the 'welfare principle' enshrined in the Children and Young Persons Act 1933; the principle of proportionality contained in the Criminal Justice Act 1991; and the aim of preventing offending, a main focus of the Crime and Disorder Act 1998. The government proposed to scrap the first two. It was envisaged (by NACRO, 2003a) that sentencers would also take into account issues such as vulnerability, public protection, optimum punishment, parental obligation, reparation and previous interventions – but that the principal aim of preventing offending will prevail. From a criminological standpoint, this would represent a move away from classicist notions of proportionality towards the positivist ideal of preventionism and sentences tailor-made to fit the criminal as opposed to the crime. Any abandonment of the long-standing welfare principle is concerning and it seems to be contrary to the focus on promotion of the well-being of the child/young person evident in *Every child matters* and enshrined in the Children Act 2004.

- *Families and communities*. The government wished to expand the use of the parenting order and other means of ensuring 'whole family' involvement in youth crime intervention, including the active encouragement of father participation and a focus on encouraging family group conferencing.

- *Policing, public order and the courts*. This included strengthening enforcement of anti-social behaviour measures via the youth court; providing YOT/local authority reports for courts regarding remand/bail recommendations; and promoting an increased understanding by children and young people of court processes (with the development of a 'young defendant's pack' to help young people and their families understand proceedings). In addition, specialist training is proposed for Crown Court judges. It is arguably not clear whether the latter measure will address the concerns expressed by the UN Committee on the Rights of the Child and the European Court in Thompson and Venables [1999] which regarded the Crown Court as essentially an adult court that was unsuitable for dealing with children and young defendants (see Chapter 1).

- *Remands*. This included proposals for greater use of bail and non-custodial remands where possible and the expansion of ISSP bail packages to support this. An extension of the use of remand foster placements is recommended, as is the possibility of remand hostels for some upper age range youth offenders.

- *Community sentencing*. This area contained arguably the most radical proposal regarding the practice of youth justice in that it recommended the scrapping of nine current community sentences and their replacement with one generic sentence which would ideally contain two or three interventions chosen from a 'comprehensive menu' of possible measures, such as reparation, drug intervention, anger management, specified activities, etc.

It was proposed that these conditions might also include residence requirements – at the family home, through expanded foster placements, hostels or local authority accommodation. Mental health treatment might also be added if necessary.

To assist implementation of these changes, there was a proposal that YOTs would be encouraged to make 'child behaviour contracts' with young people on court orders.

- *Intensive sentences and custody*. These proposals included plans to expand the use of ISSP as a high-tariff sentence and to utilise the principles of an ISSP (up to six months) as an option combined with custody in the form of a new 'intensive supervision or detention order' (ISDO) for serious and repeat offenders. It was proposed that restrictions relating to this sentence for 12–14 year olds be removed, with a maximum for this age group of 12 months.

- *Staff and organisation*. Proposals in this area related to examining the membership of YOTs, promoting further profession-specific training and investigating multi-agency links with YOTs (with a view to joined-up service provision outlined in the Children Act 2004 – see below).

Overall, the focus of these proposals was on diversion, reducing remand and custodial detention (the latter with a fortified ISSP), a reduction in the amount of community disposal options, a further focus on reparation and a move away from the welfare and proportionality principles of sentencing. NACRO pointed to the possible complexity and the risk of expansionism being created at the custodial level, but welcomed some of the diversionary measures proposed.

Within these proposals, we can see the generic youth rehabilitation order introduced in November 2009 taking shape.

Youth justice 2004: A review of the reformed youth justice system

It is worth noting the comments of the Audit Commission's review of youth justice services in 2004. The Audit Commission's general review was favourable, largely indicating that the youth justice system showed considerable improvements from the old system they reviewed in 1996 (*Misspent youth*). However, they commented upon five areas of youth justice services that still needed attention following the staged implementation of the radical reforms that flowed from the Crime and Disorder Act 1998 and the Youth Justice and Criminal Evidence Act 1999.

1. *A need to focus court work towards dealing with serious and persistent offenders*. The Commission recommended an extension of the use of diversionary practice for non-serious offenders and an extended use of the referral order – specifically the possibility of a three-month order for young people who have not appeared at court before.

2. *A need to improve court procedures*. The Commission commented upon the lack of understanding of court practice experienced by young defendants and their guardians. In addition, magistrates need further specialised training and the progress of specific cases should be regularly reviewed, with encouragement or changes made to interventions, as appropriate.

3. *A need to make sentencing practice more cost-effective*. The Commission noted that custody is the most expensive yet least efficient sentence and recommended that ISSPs should be extended.

4. *A necessity to address the wide-ranging needs of offenders.* The Commission recommended that young people's needs should be met by a holistic approach, including (a) increasing the frequency and quality of contact with supervising officers; (b) ensuring that young people are kept in/given education and training while undertaking sentencing requirements; (c) liaising with health (including mental health) services to ensure the well-being of the young person; and (d) ensuring accessible substance misuse support and accommodation provision.

5. *The need to prevent first-time offending.* The Commission noted that young people in custody often have a history of previous local authority or other service interventions. Planned and targeted early intervention is necessary, as is greater co-ordination between various services that deal with young people.

It can be seen that some of the Audit Commission's concerns (though not all) mirror a number of the proposals outlined in *Youth justice – The next steps* (above) and were addressed later in the Criminal Justice and Immigration Act 2008.

The Children Act 2004

This Act put into effect many of the proposals relating to reforms in children's services outlined in *Every child matters*. While the Act deals with issues raised in relation to the investigation into the death of Victoria Climbié and covers mainly non-youth offending matters, some areas of reform will impact upon social work practice generally. Especially notable are:

- The establishment of the Children's Commissioner for England to raise awareness of best interests of children and young people, to examine how public bodies deal with them and consider their wishes, to examine how complaints are investigated and report annually to Parliament.

- Local authorities to create Directors of Children's Services to cover education and social services.

- The encouragement of local authorities to create co-operation and to pool resources between agencies who deal with children and young people in order to improve their well-being in five key areas: health, safety, achievement, making a positive contribution and economic well-being.

- Placing a duty on key agencies to make sure that they safeguard and promote the welfare of children and young people and the creation of Local Safeguarding Children's Boards.

- The creation of databases to assist information sharing about children and young people.

- The creation of a new inspection format and regular Joint Area Reviews.

- Promoting the educational achievement of looked after children.

- Strengthening local fostering arrangements.

Youth matters

The green paper *Youth matters* (Home Office, 2005e) was published (largely following the proposals set out in the consultation paper *Every child matters*) and though it did not cover youth justice specifically, it addressed four aims in relation to youths in particular: (a) positive activities and empowerment; (b) encouraging young people to become involved in their communities (including as volunteers); (c) providing better information, advice and guidance for young people; and (d) providing better and more personalised services for young people with problems or who get into trouble.

It is the latter aim that relates to youth offending. The proposals put forward in order to achieve this aim include promoting a multi-agency, integrated approach to young people who find themselves in this category and in need of help. It recommended that an integrated package of support should be actioned for each young person, with one lead, named professional as co-ordinator of the package. The government proposed to merge a range of existing programmes that focus on specific aspects of youth services and work through children's trusts in order to address the needs of young people using a holistic approach. The issues to be tackled in this holistic manner include teenage pregnancy, young people not receiving education or training, dealing with young people with drug or alcohol problems and dealing with youth crime – the latter to help fulfil the existing duty upon local authorities under Section 17 of the Crime and Disorder Act 1998.

The proposals discussed in this paper arguably emerged with the creation of *The youth task-force action plan* and the *Youth crime action plan* in 2008 (see Ministry of Justice website).

Draft Youth Justice Bill 2005 (not enacted)

Though a youth justice bill was mentioned in the Queen's Speech for the 2004/05 session of Parliament, no formal bill arrived (despite a Draft Youth Justice Bill appearing on government websites). The bill was not mentioned in plans for the 2005/06 timetable, though it was speculated that youth justice measures might have been contained within a bill entitled Sentencing and Youth Justice at the end of 2005 or within the Police and Justice Bill released in January 2006.

The Draft Youth Justice Bill, which was not enacted, mainly proposed some of the measures that were outlined in the 2003 consultation paper, namely:

- To fix the primary purpose of youth sentencing as prevention of offending.

- To establish more effective community sentences with a simplified structure and a menu of measures from which courts can compile a suitable package for the individual with the key aim of rehabilitation.

- To develop the ISSP as a robust alternative to a custodial sentence where appropriate.

- To use DTOs when there is a need to remove the offender from the community.

- To place DTO trainees in open conditions, and allow temporary release with tagging, to improve integration of the offender back into their local community after release to prevent re-offending.

In February 2006 the Home Office published its five-year strategy, *Protecting the public and reducing re-offending.* It restated its intention to replace nine existing community orders with a single community sentence for juveniles called a 'youth rehabilitation order'.

Criminal Justice and Immigration Act 2008 and the Scaled Approach

This statute is a significant piece of legislative reform that impacted on several parts of the youth justice system, in particular it changed the sentencing structure from 30 November 2009 by introducing the youth rehabilitation order, a generic community order (with a time limit of up to three years) that replaced nine existing orders. Further, the implementation of the new sentence structure coincided with the introduction by the Youth Justice Board of 'the scaled approach' to risk assessment based upon an actuarial calculation methodology. While we will concentrate our analysis on these two major changes, it is useful to note the range of changes as charted by the Youth Justice Board (2010b) in Table 4.1.

Table 4.1 From Youth Justice Board (2010b) The Youth Rehabilitation Order and other Youth Justice Provisions of the Criminal Justice and Immigration Act 2008: Guidance for Youth Offending Teams

Name	Act reference	Description
Youth rehabilitation order	S1–8 and Schedules 1–4	Single, generic community sentence for young people, replacing existing mix of youth community sentences and combining a wide range of requirements in a targeted and flexible community sentence.
Referral orders	S35–37	Extension of discretionary court powers to make referral orders and power to revoke early, e.g. for good progress, and to extend the compliance period.
Youth conditional caution	S48 and Schedule 9	A higher-tariff pre-court disposal aimed at reducing the number of young people taken to court for a low level offence. To be piloted with 16 and 17 year olds initially.
Youth default order	S39 and Schedule 7	Will enable courts to impose an Unpaid Work Requirement (for 16 and 17 year olds only). Curfew requirement or attendance centre requirement on a young offender in lieu of an unpaid fine.
'Spent' warnings, reprimands and cautions	S49 and Schedule 10	Warnings, reprimands and conditional cautions are brought within the scope of the Rehabilitation of Offenders Act 1974; reprimands and warnings are spent at the time they are given, conditional cautions spent after three months.
Anti-social behaviour orders	S123–124	Amendments to anti-social behaviour orders and individual support orders.

Continued

Table 4.1 continued

Name	Act reference	Description
Sexual offences prevention orders	S141	Some young people will be eligible for sexual offences prevention order if convicted of an offence listed under Schedule 3 of the Sexual Offences Act 2003.
Pre-sentence reports	S12	When custody is being considered by the court for a young person the pre-sentence report *must* be in writing.
Sentences of detention for public protection	S14	S226 of the Criminal Justice Act 2003 has been amended to set a minimum detention of two years.
Extended sentences for certain violent and sexual offences	S16	S228 of the Criminal Justice Act 2003 has been amended to set a minimum detention of four years.
Automatic 28-day release on recall	S29	If a young person is recalled to custody, they will automatically be released 28 days after the day they are returned to custody, subject to meeting the eligibility criteria.
Custody credit for electronically curfewed bail	S21	A young person subject to electronically monitored curfew while on bail may have time 'credited' to reduce the time spent in custody for a subsequent custodial sentence.

The Youth Rehabilitation Order (YRO) was introduced on as a new generic community sentence for young people on 30 November. It replaced nine existing sentences and can combine several requirements (from a list of 18, outlined later in this chapter). The following 9 community sentences were *replaced by the YRO* and so no longer exist:

- Action Plan Order.
- Curfew Order (as a sentence).
- Supervision Order.
- Community Punishment Order (16–17 year olds).
- Community Rehabilitation Order.
- Community Punishment and Rehabilitation Order.
- Attendance Centre Order.
- Drug Treatment and Testing Order.
- Exclusion Order.

According to the Ministry of Justice (2009) and the Youth Justice Board (2010b) it was hoped that the changes would simplify sentencing and improve the flexibility of interventions. The YRO also allows reparation to be included, ostensibly giving further scope for victims' needs to be accommodated. Additionally, the YRO puts Intensive Supervision and Surveillance and Intensive Fostering on a statutory footing.

It was envisaged that the innovation would help to stem the increase of numbers of young people being placed into custody and the secure estate – which, according to the Youth Justice Board, had reached almost 3000 in 2008. The flexibility of options in relation to the content of a YRO could, it was argued, encourage magistrates and judges to use these robust alternatives to custody where they are available. Indeed, when sentencers choose an incarcerative sanction, the Act requires them to provide a reason if they do not use an alternative to custody for those young people who are on the custody threshold.

Drawing on advice from the Youth Justice Board's practice guidance document, let's examine the detail of the YRO.

When can a court sentence to a YRO?

- A YRO is not an available sentencing option where compulsory referral order conditions are found to exist, i.e. where a first time offender has pleaded guilty to an *imprisonable* offence and is facing sentence in a youth or magistrates court.

- To sentence a young person to a YRO, the court must consider the offence serious enough to warrant a community sentence and the restriction of liberty involved must be commensurate to seriousness of offence (Youth Justice Board, 2010b).

How many YROs can a young person have?

- As a general rule, a young person can only be subject to one YRO at any one time.

- If the young person reoffends while subject to a YRO or Reparation Order, the court cannot sentence to a new YRO, unless the existing order (including any existing Reparation Order or Referral Order) has been revoked.

However,

- If a young person is being sentenced for two or more associated offences on the same sentencing occasion, the court can impose YROs for each of the offences

- The court may impose two YROs with a different combination of ('non-intensive') requirements, indicating whether these are to run concurrently or consecutively.

- Where they are to run consecutively – the cumulative number of hours/days must not exceed the maximum specified for that particular requirement. For example, if two unpaid work requirements are to run consecutively, the aggregate length of the requirement must not exceed 240 hours (Youth Justice Board, 2010b).

The contents of a YRO

When sentencing a young offender to a YRO, sentencers have a list of 18 content requirements from which to choose. Guidance from the Youth Justice Board recommends that:

- When sentencing, a court will attach one or more requirements to a YRO and will ensure the order is proportionate to the offence for which the young person is being sentenced; and

- Youth Offending Teams, in reporting to the court (ordinarily in the form of a pre-sentence report), will recommend to the court packages of interventions which are likely to address the assessed likelihood of reoffending and risk of serious harm to others. Although there is no limit to the number of requirements a court can attach to a YRO, it is expected that only requirements that are necessary to address risk of harm to the public, reduce the likelihood of reoffending and are proportionate to the offence are included by the court (Youth Justice Board, 2010b).

Although the order itself can be made for up to a maximum of three years, the requirements can be time limited for a lesser period (i.e. only be operational for part of the YRO).

This pick 'n' mix approach to youth justice disposals is not a new creation. Indeed, the history of youth justice legislation (see Chapter 2) is littered with examples of policy developments that created choices for sentencers, generating a greater degree of flexibility in juvenile sanctioning, than that allowed in the sentencing of adults. The adaptability of sanction measures accommodates the positivist paradigm within theoretical criminology (see Chapter 3) which posits that, as crime is caused by various factors that impact upon the individual, an individualistic, bespoke package of intervention is required to 'fit' a particular defendant's needs and specifically target precipitative or risk factors. Ashworth (2000) recognised this approach to youth disposals, which he described as 'cafeteria' justice, as did Fionda (2005) who dubbed it 'à la carte' style sentencing. In Chapter 2, I described the proliferation of theoretical characterisations of youth justice policy as a 'meze' of approaches: similarly, in relation to selection of sanction content options contained within the YRO, we can see a smorgasbord methodology in operation. Below is a list of requirement options available when sentencing a young person to a YRO.

Table 4.2 Possible requirements of a YRO

The following requirements can be attached to a YRO	
• Supervision requirement (usual for all orders).	• Prohibited activity requirement (i.e. not do something for a specified time – e.g. contact someone).
• Activity requirement (up to 90 days).	• Drug treatment requirement (residential or non-residential – YP must be willing to comply).
• Curfew requirement (up to 12 hours per day up to 6 months) – could be combined with a tag	• Drug testing requirement (can only be attached to a YRO when a Drug treatment requirement has also been attached – requires that the young person must provide samples).
• Electronic monitoring requirement.	• Intoxicating substances treatment requirement (e.g. alcohol – residential or non-residential – young person must be willing to comply).
• Exclusion requirement (can't enter a specified place for a specified period).	• Residence requirement (with a specified person or specified place for a specified period – 16/17 year olds).

Table 4.2 continued

• Local authority residence requirement (e.g. children's home, foster carer for up to six months).	• Programme requirement (e.g. anger management; knife crime prevention).
• Education requirement (requires young person of compulsory school age to comply with education arrangements, e.g. PRU, college, home tuition).	• Attendance centre requirement (12–26 hours 16/17 year olds; 12–24 hours 14/15 year olds; up to 12 hours U14 year olds).
• Mental health treatment requirement – residential or non-residential (e.g. sessions with a psychologist/counsellor). Young person must be willing to comply.	• Intensive supervision and surveillance (based on the current ISSP – must be an imprisonable offence – if U15 must be a persistent offender – 90–180 days).
• Unpaid work requirement (16/17 years, 40 to 240 hours).	• Intensive fostering (must be an imprisonable offence – if U15 must be a persistent offender – max 12 months).

The scaled approach

The Youth Justice Board produced guidelines in 2009 to help practitioners understand and implement the new structured methodology of assessing risk, called 'the scaled approach'. The system

> *aims to ensure that interventions are tailored to the individual and based on an assessment of their risks and needs and should be used by the youth offending team to determine the level of intervention required when a young person is subject to YOT intervention through a Referral Order, a YRO or during the community element of a custodial sentence.*

(Youth Justice Board, 2009, p6)

The level of intervention is informed by the assessment process, and should be used to guide:

- sentence proposals made to the court;

- reports to youth offender panels;

- the intervention provided during the youth offending team's subsequent management of the order.

When youth offending team officers have to prepare a report on a young person, they must complete the Youth Justice Board's assessment framework tool, the Asset – Core Profile (available at the Ministry of Justice or Youth Justice Board's website). This is to ensure they have a good understanding of the young person's risks and needs and investigate all aspects of the young person's lifestyle, as well as their offending behaviour. This will give the officer a better understanding of the triggers for the concerning behaviour and approaches the youngster within a holistic framework (see also at the Ministry of Justice or Youth Justice Board's website, the assessment tools Onset and the Common

Assessment Framework (CAF) which are used by social workers and officers involved in prevention interventions, to try to assess risks and divert young people from coming into contact with the formal youth justice system).

The risks and needs factors identified by using the scaled approach framework should be utilised to determine the overall intervention level, which is based primarily on assessing two factors:

- Likelihood of further offending – YOT officers should add the scores from the 12 main sections of Asset – Core Profile (which relate to 'dynamic' factors affecting offending behaviour) and score four 'static' factors, to arrive at a total score between 0 and 64.

- Risk of serious harm – a full Asset – Risk of Serious Harm form (also available at the Ministry of Justice or Youth Justice Board's website) should be completed if there is a 'yes' response to any of the questions in the 'Indicators of serious harm to others' section of the Asset – Core Profile.

Although Chapter 6 contains further information about assessing young people, it is useful to outline the 'static' and 'dynamic' factors that are assessed in order to reach an actuarially based total score of risk, as noted in Table 4.3.

Table 4.3 Scoring static and dynamic factors

Asset scoring 0–64 – static and dynamic factors – see Asset at www.yjb.gov.uk	
Static factors – scored 0–4 (4 being high risk factor)	**Dynamic factors** – each scored 0–4 (4 being high risk factor)
	Living arrangements.
Offence type (e.g. burglary scores 3).	Family and personal relationships.
	Education, training and employment.
Age at first Reprimand/Warning (10–12 scores 4; 13–17 scores 2; none scores 0).	Neighbourhood.
	Lifestyle.
	Substance use.
Age at first conviction (10–13 scores 4; 14–17 scores 3; no previous convictions scores 0).	Physical health.
	Emotional and mental health.
Number of previous convictions (4 or more scores 4; 1–3 scores 3; no previous convictions scores 0).	Perception of self and others.
	Thinking and behaviour.
	Attitudes to offending.
	Motivation to change.

After completing Asset and getting a 'score', practitioners should use the framework below to determine a sentence recommendation based upon the most suitable level of intervention – see Table 4.4.

Table 4.4 Asset score correlates of risk profile and intervention level (Youth Justice Board, 2009).

Profile	Intervention level
Low likelihood of reoffending – score between 0–14(inc)	STANDARD
and	
No or low risk of serious harm.	
Medium likelihood of reoffending – score between 15–32(inc)	ENHANCED
or	
Medium risk of serious harm.	
High likelihood of reoffending – score between 33–64(inc)	INTENSIVE
or	
high or very high risk of serious harm.	

Some criticisms of the scaled approach

As I stated in Chapter 2, the actuarial risk calculation approach to youth justice has gained much momentum since the establishment of the Youth Justice Board and the development of the formal risk assessment tool – the Asset form. The creation of the scaled approach seemed to mark the wholesale adoption of the belief that an accurate, almost mathematical calculation of risk is possible. Unquestioning confidence in this type of methodology seems to negate the possibility that choice, chance and opportunity can have an influence upon youthful offending behaviour. This in turn also dismisses a major school of thought within theoretical criminology, namely the classicist's understanding that crime causation can be best understood by viewing the offender as a rational actor, who is not propelled into criminality by his/her dire circumstances (because others in similarly dire situations do not commit crime) but who chooses to commit crime because the opportunity presents itself and because they might just get away with it.

Case (2007) and Case and Haines (2009) have presented a robust critique of the risk assessment paradigm and official trust in risk factor research, which seems to have reached its zenith in the form of the scaled approach. An application of some of their concerns about this paradigm to the scaled approach assessment, can be summarised as follows:

- *Reductionism* – is it possible to reduce young peoples' lives to simple, calculable risk factors? Their lives are varied and complex.

- *Factorisation* – can complicated concepts and ideas about often multi-factor risk components really be expressed by a number?

- *Aggregation* – is it acceptable in the scaled approach to weight each very different dynamic and static factor with a maximum potential score of four (and why 0–4, why not 0–10) and when all individual scores have been allocated simply to add the scores together?

- *Generalisation* – there is an assumption that risk factors are the same regardless of sex, age, culture, background and lifestyle.

- *Homogenisation* – measures of 'offending' has been over-simplified and potential offending triggers are often viewed as impacting upon all young people to the same extent. Further, past offending might be assessed as relevant to the calculation of present risk, even though the risk factor that prompted that offending behaviour is no longer active. In essence, different factors and behaviours are measured as if they were homogenous or unvarying.

- *Ambiguity* – what is a 'risk factor'? A cause, a correlate, a symptom, a predictor? Also, what is being predicted: delinquency, anti-social behaviour, low level offending, serious offending, re-offending?

Describing young people who are being assessed by the youth justice system as 'crash test dummies', Case and Haines (2009) conclude that

> *Government claims that risk-focused policy and practice within the youth justice system have been 'evidence-based' have been founded and perpetuated on a narrow, partial, pseudoscientific misrepresentation and misapplication of the 'evidence' of risk and its relationship with offending.* (pp 307–308)

Other criticisms include:

- A young offender might receive a high score because they have multiple high level welfare needs for which they are not culpable/responsible and yet the sentence recommendation in terms of intervention level should be based on the score (Bateman, 2009, described this as 'patently unfair').

- Assessing risk factors is surely a subjective calculation? Two YOT officers might arrive at a very different score for the same offender – one Asset question even asks whether the assessor has a 'gut feeling' about the young person's propensity to violent behaviour(!).

- The method seemingly wholeheartedly embraces positivist notions of determinism, i.e. that particular factors will have certain outcomes (e.g. that school exclusion will lead to offending behaviour) – but social scientific research can never be as accurate in its predictions as natural or pure science, because people sometimes react in the most unexpected ways.

- The actuarial measurement technique focuses on the individual rather than structural causes of risk factors such as poverty, discrimination, marginalisation, unemployment, etc. (Smith, 2007).

- Using the scaled approach will potentially widen the net of criminal justice even further over vulnerable young people, without sufficiently tackling endemic social problems associated with youthful transgression (Paylor, 2010).

- The risk factors prevention paradigm fails to account for individual agency, societal or cultural contexts, motivational factors linked to personal psychology and issues of human rights (O'Mahony, 2009).

In essence, young people are being assessed for what they *might* do in the future, possibly partly due to welfare deficiencies in their lives over which they have little or no control. The idea that we can asses the risk of a youth offending in the same manner as a car insurance company measures risk by aggregating a variety of potential danger factors, perhaps appeals to simplistic notions of common sense. However, to attempt to predict the future actions of often the most vulnerable young people in this way, a way that might lead to them becoming sucked even further into systems of stigmatisation and labelling, could be viewed as a somewhat dehumanising scientific process.

Breaching a YRO

The order will be breached where the young person fails any condition on three occasions within a twelve-month period. The usual practice within youth offending teams is that the supervising officer should send warning letters on the first two failures and on the third, should refer the matter to court with a report detailing the failures. The court has the following options when dealing with a breach:

- No action.

- Fine.

- Impose another condition or amend/substitute a condition.

- Impose a new YRO with ISS (if further breach, can get up to four months custody).

- Revoke and re-sentence to any available sentence (this could be another YRO).

- If the existing sentence was a YRO with ISS or Intensive Fostering and the original offence was imprisonable the court can sentence to custody.

Sentencing guidelines

In November 2009 the Sentencing Guidelines Council published its first general guide to the sentencing of defendants under 18 years old (*Overarching principles – Sentencing youths: Definitive guide*). The release of this guide corresponded with the implementation of the youth rehabilitation order on 30 November of that year. Prior to this release, the Sentencing Guidelines Council had largely dealt with guidance for adult defendants: though piecemeal advice in relation to sexual offences and robbery matters in relation to under-eighteen year olds had been published earlier. As noted in Chapter 2, the guidelines display a mixture of theoretical approaches towards the sentencing of young people and seek to juxtapose traditional approaches to youth penology by encouraging sentencers to consider both justice and welfare aims when making disposal decisions.

The guide is essential for workers within the youth justice system (you can download a copy at www.sentencing-guidelines.gov.uk). It sets out general principles to be applied when sentencing youths and then goes on to provide advice in relation to persistent offenders and the responsibilities of parents and guardians. Specific guidance criteria for particular sentence options are then explored regarding referral orders, financial orders, the youth rehabilitation order and custodial sentences. The last section covers cases dealt with in the crown court and sets out advice in relation to homicide, grave crimes procedures, dangerous offences, offences which attract a statutory minimum sentence and guidance on remittals and issues that arise when a young person is charged alongside an adult.

The current sentencing framework and possible content of various sentencing options are examined in the chart below. However, practitioners need to be aware of the array of general principles which apply when sentencing juveniles. The guidance describes that a number of general principles apply (helpfully summarised on p8 of the guide) which are discussed in detail below.

1. First:

    Offence seriousness is the starting point for sentencing. In considering the seriousness of any offence, the court must consider the offender's culpability in committing the offence and any harm which the offence caused, was intended to cause or might foreseeably have caused. In imposing sentence, the restrictions on liberty must be commensurate with the seriousness of the offence.

    (Sentencing Guidelines Council 2009, Para 1.1)

    This aim (drawn from the Criminal Justice Act 2003) squarely reflects one of the central tenets of the classicist criminological paradigm that we discussed in Chapter 3, namely that of proportionality in relation to offence gravity and disposal.

2. The court must consider the principal aim of the youth justice system as stated in section 37 of the Crime and Disorder Act 1998, to prevent offending by children and young people.

3. The court must apply the welfare principle as enshrined in section 44 of the Children and Young Persons Act 1933, specifically that they should take account of welfare issues including the suitability of the young person's surroundings and the need to make educational or training provision. Helpfully in relation to welfare, the guide says that sentencers should be aware of the high incidence of young people with mental health problems, learning difficulties within the criminal justice system in addition to being aware of vulnerability, self harm, abuse and bereavement, language and discrimination issues. Also, it asks sentencers to reflect that adolescence is a period of change and experimentation.

4. Further, sentencers must

    be aware of obligations under a range of international conventions which emphasise the importance of avoiding 'criminalisation' of young people whilst ensuring that they are held responsible for their actions and, where possible, take part in repairing the damage that they have caused. This includes recognition of the damage caused to the victims and understanding by the young person that the deed was not acceptable. Within a system that provides for both the acknowledgement of guilt and sanctions which rehabilitate, the intention is to establish responsibility and, at the same time, to promote re-integration rather than to impose retribution.

    (Sentencing Guidelines Council 2009, para 1.3)

This principle is infact a melting pot of diverse principles and appears to want sentencers to consider everything – to take into account responsibility and culpability, the impact of the crime and victim rights, reparation, to recognise welfare-based international conventions, punishment, rehabilitation and re-integration. It is arguable that some of these aims are incompatible, giving magistrates and judges a very hard cerebral juggling act to do when sentencing juveniles.

5. Moreover, the sentence should be 'individualistic'. Echoing a major maxim of the positivist school of criminology, this principle basically recommends that the sentence should fit the offender and be tailor-made to address the risk triggers in each young person's life.

6. Additionally, courts should take into account both the chronological age of the offender (one might not expect a 10 year old to be as responsible as a 17 year old) and the level of maturity of the young person.

7. Also, somewhat confusingly, although 'a court is required to aggravate the seriousness of an offence where there are previous convictions . . . a sentence that follows re-offending does not need to be more severe than the previous sentence solely because there had been a previous conviction' (Sentencing Guidelines Council 2009, p2.4).

8. Next, culpability and harm should be considered in relation to aggravating and mitigating circumstances and whether the offence(s) reaches the sentencing thresholds should be determined:

The assessment of offence seriousness will fix the most severe penalty that can be imposed and will determine whether an offence has crossed the necessary threshold to enable the court to impose a community or custodial sentence.

(Sentencing Guidelines Council 2009, para 2.5)

However, even if, for example, the threshold is met for a custodial sentence and is so serious that only an incarcerative disposal should be given, the guide states that, 'even where the custody threshold has been crossed, a court is not required to impose a custodial sentence' (Sentencing Guidelines Council 2009, para 2.5). Basically, this seems to recommend that the starting point is the most severe disposal and then judges/magistrates can mitigate/count down from that point.

9. Furthermore, the guide states that a reduction should be given for a guilty plea (but does not state what that reduction should be).

10. In addition 'there is an expectation that, generally, a young person will be dealt with less severely than an adult offender' (Sentencing Guidelines Council 2009, para 3.1). The guide asks sentencers to consider the greater impact a sentence might have on a young person as compared to an adult, their ability to learn from mistakes and grow out of crime, the possible influence of peers and the impact of stigma on the youngster's life chances (para 3.2).

11. Lastly, the general guidance recommends that, having considered all the above principles, sentencers should reflect on the overall impact of the sentence decision they have arrived at and then consider the appropriateness of any ancillary orders (e.g. parenting order, costs, compensation, etc. – see Table 4.6).

The guide recognises that there are well documented research results that point to a correlative link between certain factors and youth crime:

Factors regularly present in the background of those juveniles who commit offences include: low family income, poor housing, poor employment records, low educational attainment, early experience of offending by other family members or of violence or abuse (often accompanied by harsh and erratic discipline within the home) and the misuse of drugs. There is also evidence that those young people who are 'looked after' have been more at risk of being drawn into the criminal justice system than other young people acting in similar ways.

(Sentencing Guidelines Council 2009, para 3.6)

However, the guide asserts that

It is clear that these factors do not cause delinquency (since many who have experienced them do not commit crime).

(Sentencing Guidelines Council 2009, para 3.7)

Crime and Security Act 2010

This statute extended the use of anti-social behaviour injunctions which came into force for adults in November 2009 (dubbed by the popular press as 'gangbos') to 14–17 year olds. These civil injunctions include prohibitions on meeting other gang members, wearing gang colours, going to certain locations or having a violent dog in a public place. Breaching the injunction could lead to either:

1. A supervision order (supervised by the local YOT). The court can impose one or more of the following:

*   a supervision requirement of up to 6 months;

*   an activity requirement of between 12–24 days;

*   a curfew requirement of up to 8 hours per day (which can be electronically monitored).

If the supervision order is breached, the court can revoke the existing order and make a new one or make a detention order.

or

2. A detention order of up to 3 months (if a supervision order is not appropriate).

The Act also stipulated that, unless exceptional circumstances exist, a parent/guardian of a young person under the age of sixteen who has breached an ASBO must receive a parenting order.

Note: The Coalition government's proposals for reforming youth justice will be examined in detail in Chapter 8.

The current sentencing framework

Issues relating to bail, remand and the diversionary disposals of reprimand, final warning and youth conditional caution are covered in Chapter 5. This section examines the current disposals available to youth court magistrates and crown court judges in relation to young people aged 10 to 17 years. Table 4.5 details the various disposals that can be used. For further details of each sentence visit www.yjb.gov.uk or www.justice.gov.uk

Table 4.5 The current disposals available in relation to young people aged 10 to 17 years

Sentence	Age range	Nature and content of sentence	Possible length of sentence
Discontinued or dismissed or withdrawn	10–17 years	The case is dropped because it is decided by the Prosecution Service that there is not enough evidence against the young person or that it is not in the public interest to prosecute.	Not applicable
Youth restorative disposal	10–17 years	Allows police or PCSO to deal with a minor matter at the scene of the crime where a young person has never received any other disposal (inc ASBO) and admits the offence. It will usually take the form of an apology to the victim during a supervised conversation. All parties must consent to this course of action. A letter will be sent to parents/guardians and local YOT will be notified and screen for risk.	Not applicable
Reprimand	10–17 years	A verbal warning given by a police officer for a minor first offence where guilt has been admitted.	One meeting
Final warning	10–17 years	A verbal warning given by a police officer for a first or second offence where guilt has been admitted. A short intervention/series of meetings takes place, usually co-ordinated by police officers attached to the local Youth Offending Team (YOT). (Note: The Legal Aid, Sentencing and Punishment of Offenders Bill 2011 plans to reform the system of reprimands and final warnings).	Up to 12 weeks
Youth conditional caution	16–17 years	Introduced by the Criminal Justice and Immigration Act 2008 (and piloted). Discretional disposal for the police or CPS to use where the 16/17 year old admits guilt and has not been previously convicted. Conditions can be attached such as completion of specified activities and/or a fine.	Up to 20 hours
Absolute discharge	10–17 years	The young person has admitted guilt or been found guilty but no formal sentencing action is taken.	Not applicable
Conditional discharge	10–17 years	The young person must stay out of trouble for a specified period. If they do, no immediate punishment is given: if they don't they can be re-sentenced.	Between 6 months and 3 years
Referral order	10–17 years	Given to a young person who pleads guilty and is appearing in court for the first time. Compulsory unless the court issues custody, an absolute discharge or the offence is non-imprisonable or fixed by law. (Content and detail noted above. In section on the Youth Justice and Criminal Evidence Act, 1999.) Amendments in 2009 gave sentencers powers to make a referral order where the young person has conviction but has not received an ARO previously; where they have been bound over or where they have received a conditional discharge. Exceptionally a second order can be made after a YOT recommendation. Also the order can be extended by up to 3 months.	Between 3 and 12 months

Continued

Table 4.5 continued

Sentence	Age range	Nature and content of sentence	Possible length of sentence
Fine	10–17 years	This should be proportionate to the crime and means are taken into account. If the young person is under 16 the parents/guardians will be responsible for payment. The Criminal Justice and Immigration Act 2008 proposed a Youth Default Order for 16/17 year olds who fail to pay fines. It was proposed that the court could impose unpaid work, a curfew or attendance centre requirement in lieu of the fine.	Not applicable
Compensation order	10–17 years	As main sentence or as an ancillary order. Paid to the victim for loss/damage. Should take into account the amount of loss/damage and the means of the offender (or parents, if under 16 years).	Not applicable
Reparation order	10–17 years	Requires that the young person makes amends for the offence either directly to the victim or indirectly via community work. Supervised by YOT.	Up to 24 hours over 3 months
Youth rehabilitation order	10–17 years	A generic community sentence for young offenders which enables sentencers to choose from a long menu of 18 requirements, namely; supervision, activities, curfew, exclusion, residence, mental health treatment, unpaid work (16/17 year olds), drug testing, intoxicating substance treatment, electronic monitering, prohibited activities, local authority residence, programmes (e.g. anger management), attendance centre, Intensive Supervision and Surveillance (ISS) and intensive fostering. It should be noted that in addition to the ISS being a possible requirement of a YRO, it can also be given as part of a bail package or as part of the community element of a detention and training order (DTO). An ISS can run for up to 12 months but often runs for 6 months, with the young person being required to undertake a high intensity phase during the first part of the order. (25 hours of activities per week.) The length and content of the order and its requirements should be appropriate to the young persons needs and reflect issues of seriousness. (See heading Criminal Justice and Immigration Act 1998 and the Scaled Approach, above, for further detail.)	Up to 3 years
Deferred sentence	10–17 year olds	After conviction, exceptionally, sentence can be deferred for up to 6 months usually to assess positive changes of circumstances or to monitor any reparation agreement.	Up to 6 months
Detention and training order	12–17 year olds	The young person spends the first half of the sentence in custody and the other half under supervision (usually by the YOT) within the community doing activities listed in the supervision order, above. The sentencing court can specify that for this second part of the order the young person should be placed on an ISS.	4 months to 2 years

Table 4.5 continued

Sentence under S90 or 91 for grave offences	10–17 years	Under the Powers of the Criminal Court (Sentencing) Act 2000 a young person who is convicted of a murder or a 'grave crime' (i.e. one for which an adult could be sentenced to 14 years in custody) can receive the same statutory maximum as an adult. They will be automatically released at the halfway point on licence (CJA 2003). YOT/probation will supervise them up to the three-quarter point. (Note: The Legal Aid, Sentencing and Punishment of Offenders Bill 2011 plans to reform the use of indeterminate sentences for both youths and adults).	Indefinite
Extended sentence for certain violent and sexual offences	10–17 years	This allows for the use of extended sentence for young people who have committed serious violent and/or sexual offences under s228 of the Criminal Justice Act 2003 (as amended by s16 of the Criminal Justice and Immigration Act 2008).	Minimum of 4 years
Sentence of detention for public protection	10–17 years	This procedure exceptionally applies where a young person needs to be detained for public protection. (S226 Criminal Justice Act 2003 as amended by the Criminal Justice and Immigration Act 2008 s14.)	Up to 2 years

If a young person does not comply with the community penalties listed in Table 4.5 s/he will be brought before the court and the relevant supervising authority (the local YOT, the probation service or the curfew monitoring body) will initiate breach proceedings. It is the practice of many YOTs to breach orders after three failures to comply/attend. If the supervising body can prove the breach (or it is admitted) the court is able to reinstate the order or to re-sentence (usually to a harsher disposal).

It is apparent from Table 4.1 that a wide range of options are available to magistrates and judges. As noted in Chapter 2, academics have commented on the vast choice and referred to a 'cafeteria' style of justice for young offenders (Ashworth, 2000). In terms of criminological theory, the sentencer is able to hand pick a 'bespoke' (Fionda, 2005) sentence requirements to fit the particular circumstances and needs of the young person. This is arguably a positivist's dream system! However, remember the problems associated with such a tailored system, that assesses individual risks in an actuarial manner, which we noted earlier in this chapter when examining the scaled approach.

Additional orders

Further to the above sentences, the following additional orders can be made. Some of these orders were introduced by the Crime and Disorder Act 1998 but were added to and consolidated by later statutory amendments (see next section, below). The orders listed in Table 4.6 include civil orders that can be sought as controlling measures for young people who have not been found guilty of any criminal offence. It should be noted that a child curfew order is a civil order that should be differentiated from a curfew order that can be used as a bail measure or as a sanction for a criminal act. The restrictive nature of these measures in terms of civil liberties is commented on in Chapter 1. Table 4.6 should be read in conjunction with the section in Chapter 8 that discusses proposed changes to anti-social behaviour legislation put forward by the Home Office in a consultation paper in February 2011.

Table 4.6 Additional orders

Type of order	Age range	Nature content of order	Time limits
Anti-social behaviour order (ASBO)	10 years and above	This is a civil order. ASBOs can be made by local authorities, the police, British Transport Police, Social Landlords and Housing Action Trusts or by other relevant authorities. An ASBO is made where the person has acted in an anti-social manner which has caused or is likely to cause harassment, alarm or distress. Individualised conditions can be attached requiring the person not to go to certain areas, near certain people, participate in certain activities, etc. Breach can amount to a criminal offence with a maximum punishment of a 2-year DTO. An interim ASBO can be obtained, pending a full ASBO hearing. The Criminal Justice and Immigration Act 2008 states that, where an ASBO is made on a youth, it must be reviewed after 12 months. If an ASBO imposed on a person under the age of 16 is breached, the Crime and Security Act 2010 stipulates that (unless exceptional circumstances exist) the parents/guardian of a young person must have a parenting order imposed.	2 years plus (no specified upper time limit)
Acceptable behaviour contract (ABC)	Any age group – primarily aimed at 10–17 year olds	This is a civil order whereby a local authority draws up an agreement that specifies that the young person must desist from certain lower-level anti-social behaviour. Intervention by a YOT or social worker may additionally be agreed. Breach of an ABC can be used as evidence for the issuing of an ASBO.	No specified upper time limit
Individual support order (ISO)	10–17 years	A civil order that is applied for by local authorities (usually the anti-social behaviour unit/team of a local authority) and intended to provide support for young people subject to ASBOs to prevent the behaviour that led to the ASBO being made. Managed by YOTs. Breach can be deemed a criminal offence with a fine of up to £1,000 (payable by parents if the young person is under 16). An ISO should be attached to an ASBO following the Criminal Justice and Immigration Act 2008.	Up to 6 months
Disperal order	No age limit	Introduced by the Anti-social Behaviour Act 2003, this order enables the police and local authority to identify problem areas where people feel threatened by groups congregating after 9pm, causing intimidation and acting in an anti-social manner. Police or community support officers can direct individuals to leave an area for up to 24 hours. Until 2005 the police had been able to take under-16s home after 9pm if they were within a designated area and not under the control of an adult. However, this power was successfully challenged in R (*On the Application of W*) v *Commissioner of Police of the Metropolis and Richmond Borough Council [2005]* EWCA Civ 1568. The police can only ask that the young person to return home. (Note proposal for reform published in 2011 by the Home Office – see Chapter 8.)	Up to 6 months
Anti-social behaviour injunctions	14–17 years	Introduced by the Crime and Security Act 2010. These can include prohibitions on meeting gang members, wearing gang colours, going to certain locations or having a dog in a public area. Breach can result in either a supervision order for up to 6 months (which could also include between 12–24 days of activity or a curfew of up to 8 hours per day) or a detention order for up to 3 months.	Not applicable but for breach: Supervision up to 6 months or Detention up to 3 months
Child safety order (CSO)	Under 10s	A civil order imposed on a child (i) who does an act that, had they been aged 10 or above, would have amounted to a criminal offence; (ii) has caused distress, alarm or harassment or (iii) has breached a child curfew order. Supervised by a social worker. Breach can result in the child being placed under a care order.	Up to 12 months
Local child curfew	Under 16 (including under 10s)	A civil order (obtained by a local authority or police) that bans the child/young person from a particular area during specified hours due to them causing distress to residents. If a child under 10 breaches this order, they can be given a child safety order (above).	Between 9pm and 6am for a period up to 90 days

Table 4.6 continued

Parenting order	Not applicable	A civil order given to parents/guardians of young people who have offended, truanted, been subjected to an ASBO, CSO or sexual offences prevention order. Parent must attend guidance sessions and could additionally be required to ensure that the child attends school, is supervised when visiting certain places and/or is home by a specified time. Failure to comply can lead to prosecution and a criminal offence. The Crime and Security Act 2010 stipulated that, unless exceptional circumstances exist, a parent/guardian of a young person under 16 who has breached an ASBO, must receive a parenting order.	Between 3 to 12 months
Costs order	10–17 years	(In existence prior to the 1998 Act.) After a court hearing where the young person has pleaded or been found guilty, they (or their parents if under 16) can be ordered to pay a contribution towards prosecution costs.	Will be given a specified time to complete payment
Compensation order	10–17 years	This can be an ancillary order (or a main order). Should take into account the financial circumstances of the offender (or parent/guardian if under 16 years old).	Not applicable

From our investigations of all the sentencing disposals and other additional measures that can be used by the state in its endeavours to control youth disorder, it is possible to understand why some academics (noted above) have indicated that the current system may amount to an over zealous system that contains a vast array of measures without a coherent, rational theoretical direction – and that some re-evaluation of the direction in which youth justice is moving is becoming increasingly necessary. As noted (above), see Chapter 8 for amendments proposed in February 2011 and Bills moving through Parliament when this book was published.

CASE STUDY

Jim (aged 15) has been convicted of an offence of Attempted Theft (found guilty after trial). In evidence, Jim admitted that he was in the area at the time of the offence with the co-defendant (aged 18) as they had been to the West End to see a film. He stated that after the film ended both he and the co-defendant made their way to the nearest tube station (which he believed was Piccadilly Circus) in order to make their way home. Jim recounted that the tube station had been temporarily closed and that guards were not allowing anyone onto the platforms, so he and the co-defendant made their way out of the tube station in order to take a bus home. Jim stated that he was then stopped by a police officer, asked several questions, and was then processed for this offence.

This version of events did not accord with the account of events provided by the Crown Prosecution Service. Jim denied observing a man withdrawing money from a cashpoint machine, denied following him into a newsagent's shop and denied making any attempts to remove any items from the man's bag or being a secondary party to any such activities. The magistrates accepted the Prosecution's evidence and found Jim guilty. However, although Jim has been found guilty for this matter, he maintains his innocence incontrovertibly and refuses to take any responsibility for this offence.

Jim is a refugee from Romania. According to Jim and his elder cousins with whom he fled Romania and with whom he now resides, they have been in the UK for about two years.

Continued

The borough's Children and Families Team now accommodates this family unit. Jim's allocated social worker is responsible for Jim's general welfare. The borough pays for the accommodation and Jim receives a subsistence allowance of approximately £142 every four weeks. His cousins are also in receipt of subsistence money. Jim has lost contact with his mother and father. His father left Romania with Jim's elder brother aged 16, and while Jim believes that his mother is still in Romania he has not been able to contact her. Jim has not had any formal schooling for approximately three years; attempts to find special educational placements for him since he has been under the guidance of the council have not yet borne fruit. In terms of career ambitions, Jim stated that he wishes to become a mechanic. Jim recounted that he spends his time watching TV and videos (which, he stated, assist him to learn English), reading English self-learning texts and playing football in a team with some friends.

Jim received a four-month referral order a year ago (which he has completed successfully) for a matter of handling stolen goods. He also received a final warning two years ago for the theft of an Ipod Nano from a shop.

- *What risk factors are in evidence?*

- *How can these be reduced?*

- *What sentence might you recommend for Jim and why?*

- *Are any ancillary orders appropriate?*

It is concerning that Jim is associating with an older co-defendant who seems to be having a negative impact upon him. There might also be issues of bullying. It is also problematic that Jim is still denying this offence, even though he has been found guilty. Other risk factors include Jim's accommodation and family circumstances – he has lost contact with his parents and is living with cousins. These factors make him vulnerable and he may have psychological issues around feelings of abandonment. Further, the fact that he is receiving no educational provision also poses a further risk factor. Additionally, his previous similar offence shows a developing pattern of offending.

Intervention to assess the suitability of his accommodation, to establish an education or training placement and to provide offence counselling are immediately necessary. As Jim successfully completed his referral order he has shown a willingness to co-operate with the Youth Offending Team. There are a range of sentence options that might be appropriate (see sentencing chart) but a Youth Rehabilitation Order of 12 months might be a sentence that would be acceptable to the youth magistrates. The requirements you might recommend be attached would possibly be a supervision requirement, an education requirement (once you have set up a placement) and perhaps an unpaid work requirement of 40 hours.

ACTIVITY 4.4

Discuss whether there are now too many options for dealing with young people who offend or take part in behaviour deemed to be disorderly or whether it is right for the government to have a variety of measures to deal with non-conforming youths. What are the implications of this expansion of youth control measures?

Future youth justice legislation

This chapter has discussed current law and practice. I review future legislation and the most recent proposals for youth justice in Chapter 8.

CHAPTER SUMMARY

In this chapter the political context and debates that led to the restructuring of the youth justice system over the last fifteen years have been discussed. We examined the rationale expressed by the Labour Government to justify sweeping reforms of the system and noted some academic commentary relating to these changes. We have analysed the content of the two main sources of contemporary youth justice laws, from 1998 to the present and examined the current sentencing options and ancillary orders available. We have further analysed other legislative enactments relating to anti-social behaviour orders and other civil orders targeted at children and young people and looked at their broader impact upon the youth justice system. We have noted the range and scope of sentencing options for young people who have committed offences and the burgeoning of other (mainly civil law) measures introduced to prevent and deter disorderly activities that do not amount to crimes.

FURTHER READING

Case, S and Haines, K (2009) *Understanding youth offending: Risk-focused research, policy and practice.* Cullompton: Willan.

Ministry of Justice (2009) *The youth rehabilitation order and the youth justice provisions in the Criminal Justice and Immigration Act 2008, Circular 2009/3.* London: Ministry of Justice.

Sentencing Guidelines Council (2009) *Overarching principles – sentencing youths: Definite guideline.*

Youth Justice Board (2010) *Youth justice: The scaled approach.* London: Ministry of Justice.

Youth Justice Board (2010) *The youth rehabilitation order and other youth justice provisions of the Criminal Justice and Immigration Act 2008: Practice guidance for youth offending teams.* London: Youth Justice Board.

WEBSITE

www.sentencingcouncil.org.uk

For the youth sentencing guidelines.

www.justice.gov.uk

For up-to-date information about youth justice policies.

www.nacro.org.uk

Their youth crime section contains research on issues of youth justice.

Chapter 5

Working within a youth offending team and in the youth justice system

Paul Dugmore

Introduction

This chapter will consider the role of the social worker in the context of the multi-agency Youth Offending Team and the wider youth justice system since the 1998 Crime and Disorder Act was passed. Working within a YOT requires an understanding of multi-agency and inter professional working and the benefits and challenges of these ways of working will be explored. The chapter provides an overview of the youth justice process indentifying the multitude of agencies involved in dealing with young people who offend and the stages a young person may go through before arriving at the door of the YOT.

Introduction to YOTs

As outlined in Chapter 2, prior to the Crime and Disorder Act (1998), the remit of working with young people involved in offending was held by juvenile or youth justice teams which were part of social services departments. These teams were staffed by a combination of social workers and unqualified workers, perhaps from a social care or youth work background. Juvenile justice teams developed following the intermediate treatment initiative implemented in the 1980's as an alternative to custody, during which time the popular view was that minimal intervention was the appropriate response as the most effective intervention was *radical non-intervention* (Pitts, 2003, p8).

This approach contrasts with the evidenced-based interventionist and correctionist approach that has been central to the Labour reforms of the youth justice system (Bottoms and Dignan, 2004).

Following an Audit Commission Inspection which led to the publication of *Misspent youth* (1996), it was perceived that the youth justice system was failing to intervene effectively with young offenders and that the same young offenders were being repeatedly processed by the courts. The report concluded that the youth justice system was ineffectual, costly and in disarray and on the basis of which the incoming Labour government set about implementing a radical overhaul of the entire system. Pilots were established to test out some of the proposed reforms which were evaluated so that evidence-based practice could be seen to be underpinning the case for change however, criticism arose when legislation, including the requirement upon each local authority to establish a multi-agency YOT, was implemented before the evaluations were complete (Holdaway et al., 2001 cited in Bottoms and Dignan, 2004).

Multi-agency working

While there had existed statutory guidance for different organisations to work in partnership, for example, *Working together to safeguard children* (1998), the duty outlined in the CDA for each local area to establish a YOT heralded the first time such a large scale multi-agency approach had been made a legislative requirement. Prior to 1998, there was evidence of some multi-disciplinary working in existence, for instance, joint health and social services ventures in which social workers were placed in Community Mental Health Teams and hospitals. The CDA set out a requirement that in each local authority area, the local authority Social Services and Education Department's must work with the Police, Probation Service and Health Authority to establish and fund a new multi-agency Youth Offending Team, stipulating that each YOT must have at least one of the following:

- A social worker.

- A police officer.

- A probation officer.

- A nominated person from the education department.

- A nominated person from the health authority.

The Act also stated that while this was a minimum requirement, other staff could also be included, from the statutory or voluntary sector. Section 37 of the act states: *It shall be the principle aim of the youth justice system to prevent offending by children and young persons.*

As well as this primary aim being laid down in statute, the Act also sets out that each local authority, in consultation with its partner agencies, has a statutory duty to formulate, publish and implement an annual youth justice plan, to be submitted to the YJB, outlining how the YOT is to be composed and resourced, its functions, how it will operate and how youth justice services are to be provided and funded. Section 38(4) defines the services to be provided as:

- Appropriate adults.

- Assessment of young people for rehabilitation programmes after reprimand/final warning.

- Support for those remanded in custody or bailed.

- Placement in local authority accommodation when remanded.

- Court reports and assessments.

- Allocation of referral orders.

- Supervision of those sentenced to community orders.

- Supervision of those sentenced to custody.

Thus, multi-agency YOTs should co-ordinate the provision of these services with YOT staff drawn from a broad range of professions associated with the care of young people in order to tackle youth crime. Subsequently, an expectation was set for YOTs to provide preventative services to target those young people who may be deemed to be at risk of offending in line with the Children Act (1989) duty on local authorities to take reasonable steps designed to encourage children and young persons not to commit offences.

Youth Justice Board

The Crime and Disorder Act also introduced the Youth Justice Board, a new body to oversee the operation and monitoring of the youth justice system, specifically YOTs and the secure estate. Section 41 of the Act prescribed the functions of the board as being:

- To monitor the operation of the youth justice system and the provision of youth justice services.

- Advising the Secretary of State on the operation of the system especially with regard to how the statutory aim could be achieved.

- Monitoring the extent to which that aim is being achieved and any set standards met.

- Obtaining information from relevant authorities.

- Publishing information.

- Promoting good practice.

- Commissioning research into good practice.

- Awarding grants to develop good practice.

At its inception, the YJB produced the *National standards for youth justice services* in 2000, updated in 2004 and 2010 (YJB, 2004b, 2010), which give guidance on the expected quality and level of service required of YOTs and the secure estate, as well as the Asset assessment framework (outlined in Chapter 6). It has also produced the *Key elements of effective practice*, guides for YOT practitioners on a range of practice areas a quality assurance process and extensive case management guidance since 2009. The YJB also has responsibility for commissioning secure beds from the secure estate and managing placements.

The youth justice process

The youth justice system is comprised of a number of agencies each performing a particular role relating to young people who offend. Figure 5.1 depicts the large number of organisations involved and how these interrelate to each other.

The police

The main functions of the police are to prevent, detect and investigate crime and maintain public order although not all of police work is crime related, rather other service work in the community. The work of the police in relation to the investigation of crimes and the detention of suspects is guided by the Police and Criminal Evidence Act 1984 and the Code of Practice accompanying the Act. If a young person is arrested on suspicion of committing, having committed or being about to commit an offence, they will be taken to a local police station where the police will start their investigation into the alleged offence. Once a person has been interviewed regarding an offence, hopefully in the presence of a solicitor and certainly an appropriate adult if the suspect is under 17, the police have a number of options open to them. These are:

- Take no further action.

- Bail the young person to return on another date.

- Issue the young person with a reprimand.

- Refer the young person to the YOT for a final warning assessment. (They can also issue a final warning immediately, although this is bad practice.)

- Charge the young person.

- Some areas operate a triage system in which a joint police/YOT decision is taken as to whether to charge or not. If the young person is not charged it is likely that they will have to undertake a restorative justice intervention.

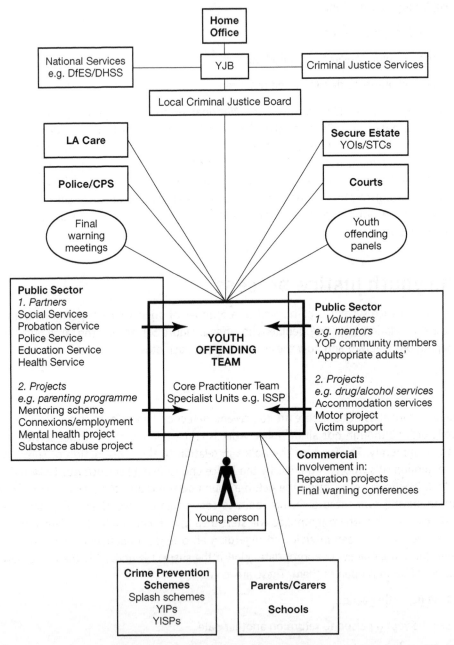

Figure 5.1 *Elements in a local youth justice system (from Appleton and Burnett, 2004, p9)*

Appropriate adults

YOTs have to ensure that an appropriate adult service is provided in the local area resourced either by volunteers or by local authority out of hours emergency duty teams. who offer 24-hour provision as young people may be arrested at any time. The role of the appropriate adult is to ensure that the young person's welfare needs are met during their detention in police custody and to facilitate communication between the young person and the police during the interview. The appropriate adult should be satisfied that the interview is being undertaken in accordance with the Police and Criminal Evidence Act 1984 and the Code of Practice. For more information on the role of the appropriate adult, there is a useful chapter in the *RHP companion to youth justice* (Bateman and Pitts, 2005).

Police bail

Young people are usually allowed home on police bail while they wait for an appearance before the Youth Court. The police may impose conditions on bail, e.g. to sleep at their home address, to report daily to a police station. The police may however, refuse bail where they believe that the person may not appear in court or may commit further offences while on bail, or for their own protection. If an offence is very serious and the police have decided to prosecute, the person may be detained until they can be brought to the earliest available court, usually the same day or the following morning. In the case of a young person being held overnight, the 'detention' should involve transfer to local authority accommodation such as a children's home, foster placement or secure unit, however recent HMIP inspection reports often highlight an acute shortage of PACE beds.

Reprimands and final warnings

The Crime and Disorder Act 1998 replaced the cautioning of young offenders (it still exists with adults) with a new system of reprimands and final warnings. Prior to the act, a young person could be cautioned indefinitely following an approach that saw young people being diverted from the criminal justice system as a way of preventing further offending based on a minimal intervention philosophy. Pitts comments on the Thatcherist approach to youth justice that consisted of *reducing costs and state intervention not dissimilar to the desire of the youth justice lobby to limit the state's intervention in the lives of young people in involved offending* (Pitts, 2003). However, as young people were being repeatedly cautioned, concern was developing that its impact was lessened and the Audit Commission (1996) criticised its use citing that cautioning was reasonably effective on no more than three occasions, and that subsequent use was not only ineffective but brought the system into disrepute (Marlow, 2005). The final warning scheme guidance (Home Office/Youth Justice Board, 2002, p5) states that:

> The final warning scheme aims to divert children and young people from their offending behaviour before they enter the court system. The scheme was designed to do this by:

- *ending repeat cautioning and providing a progressive and effective response to offending behaviour;*

- *providing appropriate and effective interventions to prevent re-offending; and*

- *ensuring that young people who do re-offend after being warned are dealt with quickly and effectively by the courts.*

Since June 2000, where there is sufficient evidence for a realistic prospect of conviction should the young person be prosecuted, a reprimand or final warning may be given, providing the person admits to the offence and consents to the reprimand or warning, and it is not in the public interest for a prosecution. Guidance on the final warning scheme states that a reprimand can only be given if a young person has not been reprimanded or finally warned before. Thus reprimands are designed for first-time offenders and the YOT must be notified when a young person is reprimanded. A final warning can only be given when a young person has re-offended having already received a reprimand. However, if the offence is serious enough to warrant it, a final warning can be given for a first offence. At this stage, the YOT must be notified so that the young person can be contacted, and assessed, using Asset (see Chapter 6) and a programme of intervention planned and offered. Compliance with this is not mandatory but if a young person fails to comply, this may be mentioned in subsequent hearings if they re-offend and are prosecuted and the police are informed of the non-compliance. If a young person offends after previously receiving a final warning, they must be charged unless the warning was given two years before the new offence was committed. A study undertaken in 2000 found that many of the young people and YOT workers saw the final warning system as 'arbitrary, unfair and disproportionate' with the way young offenders are dealt with contrasting very unfavourably with that for adults (Evans and Pugh, cited in Ball, 2004).

The Criminal Justice and Immigration Act (2008) extended the use of conditional cautions to young people as an alternative way of dealing with offending than prosecution. This meant that a 16–17 year old who had committed an offence for which they could not receive a reprimand or final warning could be offered a caution with conditions for certain offences. On the issuing of a caution, prosecution is suspended while the young person is given the opportunity to adhere to the conditions. If they do, the prosecution is dropped, however it is instigated again should the young person fail to comply with the conditions. This is currently only available in a limited number of areas.

The green paper, *Breaking the cycle: Effective punishment, rehabilitation and sentencing of offenders* (Ministry of Justice, 2010) proposes to prevent more young people from offending and divert them from the criminal justice system including simplifying the pre-court disposal system. The green paper acknowledges that under the current system of out of court disposals, young people are automatically escalated to a more intensive disposal, regardless of the circumstances or severity of their offence. This rigidity results in young people being unnecessarily drawn into the system and stifles any room for discretion by youth justice professionals. Once *Offences Brought to Justice* police targets were removed and further police discretion was allowed, a plethora of informal restorative action has developed over the past two years and this has informed the proposed new change. The proposal is to simplify the current framework by allowing police and prosecutors greater discretion in dealing with youth crime before it reaches court by ending the current system of automatic escalation so that professionals will have more freedom to determine the most appropriate response, depending on the severity of the offence and the circumstances of the young person. This may involve reparation or referrals to specialist provision to tackle offending behaviour. This departure from the current final warning system heralds the return of a similar arrangement prior to the CDA in which multi-agency cautioning panels considered cases of young people and decided whether they should be cautioned or charged. These proposals are considered in more detail in Chapter 8.

ACTIVITY 5.1

Consider the current pre-court disposals and the proposed changes outlined above. What are the advantages and disadvantages of each approach?

COMMENT

You may have favoured the proposed system of flexibility for enabling professional discretion to inform decisions made about whether to charge a young person or deal with their offending informally. Such diversion from prosecution accords with the UN Convention on the Rights of the Child as discussed in Chapter 2 and there is evidence to suggest that diverting young people away from the system can avoid stigmatising them (Kemp et al., 2002). However, you may have concluded that such informal, localised discretion also runs the risk of leading to diverging practice across the country.

Crown Prosecution Service (CPS)

The CPS is an integral part of the youth justice system, working alongside the police in making decisions about whether or not to charge a suspect. If the police are unsure whether to prosecute a young person, the CPS will advise on the appropriate action to take. In reaching a decision, the prosecutor (a qualified lawyer) will consider the case in relation to the Full Code Test, which looks at the evidence and the public interest. The Code for Crown Prosecutors, issued under the Prosecution of Offenders Act 1985 (available at www.cps.gov.uk/publications/docs/code2010english.pdf) details the evidential and public interest tests that must be applied to each case in order to determine whether or not a prosecution should be sought. In order to continue with a prosecution brought by the police, the prosecutor must be satisfied that there is sufficient admissible evidence to secure a conviction, and that it will be in the public interest. The prosecutor has to consider issues such as the defence case, reliability of witnesses and credibility of the evidence, as well as the likely outcome of a conviction, the vulnerability of the victim and the defendant's previous offending. If a decision to prosecute is made, the young person will be given a date to appear in court or be detained by the police and taken to court the following day. The CPS is also responsible for ensuring YOTs receive any documentation in relation to offences required for completion of a pre-sentence reports, consisting of evidence papers, the transcript of the police interviews with the young person, witness statements, details of previous convictions, etc.

Court

Since the passing of the Children Act 1989, young people charged with criminal offences have been dealt with by the Juvenile Court, renamed the Youth Court by the Criminal Justice Act 1991. If they are charged with an adult, they will appear in the magistrates' court, or if charged with a grave offence the case has to be committed to the Crown Court.

The Youth Court has responsibility for dealing with all young people who are charged. The Youth Court setting is more informal and is presided over usually by a panel of two or three lay magistrates, volunteers who are trained in youth matters, or sometimes by a district judge who is legally qualified and sits alone. The Youth Court deals with:

- Issues of bail and remand for young people whose cases are progressing through the court system.

- Deciding a defendant's innocence or guilt following a trial when a young person pleads not guilty.

- The committal of serious cases to the Crown Court where a custodial sentence of more than two years may be appropriate (as the Youth Court does not have the power to sentence beyond this time).

- Sentencing young people pleading guilty to, or convicted of, an offence. The Youth Court also deals with breaches of sentences when young people do not comply with the requirements of a court order. (See Chapter 4 for the sentencing framework for young people.)

If a court is unable to deal with the case straight away it has to consider what should happen to the person in the meantime. Arrangements should allow children and young people to remain living 'at home' wherever possible but it might be necessary for local authority accommodation or secure facilities to be used.

Remands to local authority accommodation

Section 23 of the Children and Young Persons Act (CYPA) 1969 gives courts the power to remand children and young people to local authority accommodation where they are charged with an offence and not released on bail. Subsection (7) of Section 23 allows the court to impose any conditions that can be imposed under Section 3(6) of the Bail Act 1976 on a defendant who has been granted bail. Some of the more common conditions are:

- To reside at a specific address.

- To observe a curfew between specified hours.

- A curfew may be enforced by electronic monitoring (a tag fitted to the leg).

- Not to enter a specific area.

- Not to associate with prosecution witnesses or pervert the course of justice.

- Not to contact other young people jointly accused.

- To comply with a YOT bail supervision and support programme which may involve numerous sessions a week.

- Bail ISSP – increased supervision and an electronically monitored curfew.

- To report to a police station.

Remand to local authority accommodation confers 'looked after' status on a young person and requires the appropriate social services department to provide accommodation for the young person. Local authority accommodation is defined by the Children Act 1989, Section 22 and may include:

- residential children's homes;

- remand foster placements;

- placement with members of the defendant's family.

The local authority has considerable discretion as to the choice of accommodation, although the court may stipulate that the young person is not placed with a named individual or at a named address. Whether a young person who is subject to a remand into local authority accommodation is placed with parents or other family or not, they are also 'looked after' children and should therefore be subject to Children Act requirements.

Another proposal outlined in the green paper (Ministry of Justice, 2010) is to introduce a single remand order for all young people aged 12–17, making local authorities responsible for the cost of court ordered remands. This would, over time and with an associated transfer of funding, relocate the full costs of all remand to local authorities. Placements of remanded young people would still be commissioned and managed by the new youth justice division within the Ministry of Justice and the local authority would be charged for this service. The green paper also proposes that local authorities gradually bear responsibility for the full cost of court ordered secure remands, in line with other moves towards payment by results in which local agencies are incentivised to reduce the use of custody.

Introducing a single remand order seeks to address the current anomaly of 17 year olds being treated as adults in remand legislation which contravenes the United Nations Convention on the Rights of the Child which provides that a child means all persons under the age of 18. Finally, it is proposed that the option of remand for young people who would be unlikely to receive a custodial sentence is removed, thus reducing the 57 per cent of young people on remand who are acquitted or receive a community sentence (Ministry of Justice, 2010).

The YOT and Youth Court panel within each authority are required to meet at least twice a year to discuss issues regarding young people at court. This can also be an opportunity for the YOT to provide training or briefings on particular aspects of practice. It is important for you to attend these where possible, as among other things magistrates will get to know you and as in all areas of work, building professional relationships across the whole youth justice system can only seek to enhance the quality and effectiveness of your practice.

Judge and jury

If a young person has committed a serious offence such as murder, rape or grievous bodily harm, the Youth Court may be of the view that the likely sentence the young person should receive will be more than the two years maximum period of imprisonment available to it. In such a situation, the case will be committed to the Crown Court for a plea and directions hearing. If the young person enters a not guilty plea, the matter will be adjourned for a trial with a judge and jury. Here, the jury, 12 randomly selected men and women, will sit through the trial, hear the evidence and have to reach a verdict, on the direction of the judge who will advise them on matters of law. If the jury finds the young person guilty of the charges, the judge could sentence there and then if it is a very serious offence such as murder. Usually, the judge will request a pre-sentence report from the YOT which will need to be completed by the date the case is adjourned to and the judge will pass sentence on the next occasion.

Appearing in court can be a very traumatic event for young people, their families and social workers, and the Crown Court is particularly intimidating with its formalities, dress code and size. Seymour and Seymour (2011) provide some useful advice on appearing in court and strategies to manage the anxieties it may present for social workers. Johns (2011) outlines the importance of preparation, practice, prediction and professionalism in order to be effective in the court arena (see Further Reading at the end of the chapter.) The youth justice system in this country has been criticised for its formal court system which does not facilitate active participation from young people and their parents/carers, and magistrates are now required to undergo training in communication skills. While some may be effective at engaging young people in the court setting, there is still huge room for improvement. The government, in responding to the European Court's ruling in the case of Thompson and Venables (V v UK and T v UK (2000) 30 EHRR 121), in the white paper *Justice for all* (Home Office, 2002) proposed changes to the way most serious trials are heard. It suggested that the current Crown Court be replaced by cases being heard by a judge and two youth magistrates in a Youth Court. However, no such changes have occurred or seem to be planned. The Thompson and Venables case did, however, bring about some changes to the way children are tried. As Bandalli (2005, p42) states:

> *Article 6 of the European Convention on Human Rights, guarantees the right to a fair trial and childhood has been recognised as having an impact on fairness. As a result, when a child or young person is charged with a criminal offence, they should be dealt with in a manner that takes into account age, immaturity and understanding. There should be less formality and attempts should be made to ensure the child understands what is happening and to make proceedings more child-friendly.*

Given the formality of the court environment, it is useful, for youth justice practitioners to visit a range of courts in order to gain some experience in how they operate. As the Youth Court is closed to the public this will only be possible if you are undertaking a practice learning placement within a YOT or children and families setting. The magistrates' and Crown Courts are not closed and it is possible to sit in the public gallery and observe proceedings.

Defence solicitors

As mentioned earlier, when a young person is arrested by the police, they are entitled to free legal advice while at the police station. If the young person is charged, this legal representation will usually be available when they appear in court. The solicitor will advise the young person in relation to the process, the evidence against them and their plea as well as issues of bail and sentence. The solicitor (or barrister if instructed by a solicitor) will also advocate on behalf of the young person in court in relation to bail and sentence. It is important for YOT social workers to liaise with the solicitor of a young person with whom they are working, as they may be required to address the court on their assessment in relation to whether the young person should be remanded into secure provision or subject to bail supervision by the YOT. The solicitor will need to see a copy of the pre-sentence report prior to the hearing so that he or she is aware of what sentence is being proposed.

YOTs

Multi-agency YOTs are designed to be part of a joined-up approach to addressing youth crime. A team comprising a number of professional disciplines is a complex operation and there needs to be a clear understanding of, and respect for, each others' role in order for different practitioners to be able to work together effectively. Most of the key agencies making up a YOT have very different philosophies, cultures, training and objectives so while able to bring a wide-ranging approach to the issue of youth crime, the potential for conflict is quite significant. Bailey and Williams (2000 cited in Burnett and Appleton, 2004) found evidence of 'turf wars' in their research into YOTs whereas Burnett and Appleton (2004) observed *cordial relations from the start and a very open attitude to the prospect of learning from each other*. Having a range of professional identities within one team can be threatening as duties are shared across other disciplines. It is important therefore to recognise the value of each discipline's contribution to the multi-disciplinary approach and the values and knowledge other professionals bring. As a social worker it is vital that you develop the skills and ability to practise within a range of professional networks to develop and maintain effective working relationships for the benefit of the young people with whom you are working.

The guidance on the setting up of YOTs suggested how each of the five key professionals may be deployed and what their areas of responsibility might be and while these are observed in practice, they are not necessarily prescribed to. It is likely that most social workers will undertake assessments and prepare reports for panel hearings and court while the issuing of final warnings will be undertaken by police officers. Social workers are more likely to attend court when young people are appearing there for sentence although most YOTs now have specific bail and remand workers. YOTs may be configured differently so that social workers may be in a team that only deals with court and report writing or one that supervises YROs. Working with young people on court orders involves planning and reviewing cases, intervening to prevent offending behaviour and working with families (see Chapter 7), liaising with others such as victims and referral order panel members. Thus, a typical day for a YOT social worker might involve a multitude of tasks and activities. Core social work tasks such as interviewing and assessing, building relationships with people, empowering, supporting and advocating on behalf of young people and challenging discrimination and injustice will all feature daily in YOT practice.

In addition to the mandatory roles within each YOT, there may be other professionals based in, or attached to, the team such as housing workers or substance misuse workers for whom funding was ringfenced in order to ensure their presence in a YOT. Historically, YOTs have had separate prevention and early intervention teams to intervene with young people at risk of offending such as Youth Inclusion and Support Panels and Youth Inclusion Programmes, although with significant budget cuts from the YJB and general cuts in public spending in the financial year 2011–12, the continuation of these are under threat. YISPs however, have been integrated into other local authority multi-agency panels.

Multi-agency working

Requiring different agencies to work together has been central to government policy for many years and the failings of such agencies in working together is often identified in inquiries into cases resulting in child deaths or where other catastrophic consequences have arisen. Recommendations from inquiries such as Laming (2003) have included the need for better partnership working. Formal ways of working together are described in a multitude of ways including multi-agency, multi-disciplinary, interprofessional, integrated working and may result in different configurations such as different agencies co-located in the same building as in the case of YOTs. Generally, such ways of working include addressing the needs of service users through services provided by more than one organisation or professional group. Working in collaboration refers to knowledge, skills and values utilised when putting this into practice (Quinney, 2006). Working in partnership requires individuals and teams to establish, maintain and review relationships so they continue to be effective. Furthermore, it is:

> not about fudging the boundaries between the professionals and trying to create a generic care worker. It is instead about developing professionals who are confident in their own core skills and expertise, who are fully aware of and confident in the skills and expertise of fellow health and care professionals, and who conduct their own practice in a non-hierarchical and collegiate way with other members of the working team, so as to continuously improve the health of their communities and to meet the real care needs of individual patients and clients.

> (Hardy, 1999, cited in Quinney, 2006, p17)

Achieving such a positive and open approach to interprofessional working is not easily achieved and given the complexities involved in bringing together professionals from a range of professional backgrounds it may result in conflict arising. The fact that different professionals undertake diverse education and training, may have different, sometimes competing agendas and priorities and work from different perspectives with distinct values, language and behaviour means that professional conflicts, rivalries and competitiveness may occur. Bringing professionals together into one team means that their professional identities may be threatened and they may feel intimidated or undervalued if their knowledge, skills and roles are shared across other disciplines.

In order to develop the ability to work in partnership with a wide range of professionals whether located in the same team or not, it is important to recognise your own contribution to multi-disciplinary practice and the specific value that you bring as well as being able to understand the values and knowledge brought by others from different agencies and disciplines. Part of your professional development as a social worker involves the need to develop the skills and ability to practise within a range of professional networks to develop and maintain effective working relationships as outlined in unit 17 of the NOS. The following factors have been identified by Barrett and Keeping (2005) (cited in Quinney, 2006) as being essential for effective interprofessional working:

- *Knowledge of professional roles – awareness of your own and others' roles.*

- *Willing participation – motivation and commitment are important if successful collaboration is to be achieved.*

- *Confidence – built on clear professional identity and a belief in the role of social work.*

- *Open and honest communication – active listening and constructive feedback seeking clarity and understanding.*

- *Trust and mutual respect – so that people feel 'safe' to deal with conflicts.*

- *Power – clear lines of responsibility and accountability.*

- *Conflict – clear ground rules and a reflective, open approach. Conflict can also produce creativity and energy.*

- *Support and commitment at senior level – change and support at all levels is essential for effective collaboration.*

- *Professional culture – language, traditions and perspectives of different professional groups may hinder or provide opportunities for new viewpoints.*

- *Uncertainty – uncertainty about new roles, boundaries and future developments needs to be acknowledged.*

- *Envy – tensions can arise from envy and rivalry especially when competing for resources and power.*

- *Defences against anxiety – Social work can create anxiety which can become displaced onto colleagues.*

   (Quinney, 2006, pp33–4)

Despite forming a central part of government policy over the last decade or two, there has been only limited research into the effectiveness of collaborative practice. Reder and Duncan state that most reforms in children's services have been in relation to the organisation and structure of services which may be ambitious as it is likely to be the attributes, skills, thinking capacities and working conditions of staff within the organisations which will bring critical improvements to everyday child protection practice. Reorganisation may emphasise, rather than reduce, interprofessional conflicts and agency mergers are no guarantee of better information sharing (Reder and Duncan, 2004, pp102–3). A research study by White and Featherstone (2005) focusing on an ethnographic study of interprofessional communication and social relations in an integrated child health service, found that professionals working at the multi-agency interface operate with robust professional identities, which are taken for granted as members of particular occupational groups, organisations or teams. They suggest that co-location does not necessarily lead to more or better communication because people do not communicate openly while aspects of their professional narratives that sustain ritualised ways of working, remain unexplored. Thus, they contend that the challenge is for conditions to be created where practice is open to challenge and scrutiny through observation of other professionals in their settings and reflexivity about professionals own identities, thus *learning to listen, communicate and understand* (White and Featherstone, 2005, p215).

In relation to YOTs, there is some research looking into the impact and effectiveness of multi-agency working. The evaluation of Pilot YOTs (Holdaway et al., 2001) found that staff roles needed to be clarified, one discipline should not dominate, that there should be a balance between generic and specialist work and that the environment must facilitate communication. On a positive note, they found that multi-agency work was cited most often as best thing in the work of staff completing survey.

Research by Burnett and Appleton (2004) which followed progress of Oxfordshire YOT for over two years found that working together was mainly a positive experience and the specific gains were the reciprocal exchange of knowledge, direct or quicker access to other services/expertise and improved referral processes. They also found that professional identities became less distinguishable with cross-disciplinary influence and shared identity developing. Another ethnographic study was undertaken by Souhami (2007) who followed a Midlands Youth Justice Team as it transformed into a YOT, during 1999 and 2000. She found that practitioners from partner agencies coming into the team blurred boundaries between agencies and that the separation of the team from social services removed the *legitimating authority of their professional body* (Souhami 2007; p184). Her research also identified that fragmentation led to inaction but also creativity and that staff from home agencies neither had clear understanding of the principle and practices of their occupation nor a straightforward attachment to them. She concluded that the development of a shared approach to youth justice in an inter-agency team paradoxically, is dependent on the acceptance and incorporation of difference.

All these research studies were undertaken during the transitional period when YOTs were being established. More recent research is needed focusing on the effectiveness of multi-agency working. As the future of the YJB is under threat and severe cuts to local authority funding are meaning that children's services are being restructured, it will be interesting to see where YOTs continue to be positioned – aside from Children's Services as many have been since their inception, or more integrated into mainstream children and families' provision.

Irrespective of where YOTs sit within a local authority, *Working together to safeguard children* (2010) states that:

- *There needs to be clear links between Youth Justice and LA Children's Social Care both at a strategic level and a child specific operational level.*

- *YOTS have a duty to ensure that their functions are discharged with regard to the need to safeguard and promote the welfare of children.*

YOTs are required by law to be part of the Local Children's Safeguarding Board and social workers within YOTs need to ensure they are familiar with local safeguarding procedures and processes so they know what action to take should a young person they are working with be at risk of or subject to harm or neglect. Government guidance, *Working together to safeguard children: A guide to inter-agency working to safeguard and promote the welfare of children* (2010) sets out the requirements of all professionals working with children to share information and collaborate and the roles and responsibilities of different organisations including criminal justice organisations. As there can often be tensions between YOTs and local authority children's services, it is essential that YOT practitioners understand their responsibilities in relation to safeguarding, particularly as they are often working with some of the most vulnerable young people and their families.

ACTIVITY **5.2**

Consider the case study below and identify the role of the YOT social worker.

Jermaine, aged 15, is arrested by the police having committed a serious offence of robbery while on bail for driving-related offences. He is interviewed by the police and on the advice of his solicitor makes no comment to any of the questions the police ask. He is given bail by the police so that they can investigate the offence further, with conditions that he lives at his parents' house, does not contact any witnesses, does not enter a certain area of the town and does not go out of the house between 7 p.m and 7 a.m. He is bailed to return four weeks later when the matter will either be dropped or he will be charged. When Jermaine returns to the police station, the police decide to charge him as they have examined CCTV footage showing him committing the robbery. Jermaine is charged and detained overnight to be taken to court the next day.

The CPS lawyer outlines the case against Jermaine and informs the court that the victim has been seriously affected by the robbery, physically in terms of bruising to his head and arms, and emotionally, scared to leave the house unless in the company of his parents. The lawyer also informs the court that at the time of the alleged offence Jermaine was on bail for driving offences for which he is waiting to be tried. The magistrates hearing the case ask you, the YOT officer present in court, to assess Jermaine's circumstances and to give them more information on whether they should be granting him bail or not.

What issues would you want to address in the 15 minutes the court has adjourned the case for?

COMMENT

You will clearly want to interview the young person in the cells to gather some basic information such as his living arrangements and education situation. Hopefully his parents/carers will also be at court so you will be able to speak to them. If not, did you think of calling them and asking them to come to court? It will be important to ascertain and assess the level of support and supervision offered to Jermaine by his family. It may be wise to ask about other extended family members who may be able to accommodate him for the duration of the court case, particularly if the victim lives near to Jermaine. The court will be concerned in making its decision that any risk of re-offending is reduced or prevented, the victim and any other witnesses are protected as well as society generally, and that Jermaine returns to court for future hearings. You will need to consider any measures that will help to secure these outcomes and a relative some distance away may prove a very valuable alternative.

Continued

How Jermaine spends his time will be an important factor to consider; if he is in school, what is his attendance like? The absence of a school place or problematic attendance means that additional supervision of Jermaine in the community will be necessary if he is to be given bail. If he cannot be placed at home safely either because parental supervision is poor or not possible, for instance due to his parents' work commitments or younger siblings, and there is no other family member that can accommodate him, the court may consider remanding Jermaine into local authority accommodation with a condition that he is not placed at home. Your response to the court must be to propose a programme of bail supervision that the court will find an adequate alternative to custody. This may include a curfew monitored electronically, bail supervision offered by the YOT or an intensive supervision and surveillance programme (ISSP), subject to resource availability (see Chapter 4 for more information on ISSP).

The secure estate

Your contact with the secure estate will occur when you work with young people who are either remanded or sentenced to a period in custody or secure accommodation. There are three types of secure settings in youth justice: local authority secure children's homes (LASCH), privately run secure training centres (STC) and prison service young offender institutions (YOI) although Ashford YOT is not privately run. All three are quite different and young people can end up in any, remanded or sentenced, subject to their age and gender.

For those on remand:

- 10–12 year olds cannot be remanded to secure accommodation/custody, so go to local authority accommodation.

- 12–14 year old boys and 12–16 year old girls cannot be remanded to custody so go to local authority accommodation which can be secure if certain conditions are met.

- 15–16 year old boys can be remanded into local authority secure accommodation or custody but will usually go to custody unless deemed vulnerable.

- 17 year olds are treated as adults and if refused bail go to YOIs.

For sentenced young people, the YJB placements strategy, as cited in Bateman (2005), states that:

- Children under 12 years of age will be placed in a LASCH.

- Children aged 12–14 years of age must be placed in a LASCH or STC.

- 15–16 year old girls should be given priority for places in non-prison service establishments.

- 17 year old girls will be allocated to a LASCH if places are available.

- 15–17 year old boys will usually be placed in a YOI although vulnerable 15–16 year old males should be considered for a placement outside of the prison service where places are available.

At the end of September 2010 there were 2,070 children (under-18s) in custody – a decrease of 453 from the same point last year. There were 1,637 children held in young offender institutions, 273 in secure training centres and 160 in secure children's homes. It is widely considered that prison service custodial establishments are inappropriate places for children so it is concerning that more children seem to be incarcerated in YOIs or privately run secure settings with less local authority secure accommodation available. However, some improvements have been noted and the Ministry of Justice and the YJB have jointly published a consultation document, *Strategy for the secure estate for children and young people in England and Wales, plans for 2011/12-2014/5*. This sets out the principles which should underpin the secure estate for children and young people:

- *A distinct, specialist secure estate for children and young people.*

- *Children and young people should be supervised and cared for by staff who are committed to working with them and who have received appropriate training.*

- *The built environment should be conducive to working effectively with children and young people and living units should be relatively small (even if within larger establishments).*

- *Children and young people in the secure estate should not be disadvantaged on the grounds of gender, ability, sexual orientation, race, ethnicity or religion.*

- *Staff should proactively engage with all young people to identify and meet the specific needs of all young people placed in custody.*

- *Children and young people should be placed in the establishment that is best able to meet their needs and give them the maximum opportunity to address their offending behaviour.*

- *In accordance with existing legislation, secure establishments should minimise the likelihood of harm to young people through rigorous safeguarding measures which will:*

  - *have regard to the need to safeguard and promote the welfare of children and young people;*

  - *protect them from harm from self;*

  - *protect them from harm from adults;*

  - *protect them from harm from peers;*

  - *actively seek and incorporate the views of children and young people into existing practice.*

- *An early and comprehensive assessment of need should be undertaken. This will then allow establishments to target resources at offending behaviour and any wider identified needs, thus enabling the successful engagement of young people in custody. The assessment should also lead to the development of stable resettlement arrangements.*

- *Children and young people should have access to a full and purposeful day which equips them to become engaged in sustainable education, training and employment on release.*

- *Children and young people should receive appropriate physical health, mental health and substance misuse services.*

- *Children and young people should attend programmes designed to address their offending behaviour.*

(Ministry of Justice/YJB, 2011)

These principles are considered to be an essential platform for protecting the rights of young people and ensuring the safety and well-being of young people in secure establishments and are cognisant of the Munby judgement which established that children in custody have the same rights and entitlements as those children in any other setting under the 1989 and 2004 Children Acts and the Human Rights Act (1998) and the United Nations Convention on the Rights of the Child (1989). At the time of writing, this strategy was out for consultation and likely to be completed by the end of 2011.

Both YOIs and STCs have attracted criticism from the United Nations Committee on the Rights of the Child, Her Majesty's Inspectorate of Prisons, prison reform groups such as the Prison Reform Trust and the Howard League for Penal Reform and the Commission for Racial Equality. Given such a wealth of criticism of a system that is largely ineffectual, with recidivism rates for those leaving custody approximately 75–80 per cent (Ministry of Justice, 2010, Howard League, 2008) it is concerning that the UK still has one of the highest rates of young people in custody in Europe. Added to that the fact that within the incarcerated youth population around one third of children have been in care, 15 per cent have special educational needs, 80 per cent have been excluded from school, over 40 per cent are classed as vulnerable and 30 children have died since 1990 (cited in Muncie, 2009) the fact that this is the favoured approach to dealing with a group of troubled children makes one question how civilised a society we must be if this is how we treat our most vulnerable.

If a young person is remanded into custody, the YOT should be present in court, although if it is by an adult court, this is not always the case. However, the YOT should at least be notified. National Standards require that remanded young people are seen within five working days and a remand plan be drawn up that must then be reviewed within timescales. Once a young person receives a custodial sentence, a post-court report needs to be completed that accompanies the young person to the secure establishment, and any concerns about their welfare need to be clearly identified on this. Again, sentenced young people must be seen in custody within five working days so that a sentence plan can be drawn up that outlines what they will be doing while serving the custodial part of the sentence. The young person and parents/carers should actively contribute to this process and the plan has to be reviewed regularly. In all cases, a key worker will be allocated to the young person in secure settings and it is important that you communicate regularly with this worker and share information accordingly. Planning for resettlement should ensure a seamless response between custody and community. Research (Goldson, 2002) identifies the vulnerability of children in custody and the lack of communication between staff in the secure estate and in the community. It is therefore crucial that you ensure your assessments and any other relevant information are always forwarded to the relevant institution and that visiting young people in custody and attending planning meetings is prioritised.

Given that the recidivism rate is still high, 71.9 per cent (YJB and Ministry of Justice, 2011), planning for a young person's release from custody is fundamental to reducing the risk of their reoffending.

ACTIVITY 5.3

When working with a young person serving a custodial sentence, when would you need to start thinking about his/her resettlement?

What might you need to address to ensure effective resettlement?

COMMENT

Hopefully you will have identified that resettlement work begins at the assessment and report writing stage, prior to sentence, as you will have been assessing factors such as family and living arrangements and education, training or employment.

Once a custodial sentence is made, it is important that work focuses on the young person's links with his or her community throughout the duration of the time spent in custody. This may involve facilitating contact with family members, liaising with the education or training provider or employer, or children and families teams if the young person is looked after or deemed a child in need. It may well be the case that the custodial sentence contributes to the young person being a child in need which then places responsibilities upon the local authority. One of the key roles of the YOT social worker during a custodial sentence is to ensure good communication among all relevant professionals, agencies and the family and ensuring all contribute to the sentence planning process. NACRO has produced useful guidance in relation to children entering custody who are looked after. This includes the continuing responsibility of the local authority when a child on a care order enters custody for assessment, planning, intervention and review. Social workers with responsibility for looked after children are also required to maintain and carry out their statutory duties while a looked after child is in custody and be actively involved in planning for return to community. NACRO suggest that Children's Services and YOTs should ask:

- Are we ensuring review and planning continues if a child on a care order receives a custodial sentence?

- What action is required by the local authority to keep in touch with the child?

- What action is taken to ensure the throughcare needs of children not subject to care orders are met?

- Is there sufficient accommodation to ensure real placement choice for looked after children who offend?

- Is there proper post-transfer planning of all services for those in custody?

- Are children not looked after who are in custody treated as children in need and provided with services?

(NACRO, 2005, p39)

CHAPTER SUMMARY

This chapter has looked at the complex system that operates to deal with the detection, prosecution, sentencing and rehabilitation of young people committing crimes. Being a social worker in a YOT means being able to work closely with a range of other professionals based in the same team as you, but having also to work with other agencies such as the courts, lawyers and the prison service. We have identified the functions of some of these agencies and you have considered these in relation to case studies. Hopefully it has been made clear that in order to be an effective social worker within the field of youth justice, developing key skills in multi-agency and inter-professional working and having a greater understanding of the complex system, is likely to result in improved practice.

FURTHER READING

Bateman, T and Pitts, J (2005) *The RHP companion to youth justice*. Lyme Regis: Russell House Publishing.

A very readable and comprehensive overview of youth justice with contributions from a range of academics and practitioners in the field.

Burnett, R and Appleton, C (2004) *Joined-up justice: Tackling youth crime in partnership*. Lyme Regis: Russell House Publishing.

This book identifies some of the challenges faced by YOT practitioners and the impact of the recent reforms based on research into a YOT.

Johns, R (2011) *Using the law in social work*, 5th edition. Exeter: Learning Matters.

This text offers useful advice on appearing in court.

Seymour, C and Seymour, R (2011) *Court room and report writing skills for social workers*. Exeter: Learning Matters.

This text offers useful guidance for students on appearing in court and writing court reports.

WEBSITE

www.cps.gov.uk

This website contains the Code for Crown Prosecutors which gives more detail about the evidential and public interest tests that have to be met if a prosecution is to be considered.

www.dca.gov.uk

This website provides information about the legal system, the courts and judiciary.

www.ministryofjustice.gov.uk

The Ministry of Justice website contains a number of relevant publications on all aspects of crime.

www.youth-justice-board.gov.uk

This website provides information on all aspects of YOTs, the secure estate, sentencing and contains many documents that can be downloaded. However, the website will close in 2012 when the YJB transfers to a new unit within the Ministry of Justice.

Chapter 6

Assessing young people

Paul Dugmore

Introduction

In all areas of social work, assessment is often considered to be the initial part of social work involvement, in order to assess need and risk and access resources and services. This is particularly apparent in youth justice with the National Standards stating that *All children and young people entering the youth justice system benefit from a structured needs assessment* to identify risk and protective factors associated with offending behaviour to inform effective intervention (YJB, 2010d, p5).

This chapter will consider the purpose of assessment in relation to young people who offend and provide a brief overview of different types of assessments in youth jutsice practice. Asset, the assessment tool used by YOTs is discussed and the relationship between assessment and reports (for court and referral order panels). The chapter will conclude by considering the relationship between assessment, risk and need focusing specifically on the interface with safeguarding and mental health.

What is assessment?

Within a social work context, assessment is often described as an activity undertaken in order to identify a person's needs or problems so that the appropriate intervention can then be provided in order to meet the identified needs or problems. Assessment is largely an information-gathering exercise undertaken to establish what the presenting and underlying factors are in a service user's life, by working in partnership with the service user, their family, and other professionals who may be involved. However, it is not only about the gathering of information, but should be seen as *a holistic process that involves gaining an overview of the situation* (Thompson, 2005, p64) and analysing the information in order to inform the appropriate course of action. An assessment might be carried out as a one-off event and as such may be static, or it may be a fluid process occurring more than once, depending on the situation. In youth justice, it is likely to be more than a one-off event.

According to Middleton (1997), cited in Parker and Bradley (2010, p5), assessment is:

> *The analytical process by which decisions are made. In a social welfare context it is a basis for planning what needs to be done to maintain or improve a person's situation . . . Assessment involves gathering and interpreting information in order to understand a person and their circumstances; the desirability and feasibility of change and the services and resources which are necessary to effect it. It involves making judgements based on information.*

More specifically, in relation to youth justice, Baker et al. (2011, p12) define assessment as:

> *A dynamic, multi-faceted process of information gathering and analysis that leads to in-depth understanding of a young person's offending behaviour. It provides the basis for the planning of interventions in order to:*
>
> - *Help a young person avoid reoffending.*
> - *Assist a young person to achieve their potential.*
> - *Help to protect victims and communities.*

Thus, assessment is not simply about the collation of information, it is, equally importantly, about making sense of that information, analysing it and weighing it up.

Wilson et al. (2008, p272) contend that assessment definitions need also to explicitly state the *constructed and relational nature of the assessment process* acknowledging the *demanding, personal and affective nature of the task*. They refer to a definition by Walker and Beckett (2003, p21) that includes *having the personal integrity to hold to your core values and ethical base while being buffeted by strong feelings*. Such a wider definition also allows for a consideration of what the assessing practitioner brings to the assessment and the relationship between the assessor and the person being assessed. An ability to reflect upon this relationship and consider issues of transference and counter-transference is also important (Preston-Shoot and Agass, 1990). Supervision is vital to enable practitioners to be cognisant of unconscious processes that may be at play during an interaction with a service user. These kinds of data can also be helpful in providing additional intelligence to the practitioner about what may be going on for a young person and an awareness that feelings may be transferred from the past may help one to look at the situation more objectively. This awareness may in turn help the assessing practitioner to resist colluding with or being manipulated by the young person (Salzberger–Wittenburg, 1970).

ACTIVITY 6.1

Think about undertaking an assessment of a young person coming to the attention of the YOT.

- *Identify different kinds of assessment that might be undertaken in a youth justice setting.*

- *What are important factors in carrying out a good assessment?*

- *What might impede a social worker in undertaking an effective assessment?*

COMMENT

You may have acknowledged that in order to ensure an assessment is effective, it is important that as the social worker you are clear about the purpose of the assessment, that is, what it is you are assessing and why. In the gathering of information, the obvious starting point is an interview with the young person. However, it may be more useful if you have obtained information from other sources, where possible, prior to the interview as this may help determine the areas for discussion. Skills required here include active listening, effective communication and observation in order to pick up on non-verbal cues, as well as the ability to clarify meaning.

Assessments should also be balanced so that as well as identifying problematic behaviour or risks, positive factors and strengths are also highlighted. Assessment tools are often criticised for focusing on the negative aspects of service users lives or behaviour. Adopting a strengths-based approach that involves the social worker focusing on the strengths and resources of the service user, rather than the problems or deficits, enables solutions to be identified that harness the strengths as a way of addressing the problems. Strengths can refer to individual strengths such as aspirations, competencies or confidence or relate to communities and include opportunities, social networks, and resources (Kondrat, 2010).

The decisions made in an assessment may have a huge impact upon the outcome for the young person relating to which services or intervention they receive or the potential loss of liberty for instance.

As discussed in Chapter 1, locating the assessment task within a value-based framework is essential as is an awareness of how one's own background and value base may impact on the young person/family and circumstances being assessed, therefore in challenging assumptions it is vital to be as objective as possible. While assessment is about making judgements about a set of circumstances or facts based on evidence gained, it is not about making value judgements. Milner and O'Byrne provide a helpful distinction between facing the challenge and responsibility of making judgements but refraining from the prejudice and blame implicit in being judgemental (Milner and O'Byrne, 2002, p170).

Framework for assessment

Milner and O'Byrne (2009, p62) suggest a comprehensive framework for assessment that has five key stages and is applicable across all social work settings:

- *Preparation* – this refers to the purpose of the task and establishing what is relevant.
- *Data collection* – undertaken with an open mind and in line with core social work values of empowerment and respect.
- *Weighing the data* – identifying if there is a problem and if so how serious it is within a theoretical and evidence-based framework, identifying themes but also gaps in the data.
- *Analysing the data* – interpreting the data using theoretical perspectives to identify the required intervention.
- *Utilising the analysis* – finalising judgements and preparing an intervention plan.

    Milner and O'Byrne (2009), p62

This model is adapted to a youth justice context by Baker et al. (2011) which is helpful considering some of the issues faced when assessing young people who offend.

Types of assessment

Smale and Tuson (1993) advocate that an 'exchange model' should ideally be adopted when undertaking an assessment. This views service users as experts in their own lives with assessment as a mutual process where the social worker follows what is said by the service user rather than attaching their own interpretation. The social worker focuses on the service user's internal resources and strengths to reach jointly agreed objectives. They suggest that a questioning model is more likely to be used when risk factors inform the main emphasis of the assessment whereas the procedural model is more common when resource constraints underpin the assessment process. The challenge for practitioners is to use an exchange model within a context that is pre-occupied with risk and in which resources are severely limited or lacking.

Assessment in youth justice

In more recent years, particularly following concerns about social workers' abilities in relation to high-profile child protection and mental health cases (Victoria Climbié and the Laming inquiry of 2003; Christopher Clunis and the Ritchie inquiry, 1994), there has been a rise in the concept and practices of risk assessment and management. As a result, government policy and legislation has ensured assessment has been at the heart of social work activity in relation to community care, children and families and youth justice. The Department of Health's *Framework for the assessment of children in need and their families, provides a systematic way of analysing, understanding and recording what is happening to children and young people within their families and the wider context in which they live* (DoH, 2000. pviii).

This structured assessment framework has been mirrored to some extent in youth justice with the introduction of Asset in 2000. Following the implementation of the Crime and Disorder Act 1998 and multi-agency YOTs, one of the first tasks of the newly established Youth Justice Board (YJB) was to commission the development and introduction of a national assessment tool to be rolled out across England and Wales. This was significant as prior to the Crime and Disorder Act 1998, there was no standardised assessment tool or process being used by youth justice teams; and so practice was variable. The research and design of the assessment tool was carried out by the Oxford University Centre for Criminological Research involving an extensive review of the research literature relating to risk and protective factors for offending young people. Asset was also adapted from assessments used by the probation service with adults for appropriate use with children and young people.

In 2005 the YJB issued the *Key elements in effective practice in relation to assessment, planning interventions and supervision (APIS)* and this was updated in 2008. These were accompanied by background source documents to provide a guide to youth justice practitioners and managers on the current state of the evidence base on effective interventions and services. The most recent version is available at: http://yjbpublications.justice.gov.uk/Scripts/prodView.asp?idProduct=384&eP

The assessment framework implemented by the YJB has been informed largely by the risk-factor prevention paradigm which identifies key factors that contribute to the likelihood of a young person committing an offence. Baker et al. (2011) suggest that assessors need to be mindful in identifying not only the relevant risk or protective factors but also to consider their significance for the individual young person being assessed. The types of risk and protective factors encompassed in the risk-factor prevention paradigm have been identified from research-based, longitudinal studies (Farrington, 2007) and include those already mentioned in previous chapters, grouped in the categories of family, school, community and personal.

Research findings demonstrate the following factors contribute to offending by young people:

- *Children whose parents are inconsistent, neglectful and harsh are at increased risk of criminality as young people* (Newson and Newson, 1989).
- *Family conflict – quality of parent–child relationship, parental supervision and discipline, family income, the nature of relationship breakdown between parents* (Utting et al., 1993, Graham and Bowling, 1995).
- *Family history of criminal activity* (Farrington, 1995).
- *Low income, poor housing and large family size* (Utting et al., 1993, Farrington, 1992).
- *Aggressive behaviour and bullying* (Rutter et al., 1983).
- *Hyperactivity and impulsivity.*
- *Low intelligence and cognitive impairment.*
- *Alienation and lack of social commitment.*
- *Early involvement in crime and drug misuse.*
- *Delinquent peer groups.*
- *School factors – low achievement, negative experiences at school, frequent changes of school and truancy.*
- *Disadvantaged neighbourhood, population instability.*
- *Substance abuse and alcohol use.*
- *Low self-efficacy, high self-esteem.*

    (YJB, 2008)

Research has also identified certain protective factors that can reduce the likelihood of a young person offending:

- *Positive temperament.*
- *Educational motivation.*
- *Intelligence.*
- *Parenthood.*
- *Stable relationship with at least one family member.*
- *Good experiences at school and positive attitude towards education.*
- *Presence of biological father.*
- *Emotionally supportive home.*
- *Positive peer relations but also lack of friends.*

    (YJB, 2008)

While it is important that youth justice practitioners are aware of the research evidence base and that this forms part of the knowledge base that informs their practice, it is essential that consideration is given to particular factors that may be relevant to specific types of behaviour such as sexual or violent offending or gang membership.

The YJB APIS model is informed by the Risk, Need and Responsivity (RNR) model outlined by Andrews et al. (1990) which is built on three key principles for working with offenders that reflect general personality and social psychology theories of crime (Andrews et al., 2006, cited in YJB, 2008):

1. *The Risk principle* – The most intensive interventions should be reserved for those people posing the highest risk of recidivism. It is based upon evidence that indicates recidivism rates are reduced most when programmes are delivered to this group of offenders.

2. *The Need principle* – Interventions should target the issues or needs most associated with the perceived causes of the offending.

3. *The Responsivity principle* – Planned interventions should be matched with the personality, motivation and ability of the individual as well as their age, gender and ethnicity as this is more likely to produce a positive response.

The RNR model assumes that assessment is based on actuarial assessment tools and the risk factor–prevention paradigm. Criticisms of the paradigm include the lack of attention paid to young people's own perceptions of the risk and protective factors in their lives; the individualisation of wider, structural political and social factors that places the responsibility on the young person negating any responsibility of society or government; and that risk and protective factors are not sensitive to individual or social difference such as age, gender, ethnicity class or context (Case, 2007, O' Mahoney, 2009). In addition to this, other factors than risk will account for the success of an intervention and credit needs to be given to the characteristics of offenders in relation to recidivism (Lowenkamp and Latessa, 2004, cited in YJB, 2008.)

Baker et al. (2011) maintain that given risk is likely to be a feature of youth justice practice, it is important that assessments ensure risk and protective factors be considered relevant to each individual young person's specific context and set of circumstances. Furthermore, finding out about the young person's aspirations and goals and taking these into consideration alongside risk, will build up a clearer, more accurate picture. Any actuarial assessment which classifies young people on the basis of risk may lead to young people being assessed at a similar level in spite of significant differences. Therefore, the assessor needs to ensure they adopt an individualised approach to each assessment that draws out the specific needs, circumstances, priorities, abilities and attributes of the young person. This can be a challenge when assessments are usually required to be completed within specified timescales where the temptation may be to use the assessment tool as a means of gathering information without using that information and analysing it to try and understand what is underlying the offending behaviour.

Wider social work practice beyond the youth justice sphere has been subject to significant reform in recent years, often implemented following a serious case review into a child death. Such reforms have tended to create additional procedural guidance and detailed assessment mechanisms which, as identified by Munro (2011, pp121–2), *tell the social worker what data about families to collect, how quickly to collect it and what categories to use in recording it*. She suggests that while such information is needed, front line staff have not been sufficiently helped in knowing how to collect and analyse it. She has highlighted the importance of social workers moving away from procedural manuals and knowing how to collect data, through creating relationships, asking challenging questions and understanding individual's experiences, worries, hopes and dreams, and helping them change (Munro, 2011). Writing over a decade before, Howe (1996, p88) contends that postmodernist, neo-liberal reform of the public sector and social work practice have become analytically more shallow and performance orientated. Within this context, he maintains that:

> *Behaviour is no longer analysed in an attempt to explain it. Rather, it is assessed in terms of administrative procedures, political expectations and legal obligations. Social workers now ask what clients do rather than why they do it – a switch from causation to counting, from explanation to audit. Depth explanations based on psychological and sociological theories are superseded by surface contradictions.*

Furthermore, Howe suggests that within a criminal justice context the focus has moved away from the psychological and social condition of the offender as the offence becomes the focus of concern in the shift from welfare to justice approaches. He gives the example of someone who is emotionally impulsive stemming from a difficult childhood where treatment is not informed by understanding the origins of the anger but instead they are taught to 'manage' their anger rather than reflect on the loss of control. Morrison (2007) maintains that current assessment frameworks such as Asset give limited attention to the importance of history or understanding the interaction between current problems and experiences of loss, trauma and bereavement. He refers to a survey of 1,000 young people supervised by YOTs which found 90 per cent had significant experience of loss or rejection and identified emotional literacy as a key variable affecting change (Youth Justice Trust, 2003). Morrison (2007, p255) further contends that those undertaking assessments may often suppress emotional information due to *personal discomfort or cultural, organisational and professional beliefs which fail to distinguish 'being emotional' from using emotion*. A lack of self-awareness of emotion can result in important information being missed in relation to potential dangers associated with a client or about intrusions from the worker's own experience which may distort observation and assessment.

These kinds of arguments expose the complexity involved in assessing people and the external and internal factors that can impact upon the assessment process such as government policy, agency procedures and the undercurrent at play in the assessor's own psychological world.

Asset

Figure 6.1 shows how Asset has been designed based on the availability of research evidence. The assessing practitioner is required to complete all the sections identified below in order to assess the likelihood/risk of the young person re-offending. Each section is then rated from 0 to 4 giving a total up to a maximum of 48, the higher the rating the higher the risk of the young person re-offending. This figure is then used to establish which category within the Scaled Approach, the young person falls into which determines the corresponding level of intervention they receive.

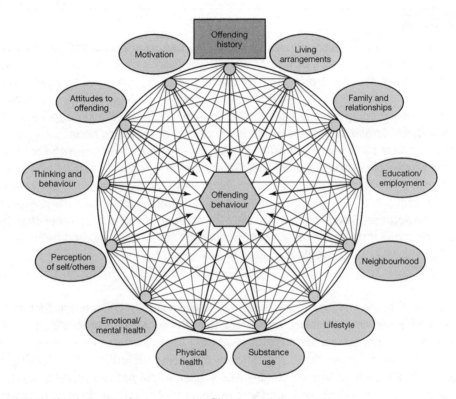

Figure 6.1 Components of Asset *core profile*

© *Dr C H Roberts, Probation Studies Unit, Centre for Criminology, University of Oxford*

Asset is designed to be used with every young person coming into contact with a YOT at the final warning, referral order and pre-sentence report (PSR) stages, as well as with young people appearing in court where bail is an issue. It is a tool that facilitates the systematic assessment of the circumstances and characteristics of offending young people with each factor scored according to its degree of association with the offending behaviour, providing an overall score of the risk of each young person re-offending (Burnett and Appleton, 2004).

It is important to bear in mind that assessments in youth justice are generally carried out following court mandated action with young people generally presenting involuntarily. It is anticipated that Asset will be carried out by the practitioner in consultation with a range of other people. The core profile is the Asset that is used in most cases.

ACTIVITY *6.2*

List the people/sources of information that you might need to speak to or access in order to complete a thorough assessment of a young person and their offending behaviour and any barriers you may encounter in carrying out an assessment.

COMMENT

You will have no doubt considered that the young person will need to be interviewed in order that you can gain a picture of what is going on in their life, why they carried out the offence that has led to their contact with the YOT and how they feel about this. You may have established that this would need to be take place over a number of meetings, including a home visit, so that you can verify information obtained, seek more information and make sense of this in the context of the young person's life. As the young person is still a minor you probably also considered that contact with the young person's parent(s) or carer(s) is vital. If the young person is known to a social worker in a children and families team it would also be important to speak to them, and to a relevant teacher from school. Did you think about looking at the evidence from the police and Crown Prosecution Service so that you have an account of the offence other than the young person's? If the young person has offended previously, they may also be known to the YOT and case records would then need to be referred to.

It is crucial that the assessment process is not carried out in isolation but in partnership with all other relevant individuals, with information shared where appropriate and necessary. It may be that other assessments have already been completed on a young person, and it is possible to obtain these. The criticisms by Laming (DoH/HO, 2003) following the inquiry into the death of Victoria Climbié where agencies did not work collaboratively or share information highlight the importance of doing so. The setting in which the assessment is undertaken is also important and it is often useful to see if a young person responds differently when they are at home for instance.

Undertaking an effective assessment

In order for an assessment to be of good quality, it is important that adequate preparation for the first interview is undertaken. Being aware of the purpose of the assessment process so that this can be explained clearly to the young person by using language they understand and that is appropriate to their age and developmental stage is also essential. A study by Cleaver et al. (2004) involved eight young people being interviewed about their experience of being assessed and found that only two of them could remember the social worker explaining why the assessment was being undertaken and what it would consist of. Asset is designed for use with young people aged 10 to 18. Clearly this is a wide age range and young people will have differing levels of cognitive development. Given that research shows that 23 per cent of young offenders have very low IQs of less than 70, and 25 per cent have special educational needs (Talbot, 2010) the individual needs and abilities of the young person need to be considered as this may influence their response to the assessment process. There is evidence emerging which demonstrates that significant changes in brain function occur between puberty and adulthood which affect parts of the brain responsible for functions such as self-control, judgment, emotions, and organisation (Johnson et al., 2009). This may help to explain certain teenage behaviours such as poor decision-making, risk taking, and emotional outbursts where vulnerable young people with communication problems may be unable to express themselves effectively, resulting in disruptive and aggressive behaviour which may lead to involvement with the police. Research by Moseley et al. (2006) found that offenders gaining oral communication skills qualifications were 50 per cent less likely to re-offend in the year after release than the national average, however the availability of such provision is patchy both within YOTs and the secure estate.

The Bercow Review (2008), *A review of services for children and young people (0–19) with speech, language and communication needs*, suggests that policy makers, professionals and service providers lack understanding of the centrality of speech, language and communication. The report refers to clinical opinion about the value of early intervention and suggests that if this is not in place there are multiple risks of lower educational attainment, behavioural problems, emotional psychological difficulties, poorer employment prospects, challenges to mental health and a descent into criminality. The Bercow Review makes various recommendations, some of which are specifically relevant to youth justice:

- *That the commissioning framework includes advice on how to identify the right skills and capacity mix required in the children's workforce to deliver services and agreed outcomes, including staff with specialist skills able effectively to assess and support children and young people with speech language and communication needs (SLCN) (p4)*

- *That the Government's forthcoming Youth Crime Action Plan and the follow-up work on young offenders' health should consider how best to address the SLCN of young people in the criminal justice system, including those in custody (p5).*

Thus, as research evidence continues to emerge, it is important that practitioners are cognisant of such issues when undertaking assessments and that additional, specific assessments can be accessed by specialists in SLCN where required.

Discussions about the YOT's confidentiality policy and its limits should also take place, particularly important given the multi-agency nature of YOT's and the legislative requirement the different agencies have to share information.

Jones (2003, p65) identifies a list of qualities and skills needed by professionals involved in assessing children and young people:

- *Listening to the child.*

- *Conveying genuine interest.*

- *Empathic concern.*

- *Understanding.*

- *Emotional warmth.*

- *Respect for the child.*

- *Capacity to manage and contain the assessment.*

- *Awareness of the entire transaction between interviewer and child.*

- *Self-management.*

- *Technique.*

Issues relating to values and ethical practice as introduced in Chapter 1 are relevant in assessment. It is important that assessing social workers are aware of their value base and how this might impact on the questions asked and impressions and judgements made. For instance, when assessing young people from different ethnic or cultural backgrounds social workers may make assumptions based on stereotypes about particular cultural groups. Similarly, in assessing a young person with a similar cultural identity, it is important not to engage in collusion. Interpreters should also be used, if required, by either the young person or his/her parents/carers and care should be taken that eye contact and body language is maintained with the people being interviewed rather than directed towards the interpreter.

The work of Egan (2002) is relevant here in relation to effective communication skills such as active listening, probing, clarifying and summarising. Knowledge of unconscious processes and psychodynamic concepts such as transference, counter-transference and defence mechanisms such as projection and splitting are also an important source of knowledge on which to draw in the assessment process in order to try and understand what may be going on. This can help in enabling the assessing social worker to be aware of their own feelings so that these do not prevent him/her from getting to know the young person as an individual. Salzberger–Wittenberg (1970) suggests that caseworkers may be so preoccupied by an eagerness to be helpful, or by what their supervisor may say, or proving how successful they are, that such distractions may overshadow the interview and distort their perceptions and reactions. She suggests that working over these feelings beforehand and then keeping them in check during the interview, enables the worker to be *freer to observe and take in what is going on here and now* (p4). Morrison (2007) asserts that information relating to emotionally or morally loaded material such as trauma and loss or substance use, is largely influenced by how empathic and non-judgemental the assessor is. Beyond this level of awareness it is also fundamental that social workers engage in the reflective and reflexive aspects of their work. Reflexivity is defined as:

> *A way of working that grows from reflective practice, it is a circular process, of meditating upon the involvement you have with service users, and the changing interactions between you and them. It takes into account the structural forces (such as power and oppression) inherent in the interview situation, as well as examining the psychological issues that may also have an impact on the process. You then evaluate and examine your and others' reactions, to see how future involvements may be changed.*

(Allen and Langford, 2008, p15)

Engaging reflexively following an assessment interview with a young person may lead the assessing social worker to ask:

- What does this young person make me feel like?

- What does this tell me about him/her?

- What does this tell me about the nature of our relationship?

- What does this tell me about the effect s/he has on others?

- Is this a valid response in terms of what the young person is communicating?

- Am I reacting in terms of what I am bringing to the situation?

  (Adapted from Salzberger–Wittenberg, 1970, p19)

The Asset assessment tool includes a self-assessment tool specifically designed for young people to complete which could be used at the start of the first interview. This is a valuable opportunity to engage the young person in the assessment process, to attempt to empower the young person and redress the inherent power imbalance in the relationship. Baker et al. (2011) suggest that how seriously a young person's views are taken by the assessor will be determined by the extent to which they reflect on the issues raised and differences in perspectives explored. Using the self-assessment as a means of individualising the assessment may also seek to counter some of the criticisms of assessment tools and the risk factor prevention paradigm discussed previously.

The core Asset profile should not be completed section by section in the interview, rather, each section should be addressed over the course of interviews, through contact with other relevant people and sight of other documentation such as education reports and CPS documentation, for instance. By the end of the information gathering, it should be possible to complete each of the sections, record the evidence and award an appropriate rating for that section. As well as focusing on the criminogenic (risk) factors, which comprise the vast majority of the core profile it is important to look at the positive, protective factors relating to the young person and his/her life which make up the following three pages. However, rather than just identify protective factors, it is important that an analysis goes beyond their presence to consider what impact they have on a young person. They may, for instance:

- Reduce sensitivity to risk factors.

- Reduce the impact of risk factors.

- Promote self-esteem and self-efficacy.

- Open up new and positive opportunities.

- Neutralise or directly counter risk effects.

  (YJB, 2008)

Criticisms of Asset

Completing Asset for the first time can be quite difficult, particularly deciding which rating to give to each section. While many practitioners find Asset to be a valuable tool in structuring a complex assessment process, ensuring that all areas are addressed, others (Smith, 2007; Pitts, 2003), are critical of the routinisation it causes, seeing it as a management tool both locally and nationally. Criticism is also made of the 'tick box' nature of Asset and its over-reliance on negative risk factors to the negation of positive strengths, which is inconsistent with more recent government thinking on assessment and service-user involvement (*Framework for assessment of children in need and their families, National service framework for older people*, the Common Assessment Framework). Smith (2007, p114) summarises the concerns of practitioners in research carried out by Roberts et al. (2001) as follows:

> *The concerns of YOT members about the spurious accuracy of an apparently objective scoring system focused on a number of specific points: uncertainty about what a particular score might mean; lack of flexibility to 'weight' elements which might be more or less relevant in some cases; the negative consequences of finding out more about a young person (especially significant because of the overall negative bias in this direction of the ASSET document); and possible misuse of the aggregated data by the YJB.*

This perspective is not uncommon in relation to standardised assessment tools with clinical assessments perceived as enabling practitioners to exercise more skill and professional judgement. Proponents of such tools argue, however, that they are rooted in empirical data and their predictive value can be researched and evaluated. For more of a discussion on the problems with actuarial assessments see Annison (2005), Case (2007) and O'Mahoney (2009). Baker (2004) argues that the effective use of Asset 'requires the use of considerable professional skill and expertise' as 'practitioners are asked to make decisions about a wide range of issues, from practical assessment of the suitability of a young person's accommodation arrangements to judgements about their self-perception, levels of victim awareness and motivation to change' (Baker, 2004, p81). She suggests that the ratings are based on practitioners' own clinical judgements rather than arrived at by the number of boxes ticked in a particular area. Students and practitioners may wrestle with the prescriptive nature of Asset that may seem to contradict the importance of critical thinking skills developed during professional training. As practice develops, it is crucial that practitioners ability and confidence to use Asset as a tool to enhance practice increases while approaching every assessment critically and treating each young person uniquely to ensure the right questions are asked in order to elicit accurate, relevant information. Asset, while comprehensive, cannot cover every eventuality so deep probing into areas in more depth than it may indicate, is required, such as when trying to uncover the trauma experienced by a young person seeking asylum. While it requires an element of ticking boxes Asset also requires practitioners to move beyond this and use their professional discretion to determine how to apply the structured framework to the complexities and diversity of the world of the young person being assessed.

It is suggested that in order to improve analysis in assessments that a long-term view of a young person and their behaviour is taken, rather than viewing offences in isolation (Sheldrick, 1995, cited in YJB, 2008) and that assessors develop *whole case hypotheses* which endeavour to bring together different issues (Sheppard et al., 2001, in YJB, 2008). Assessment in youth justice is a multifaceted, detailed, time-consuming process, laden with professional dilemmas and ethical issues. Therefore it is important that assessment issues are reflected upon regularly and discussed with other colleagues and in supervision. The decisions made on the basis of an assessment can have a profound impact upon a young person's life so ensuring all sources of information have been gathered and any gaps acknowledged, before engagement in thoughtful, reflective, critical analysis of the information in order to make evidence-based decisions is key if an assessment is to stand any chance of being fair.

It is within the context of such criticism of Asset, alongside other factors such as the risk and protective factors paradigm being contested (as discussed in Chapter 4) and reviews of practice following deaths and serious incidents in the secure estate and the community, that the YJB has embarked on a review and overhaul of the assessment framework. In doing so, it is acknowledging that the current system, while bringing some benefits to practice, is not fit for purpose. Linked to this is the issue of front line practice outlined in the Justice green paper which highlights the need to reduce the amount of time youth justice practitioners spend working at computers in order to devote more time for direct work with young people. This is consistent with the Munro *Review of child protection* which similarly identified the significant time social workers spend in front of computers as a barrier to engaging with children and families (Munro, 2011). Additionally, a Public Accounts Committee criticised the current assessment framework's ability to identify communication difficulties in children and young people. As a result of all these factors, a statement of intent – proposed framework was published (Teli, 2011) paving the way for a consultation exercise which has now been undertaken. A new model has been developed and a decision on whether the proposed reform will be developed further and fully implemented is awaiting confirmation. Some of the key principles of the model include:

- *Increased emphasis on strengths.*

- *Clearer distinction between the identification of need and the likelihood of reoffending to help ensure appropriately targeted interventions around offending behaviour and accurate referrals to universal services.*

- *Greater clarity about definitions relating to risk and the use of predictive measures.*

- *A variety of ratings and measures rather than one score.*

- *More iterative and dynamic assessments.*

- *The level of assessment reflecting the complexity of the young person's personal circumstances/behaviour.*

- *Ability for appropriate information to be transferred at key points such as custody transitions.*

- *Greater alignment to external children's assessments such as CAF.*

- *Clearer relationships between assessments and intervention plans.*

- *The need to take account of young person's speech, language and communication needs.*

- *Improved self-assessment tools and processes and a specific tool for parents and carers.*

- *The framework will be used across all parts of the youth justice system – from prevention through to custody.*

    (YJB, 2011, pp9–10)

This new framework has been tested with a number of YOTs, a YOI and a STC and feedback was positive. A review has also been undertaken into the Scaled Approach following the first year of its implementation. This has identified the following strengths:

- *Improvements in the quality of youth justice reports, assessments and plans.*

- *A clear rationale for allocation of scarce resources, easily understood by practitioners and perceived as fair by young people.*

- *A clear methodology for distinguishing between statutory and voluntary contacts.*

- *The potential for impacting positively upon key youth justice outcomes, in particular the reduction in risk posed by young people in relation to offending and serious harm.*

- *A structured system of contact which follows effective practice principles while allowing enough flexibility to allow for individual diversity.*

The review also identified the following criticisms:

- *The 'jump in' contact requirements between the enhanced and intensive is too great and carries the potential for increased breach for young people within the intensive banding.*

- *The drop in contact requirements at the three-month stage for those managed in the intensive banding is too great and does not facilitate good continuity in case management.*

- *The professional judgement in setting intervention levels has been used minimally despite being a key feature of the model, resulting in some young people being managed at the wrong intervention level.*

The proposed assessment framework includes revising the Scaled Approach model:

- *Practice advice will clarify that contact levels are minimum and that practitioners will be free to select a higher level of contact up to the threshold of the next intervention band.*

- *The model will provide an indicative intervention banding based on a combination of the improved static prediction tool and risk ratings.*

- *Practitioners will take account of all the information in their assessment of the young person and will actively select the appropriate intervention level and number of contacts.*

- *The minimum requirement for young people in the intensive banding will be reduced to ten contacts per month for the first three months and revert to four per month thereafter.*

- *Professional judgement will be enhanced by removing the centrally dictated requirement for management oversight of decisions to vary intervention levels.*

This proposed assessment framework appears to address much of what was deemed deficient in the current system by practitioners and academics. Whether the proposed changes will be implemented remains unclear during the uncertain territory of the demise of the YJB and transfer of its functions to the Ministry of Justice and during difficult economic conditions and severe public sector funding cuts imposed by the Coalition government.

ACTIVITY **6.3**

Based on the information in the continuing case of Jermaine below, introduced in the previous chapter, applying your knowledge and skills of assessment, look at each section of the core Asset to assist you in completing a report from the court. The full Asset core profile can be obtained from the following link: www.justice.gov.uk/guidance/youth-justice/assessment/asset-young-offender-assessment-profile.htm

Consider what issues you would want to address specifically in this assessment. What kind of questions would you want to ask Jermaine and who else would you want to speak to?

You are allocated the case of Jermaine to prepare a pre-sentence report for three weeks' time. He has pleaded guilty to the driving offences: taking a vehicle without consent, having no insurance and no licence and failing to stop for the police. The PSR request paperwork states that Jermaine is aged 15 years, 7 months, lives at home with his mother, stepfather and younger brother (12) and sister (9). He sees his birth father periodically. Jermaine attends the local secondary school and is a member of the football team. He has a reprimand for theft from 18 months ago. He was on bail supervision for three months in relation to a robbery charge that was committed to the Crown Court.

COMMENT

In approaching this assessment you would hopefully have accessed the evidence papers detailing the offence that Jermaine has pleaded guilty to so that you can interview him in order to ascertain his actions and intentions. You would want to know details of the offence – and exactly what role Jermaine played. You may have explored whether any planning took place, whether the victim was targeted and if Jermaine had been under the influence of any substances at the time and identified if there were any inconsistencies in Jermaine's intentions and actual behaviour. You would also want to consider any factors that make the offence more or less serious, known as aggravating or mitigating circumstances and a victim impact statement might have been available via the YOT police officer. You will need to comment on what level of remorse, if any, he has demonstrated, gain an understanding of why Jermaine committed the offence and knowledge of his personal and social circumstances will inform your thinking as well

Continued

as any motives he may have had. You would want to locate this instance of offending within Jermaine's overall behaviour and therefore details of any previous offences or patterns emerging in any response to previous involvement in the youth justice system need to be addressed. Remember that you are supposed to be providing an analytical account that goes into detail rather than just giving a description of events. Your thinking should be firmly located in the theoretical framework outlined in Chapter 3 and also informed by psycho-social approaches which take into account internal, psychological factors as well as external, structural factors such as poverty and class.

It is important to remember that you are looking for evidence relating to protective factors, not just those associated with risk, so that you are giving a balanced view and that the proposed intervention resulting from your assessment focuses on his strengths as well as any problematic areas.

Pre-sentence reports

The pre-sentence report that would need to be prepared in a case such as Jermaine's should be in accordance with the YJB National Standards, 2010 (YJB, 2010d) which requires YOTs to ensure that pre-sentence reports assist courts in determining the most suitable method of dealing with a young person by ensuring that they are based on:

- an Asset assessment;
- a minimum of one interview with the child or young person;
- an interview with at least one parent/carer, where possible;
- a home visit, where possible (if not possible give reasons why);
- CPS advanced disclosure information;
- an assessment of the victim's wishes regarding, and willingness to engage in, reparation and restorative justice interventions;
- an assessment of the consequences of the offence, including what is known of the impact on any victim, either from the CPS papers or from a victim personal statement;
- information from other relevant sources such as YOT case records, specialist assessments, or information from other agencies.

The standards also require the following format to be used:

- *Front sheet* setting out basic information relating to young person and the court hearing.
- *Sources of information* where the people spoken to and documents referred to are stated.
- *Offence analysis* which provides the court with an analysis of the offence, its context, impact upon the victim and an understanding of why it happened.

- *Offender assessment* which looks at the circumstances of the young person in relation to family, education, previous offending, including any mitigation and provides an assessment of the young person, leading to a proposed intervention level and an assessment of the need for parenting support.

- *Assessment of risk* where an assessment of the risk of the young person re-offending is made. The focus here should also be about the assessment of risk to the community and the risk to the young person including the risk of serious harm to others, and an assessment of dangerousness if appropriate.

- *Conclusion* that summarises the main issues and includes a realistic proposal for sentencing.

The importance and value of pre-sentence reports is perhaps best evidenced by research findings that demonstrate that high quality reports have a significant impact on resulting sentences. A study by the YJB (2000) cited in Bateman and Pitts (2005) found that *PSR's in low custody areas achieved a higher score in a quality audit than areas with a higher level of incarceration* (Bateman and Pitts, 2005, p116). However, research also shows that reports written within youth justice are often lacking in analysis and provide a descriptive, repetitive outline of information already presented (HMIP, 2006).

RESEARCH SUMMARY

Effectiveness and evaluation of Asset

Burnett and Appleton (2004) undertook research at Oxfordshire YOT, one of the few 'pathway' YOTs designated by the YJB to trial the new legislation and policy changes. The researchers followed the progress of the YOT for two and a half years, focusing on a wide range of issues including Asset. Feedback on the implementation and use of Asset was varied, with some practitioners finding it a useful structure to follow while other, more seasoned staff were more critical:

Some dissatisfaction with Asset was linked to perceptions of it as needlessly detailed, not to benefit practice but to serve as a research tool for performance monitoring and to supply statistics to the YJB. The most critical practitioners objected that their judgements were being forced into tick boxes to feed the government information machine. Managerial staff in the YOT, however, found that the tool generated invaluable aggregate information, added to the YOT's database, for monitoring work and for estimating resource requirements. (*Burnett and Appleton, 2004, p33*)

The Youth Justice Board commissioned research into the validity and reliability of the Asset assessment for young offenders, which looked at findings from the first two years of the use of Asset. This evaluation took place over 18 months with 39 YOTs nationwide. The data sample consisted of 3,395 Asset completed profiles with 82 per cent male and 18 per cent female and 10 per cent from ethnic minorities. It also included 627 'What do you think' Assets. The study presents information in relation to the range of factors included in Asset, such as the young person's living arrangements, education and vulnerability. It also shows

Continued

that the current Asset rating score predicted reconviction with 67 per cent accuracy which was maintained with specific groups such as females, and it was found to be predictive of frequency of reconviction and sentence at reconviction. Results in relation to reliability were seen as encouraging with a generally good level of reliability between teams within YOTs and between staff from different professional backgrounds and a high degree of consistency in the ratings of individual assessors (Baker et al., 2003, p7).

This research was extended to analyse data for a 24 month period in order to assess the accuracy of Asset on measuring change over time.

Key findings were:

- Predictive validity (in relation to whether a young person was reconvicted or not) increased over time. Using the 'per cent correctly predicted' method the accuracy figure was 69.4 per cent (compared to 67 per cent at 12 months). The 'area under curve' measure also improved slightly.

- Accuracy in predicting frequency and seriousness of reconviction was maintained at 24 months.

- Predictive accuracy for population sub-groups (female offenders, ethnic minorities and younger offenders) was maintained at 24 months.

- Current Asset performed reasonably well in predicting reconviction among Final Warning cases at 12 months but was less accurate at 24 months.

(Baker et al., 2005, p4)

Assessment of risk or need

In the youth justice arena, risk assessment is a multi-layered affair consisting of assessing the risk of re-offending of each young person, the risk to the young person in terms of their vulnerability and any risk of harm they may pose to the public. Each of these areas is addressed by Asset: the risk of re-offending and vulnerability within the core profile, and the risk of harm warranting its own additional assessment for those who trigger a positive answer to certain questions.

Vulnerability

The 'Indicators of vulnerability' section of the Asset core profile focuses on the possibility of harm being caused to the young person. It requires practitioners to assess whether there are indications that the young person is at risk of self-harm or suicide and if there are any protective factors that may reduce this vulnerability. It also considers whether the young person is likely to be vulnerable as a result of factors such as the behaviour of others; other events or circumstances; or their own behaviour.

If a young person has been assessed as medium, high or very high risk of vulnerability in the core Asset profile a Vulnerability Management Plan is required to be completed. This is a separate document to the intervention plan but should include specific proposals related to reducing vulnerability and should be integrated with any other plans for the young person such as a care plan or pathway plan if they are looked after.

As with all sections of Asset, completion of this section requires that evidence is given to justify the particular rating boxes that are ticked. Given that this assessment and the Vulnerability Management Plan could accompany a young person to the secure estate if they are remanded or sentenced to a period in custody, it is vital that such information is as accurate and detailed as possible as the young person may require close monitoring to ensure their own safety. Unfortunately, research shows (Goldson, 2002) that many young people in custody have a history of problems, abuse, mental health issues, educational and social exclusion, for instance, so it is highly likely that any time spent working in a YOT will include dealing with vulnerable young people, some of whom are imprisoned. With such high numbers of young people incarcerated in the UK, it is perhaps not surprising that tragedies still occur, such as the death of Gareth Price, aged 16, on 20 January 2005, who was found hanging in his care and separation cell, Gareth Myatt, aged 15, who died on 19 April 2004 after losing consciousness while being restrained by staff at Rainsbrook Secure Training Centre, or 14-year-old Adam Rickwood, the youngest person to die in custody in the UK in August 2004 at the privately run Hassockfield Secure Training Centre, 100 miles from his home. It was his first time in custody and it is said he had threatened to kill himself a few days beforehand, as he was finding it difficult being so far from his family and home. While this concerns the wider issue of whether custody is suitable for many young people, it also emphasises the importance of high-quality assessments informing court reports so that courts have all the information at hand before making decisions, as well as the need for the assessment to be shared with the secure estate.

Research commissioned by the YJB in 2005 involving 301 young people from 6 YOTs and 6 custodial units, found that 31 per cent had mental health needs. This included:

- 18 per cent experiencing problems with depression;
- 10 per cent suffering from anxiety;
- 9 per cent suffering from post-traumatic stress disorder (PTSD);
- 7 per cent having problems with hyperactivity;
- 5 per cent reporting psychotic-like symptoms.

(Youth Justice Board, 2005, cited in Perry et al., 2008)

Thus, it is vitally important that mental health issues are identified as part of any assessment process of young people in the youth justice system so that these can be addressed. The core Asset profile includes a section on emotional and mental health so that the assessing practitioner is required to take into account whether such issues are prevalent. YJB guidance indicates that where a young person is rated as 3 or higher in this section of the core Asset, the second stage of the screening process should be instigated using the Screening Questionnaire Interview for Adolescents (SQUIFA) tool.

SQIFA is used to screen for eight common mental health problems in adolescence:

- alcohol use;
- drug use;
- depression;
- traumatic experiences;
- anxiety and excessive worries/stress;
- self-harm;
- attention deficit hyperactivity disorder (ADHD);
- psychotic symptoms.

SQUIFA requires a rating of 0–3 to be applied to the different categories assessed. The assessing YOT practitioner should consider repeating the questionnaire in 4–6 weeks or if the circumstances change if a score of 2 is obtained. A score of 3 or more on the SQUIFA requires that the young person is referred to the health worker or a suitably trained worker in the YOT in order that the third stage screening interview, the Mental Health Screening Interview for Adolescents (SIFA) is completed. If a young person screens as positive a referral to the Child and Adolescent Mental Health Service (CAMHS) is required. A negative screening is recommended to be followed up within six weeks accounting for the changing needs of young people. While it is important that the mental health needs of young people are considered carefully it is also essential that they are done so within the context of the young person's development during adolescence which is known to be a turbulent and difficult time for most young people as they struggle to cope with the huge physical changes they experience while establishing their identity. Referrals to CAMHS may cause huge anxiety for young people and they will need support from their YOT worker in both accessing and engaging with such services.

For some young people their vulnerability will stem from their experience of neglect or abuse from their parents or carers. While some young people experiencing such adversity may already be known to children and families social work services, in which case, good collaboration is crucial with the relevant team, many may not be previously or currently known to such services. Should an assessment of a young person identify issues of safeguarding, the YOT practitioner must be clear with the young person in relation to limits regarding confidentiality and ensure these concerns are raised with the relevant referral and assessment team within children's services. Local arrangements will be in place which will be informed by *Working together to safeguard children* (2010 and due for revision in 2012 following the Munro Review, 2011), local child protection procedures and Local Safeguarding Children's Board (LSCB) guidance. This may involve completing a Common Assessment Framework (CAF) which was introduced following the green paper, *Every child matters* (2003a) to assist all practitioners working with children in universal and specialist services to assess children's needs earlier and more effectively.

Piper (2004), suggests that one advantage of the CAF could be developments that breakdown the 'insularity' of the youth justice system. For instance, if a young person offends who is also the subject of child protection concerns, s/he should also be referred to a

Children and Families Team where another assessment will be undertaken under s47 of the Children Act 1989, using the *Assessment Framework*. Piper cites a NACRO briefing that suggests YOT staff should receive training on child development and welfare if they are to effectively share corporate parenting and associated aims and objectives and that the CAF may assist in bridging the gap between the separate assessment tools and systems as well as the differing professional cultures in the child protection and youth justice systems.

Risk of serious harm

The 'Indicators of serious harm' section of Asset focuses on the possibility of the young person causing serious physical or psychological harm to someone. Practitioners completing it have to state whether there is any evidence of:

- behaviour where serious harm was planned or caused or other (reckless) behaviour that may have led to serious harm being caused.

The assessor is required to consider issues such as:

- use of weapons, whether the young person is involved in targetting any individual or group, has concerning motives or discriminatory beliefs.

Finally, the assessor must identify whether there are any concerns about other disturbing or harmful expressed behaviour by the young person or other people or any intuitive feelings about possible harmful behaviour.

Due to difficulties attached to predicting violent or harmful behaviour it is acknowledged that while empirically based assessment frameworks informed by research can be used, the ultimate decision warrants clinical judgement (Borum et al., 1999, YJB, 2008).

If any of the above questions warrant a 'yes' by the assessor, a 'Risk of serious harm' (ROSH) Asset must be completed. Specific YJB guidance is available in relation to the completion of this form and is available at: www.justice.gov.uk/guidance/youth-justice/assessment/asset-young-offender-assessment-profile.htm

The guidance advises that an analysis of the information recorded in the core Asset profile and other completed assessments is required, along with additional information to fill any gaps or unanswered questions to make a comprehensive assessment of risk of serious harm. The full ROSH Asset includes sections on evidence of harm-related behaviour, which is defined broadly as 'behaviour that has actually resulted in serious harm to others, and behaviour where there was a real possibility of such harm occurring'. Current risk indicators are also addressed, as is future harmful behaviour, with a concluding section in which an assessment of low, medium, high and very high risk needs to be made. On the basis of this classification, an indication is then required as to which Multi-Agency Public Protection Arrangements (MAPPA) level the young person is assessed as being at. There are three levels: level 1 where risk management should be dealt with by the YOT through normal supervision procedures; level 2 requires local interagency risk management and attendance at level 2 Strategic Management Board meetings; and level 3 requires an automatic *referral to the Multi-Agency Public Protection Panel where a structured and detailed risk management plan is developed* (YJB Risk of Serious Harm guidance, p8). The YJB has also issued *Dangerous offenders – Guidance on Multi-Agency Public Protection Arrangements* – available at: www.youth-justice-board.gov.uk

If a young person has been assessed as medium, high or very high risk in the conclusion section of the ROSH a Risk Management Plan is required to be completed. This needs to address the type of behaviour causing concern, its potential impact and the likelihood of it occurring. It should also be integrated with any other plans such as the supervision plan, care plan or pathway plan involving all relevant professionals so the risks are clearly identified and strategies in place to mitigate them. It is important that the assessment is reviewed and updated regularly in the light of any changes.

While assessing and managing risk is an extremely important part of the work of a Youth Offending Team social worker it is important also to bear in mind that most young people you will be working with will not be assessed as dangerous. Completion of the ROSH Asset will only be required in a minority of cases and it is imperative that young people are not identified and labelled a serious risk unless there is significant evidence to support such a claim.

CHAPTER SUMMARY

In this chapter we have considered what the purpose of an assessment is, when assessments are used and what makes a good assessment. We have identified that ensuring assessments are thorough information-gathering exercises with concrete evidence provided and used in making analyses, judgements and decisions is extremely important. The assessment tool, Asset, used in youth justice, has been examined as well as the research that has informed its development. We have looked at the complexities and difficulties involved in carrying out an assessment and considered the issues raised in a case study. We have examined the concept of risk assessment and the importance of ensuring assessments are carried out properly to ensure accuracy. In the next chapter we will begin to consider applying the assessment to the planning, intervening and evaluating work with young people.

**FURTHER
READING**

Baker, K, Kelly, J and Wilkinson, B (2011) *Assessment in youth justice*. Bristol: Policy Press.

Provides a comprehensive account of theory and practice in relation to assessment and planning interventions in a youth justice context.

Milner, J and O'Byrne, P (2009) *Assessment in social work*. 3rd edn. Basingstoke: Palgrave Macmillan.

This book summarises a range of theories relevant to the assessment process.

Chapter 7

Working with young people

Paul Dugmore

ACHIEVING A SOCIAL WORK DEGREE

This chapter will help you begin to meet the following National Occupational Standards.

Key Role 2: Plan, carry out, review and evaluate social work practice, with individuals, families, carers, groups, communities and other professionals

- Respond to crisis situations.
- Interact with individuals, families, carers, groups and communities to achieve change and development and to improve life opportunities.
- Prepare, produce, implement and evaluate plans with individuals, families, carers, groups, communities and professional colleagues.
- Support the development of networks to meet assessed needs and planned outcomes.
- Work with groups to promote individual growth, development and independence.
- Address behaviour which presents a risk to individuals, families, carers, groups and communities.

Key Role 3: Support individuals to represent their needs, views and circumstances

- Advocate with, and on behalf of, individuals, families, carers, groups and communities.
- Prepare for, and participate in decision making forums.

Key Role 4: Manage risk to individuals, families, carers, groups, communities, self and colleagues

- Assess and manage risks to individuals, families, carers, groups and communities.
- Assess, minimise and manage risk to self and colleagues.

Key Role 5: Manage and be accountable, with supervision and support, for your own social work practice within your organisation

- Manage and be accountable for your own work.
- Contribute to the management of resources and services.
- Manage, present and share records and reports.

Key Role 6: Demonstrate professional competence in social work practice

- Research, analyse, evaluate, and use current knowledge of best social work practice.
- Work within agreed standards of social work practice and ensure own professional development.

It will also introduce you to the following academic standards as set out in the social work subject benchmark statement:

5.1.4 Social work theory.
5.1.5 The nature of social work practice.
5.4 Problem solving skills.
5.5.4 Intervention and evaluation.
5.6 Communication skills.

Introduction

This chapter will focus on how to intervene and provide services to young people who have offended or are at risk of offending. The importance of relationship-based practice based on establishing clear professional boundaries and the need to engage young people will be explored and issues of diversity, equality and working with difference. Following on from the previous chapter and the need for assessment to be integral to the social work process, the importance of planning, reviewing, ending and evaluating interventions with young people and the frameworks in place for achieving this will be considered. Finally the chapter will examine the different approaches to working with young people such as one-to-one work, group work and restorative justice, having critiqued issues relating to evidence-based practice.

Building a relationship

Being able to form professional relationships is fundamental to good social work practice and the importance of being able to do so is enshrined in the National Occupational Standards and GSCC Code of Practice for Social Care Workers. This is equally as relevant for social workers in youth justice who occupy a clear position of authority, act as officers of the court and work with young people who are often disadvantaged, progressing through troubled adolescence, resistant to authority and who possibly have experience of abuse, emotional and/or behavioural problems and a range of social problems. YOT social worker's first point of contact with a young person is likely to be during a time in which they may well be anxious, overwhelmed and scared about the ensuing process and possible outcomes.

Being able put a young person and their family at ease, demonstrating warmth and empathy and having clarity about their role are all important factors in establishing a good working relationship.

Overall, studies show that the key characteristics that children look for in a social worker are: a willingness to listen and show empathy; reliability; taking action; respecting confidences; and viewing the child or young person as a whole person and not overly identifying a child with a particular problem (Hill, 1999; Morgan, 2006; Curtis, 2006, cited in Oliver, 2010, p8). Additionally, research by Hill, (1999) and de Winter and Noom (2003) found that where young people have been asked what they value in a social worker they said being actively involved in decision making; keeping promises, being available, punctuality, privacy and communication that does not stress power differentials. Therefore, it is important to remember that we are working with children with problems rather than problem children.

Given that you will often be working with young people for whom relationships have often broken down, creating a trusting environment where there is room for development is crucial (de Winter and Noom, 2003). It is also necessary to sustain support even when the young person makes mistakes. Other research (de Winter, 2003, Hill, 1999, Barry, 2000) suggests that dialogue and a participatory approach where you and the young person identify the main problems, look for causes and solutions and assess development will yield more positive outcomes. This ties in with the importance of establishing, harnessing and working with a young person's positive (protective) factors rather than just the problematic areas of their life.

ACTIVITY **7.1**

What do you think are the key considerations in starting a new professional relationship with a service user? Are these any different when the service user is (1) a young person? (2) a young offender? Practise introducing yourself as a social worker to a young person you are meeting for the first time.

COMMENT

You may have identified the importance of first impressions, of being warm and friendly, listening to the young person, discussing expectations and boundaries and getting to know them and their interests.

Traditionally, social work practice was based on the concept of the relationship and psychoanalysis provided an important theoretical framework (Bower, 2005). The rise of Marxist, sociological theory that considered wider social structures as impacting on the lives of clients rather than their own internal difficulties diluted the influence of psychoanalytical thinking upon social work. A psychosocial approach to casework was developed by Hollis (1972) whose *Psychosocial Therapy* stressed the need of the case worker to intervene in the client's immediate environment in order to reduce pressures or access resources. For Hollis, casework as a psychosocial treatment method recognised *the interplay of both internal psychological and external social causes of dysfunctioning* (Hollis, 1972, p9). In the last chapter the rise of managerialism or the rational–technical approach to public sector services was discussed which brought with it an *emphasis on paperwork, procedures, 'quick fix' solutions and approaches that will eradicate risk at the expense of the professional relationship* (Wilson et al., 2008, p5). Howe purports that as relationships between social workers and clients change from supportive and therapeutic to transactional and service-orientated, the personal relationship, necessary in order for successful outcomes to be achieved, is *stripped of its social, cultural, emotional and interpersonal dimensions* (Howe, 1996, p77).

Recent reports by the Social Work Taskforce (2009), Reform Board (2011) and Munro (2011) have all been critical of the managerialist culture that has evolved in recent decades, its rational-technical approach to social work and its preoccupation with performance indicators. Munro identified that the heavy prescription that has evolved has obscured the need to form relationships with families in order to understand them and has recommended this be reduced to enable social workers to exercise more professional judgement (Social Work Taskforce, 2009, Munro, 2011).

While the current reviews of the social work profession may lead to strategies implemented to improve practice and return to traditional forms of social work, the challenge for social workers is to strive to adopt relationship-based practice in their work with clients while rational-technical approaches still inform the systems and policy that shape practice. Wilson et al. (2008) propose a model of relationship-based practice that comprises the following characteristics:

- It recognises that each social work encounter is unique.

- It understands that human behaviour is complex and multi-faceted – people are not simply rational beings but have affective – conscious and unconscious – dimensions that enrich but simultaneously complicate human relationships.

- It focuses on the inseparable nature of the internal and external worlds of individuals and the importance of integrated – psychosocial – as opposed to polarised responses to social problems.

- It accepts that human behaviours and the professional relationship are an integral component of any professional intervention.

- It places particular emphasis on the use of self and the relationship as the means through which interventions are channelled.

(Wilson et al., 2008, p8).

This model highlights the importance of being open to the emotional experience of other people, ourselves and able to distinguish between the emotions of others and our own. An understanding of psychodynamic theory can help social workers to explore and disentangle what is going on in a situation for the person in need of help as well as for the social worker who cannot fail to be affected by the emotional intensity of practice. Thus, knowledge of types of psychological defence mechanisms such as projection and splitting, are useful to identify when an individual projects their bad thoughts and feelings into someone else as well as transference, where the client's feelings, images and experiences from their internal world are transferred onto another person. This person is then treated as if they were an object from their own internal world. This can be useful in social work as it enables the practitioner to become aware of, and make sense of, what has been projected into them by a service user.

If you are allocated a case of a young person you have previously assessed, it is generally easier to build a working relationship as you will have already started the process. If you start working with a young person who is previously unknown to you, it is vital that you develop a relationship based on some clear ground rules very early on.

If you find this task difficult, it may be helpful for you to think back to when you met a professional for the first time as a service user, such as going to see your doctor or bank manager. How was it? How do you expect to be treated? The things that are important to you are probably important to other people too.

Initial contact

It is essential that thorough preparation is carried out before commencing work with a young person and this involves reading information already held on a young person's file. Research shows that children often report that a frequent change of social worker led to frustration and upset at having to re-tell their stories and difficulties in forming a relationship of trust (Blueprint Project, 2005). It is crucial to be clear about the purpose of any involvement or intervention with young people so that they understand this. It is also useful to bear in mind that information held on file may be inaccurate, negative or another person's view. For instance, the young person may have been very uncommunicative in a previous interview with a colleague due to an incident that happened at school or home before the interview. The colleague may not have known about this and therefore may have perceived the young person in a particular way. Thus, in establishing a new relationship the social worker needs to be open-minded about prior information and form their own opinions. Although questioning is an important part of the relationship building phase as research identifies, the need for the young person to retell their life stories repeatedly should be avoided.

First impressions play an important part in establishing any relationship and given that a young person attending a YOT may have a multitude of feelings about social workers ranging from ambivalence to mistrust, it is important to be aware of these.

Koprowska (2010), in writing about the significance of first impressions in social work practice offers four principles:

1. *Be clear* – use simple language, free from jargon and pompous phraseology.

2. *Be concise* – prepare yourself so you know the key issues in any situation, and can communicate them succinctly.

3. *Be comprehensive* – keep in mind all the key issues, and watch out for sidelining information that makes you feel uncomfortable.

4. *Be courteous* – courtesy is much more than good manners, though these are essential, and a certain level of polite formality is important when communicating with people new to us. Courtesy is also the way in which the underpinning values of social work are communicated – our respect for individuals and their uniqueness, and our commitment to anti-discriminatory and anti-racist practices and hence our respect for diversity.

   (Koprowska, 2010: 55–6)

Some criminological theories such as subcultural and Marxist approaches, outlined in Chapter 3, would suppose that young people offending will perceive YOT social workers as part of the state/authority and therefore as agents of social control. This may mean you are viewed with suspicion. While being clear about your role and purpose, and the authority mandated by legislation, you should also be able to demonstrate that you are aiming to work in the young person's best interests. Practical examples of this, such as demonstrating respect and understanding, will hopefully start to develop trust. Such theories may also attribute possible notions of collusion where there are shared identities such as class or ethnic grouping. This can pose a challenge, as you have to retain professional boundaries while perhaps demonstrating some level of personal understanding or empathy.

It is important that young people understand why they have to attend the YOT and what the role of the social worker will be in working with them. This is a good time to talk about your expectations of the young person in terms of agency policy, the requirements of their order, and National Standards for instance. It is also necessary to establish if there are any expectations the young person may have of you or the service, and questions they may have about your role and what they might want from the intervention, as this can then form the basis of contract setting or planning that you will work towards over the course of the intervention. This should include:

- Giving information about the office opening hours.

- Contact arrangements and details.

- Establishing the best time for appointments to be made with the young person, taking into account religious observances.

- Informing the young person of the enforcement procedure and what happens when appointments are missed.

- Ensuring that the young person is aware of the complaints procedure.

- Explaining how confidentiality works, particularly in a multi-agency team.

- Introducing the young person to the notion of partnership.

- Outlining that work will also include close contact with parents/carers.

A welfare approach to working with young people

Core social work values such as respect, empathy, acceptance and partnership should underpin practice with young people and their families. The discussion that took place in Chapter 1 is relevant here, as how you view young people who have committed offences will contribute greatly to your ability to forge strong, positive and supportive working relationships with them. As well as being mindful of their age and stage of emotional, physical and intellectual development and their social circumstances, it is also essential that their experiences to date are taken into account in terms of shaping who they are and why they might be displaying certain criminal or negative behaviours. Thinking back to Chapter 3 and the different criminological theories to help identify the cause(s) of criminal behaviour should help. Research looking into the links between risk factors and offending behaviour, carried out by Liddle and Solanki (2002), found that the young people in their sample had an average of about six risk factors, some of which included:

- Only 14 per cent were living with both biological parents, 66 per cent lacked a good relationship with one or other parent.

- 22 per cent had suffered bereavement, 39 per cent family breakdown or divorce and 34 per cent had lost contact with significant people.

- 44 per cent had experienced neglect or physical, sexual or emotional abuse, or had witnessed violence in the family.

- 22 per cent were looked after by social services, 27 per cent had been previously.

   (Liddle and Solanki, 2002, p1)

While this is only one study, there are many more that show similar findings (Goldson, 2000; YJB, 2007; NACRO, 2003b). Faced with such data it is important to bear in mind that building a relationship may be extremely difficult with some young people; they may not have experienced much boundary setting in their lives or have not been treated with respect or listened to. As a result, they may experience the supervisory relationship as difficult, leading them to attempt to sabotage it in a number of ways. Remaining clear about your purpose, reflecting on your practice and demonstrating understanding but firmness will all be crucial in determining a successful outcome.

However, it is perhaps easy to lose sight of the fact that you are dealing with children and young people when the system you are working within operates according to principles of responsibility, where *doli incapax* has been removed and opportunities to adopt a 'child first' philosophy (Haines and Drakeford, 1998) have been reduced. Indeed, research undertaken in YOTs in Wales by Cross et al. (2003) found that social work students on placement in YOTs found that young people tended to be perceived as young offenders. One student commented:

> *That was something I was very conscious of coming into it. There's not as much recognition of them not being adults – and they're children not adults. The wording is all around offenders rather than young people.* (Cross et al., 2003, p159)

Thus, it is important that as a student and a newly qualified practitioner in youth justice you strive to retain your social work identity within a multi-agency environment and keep an analytical approach to the systems and processes you work in. Youth justice, like all other areas of social work, continues to move towards more managerialist, performance-led practice. This approach, combined with the justice components of New Labour reforms, sometimes makes it difficult to remain child-focused in what can be a demoralising world. As identified in Chapter 2, the youth justice system is fraught with competing tensions between justice and welfare approaches and you need to be able to maximise the opportunities for practising a welfare approach. You may struggle to do this when you are working with colleagues who adopt a justice approach and a system that draws on competing philosophical approaches. This is where the importance of building a trusting relationship with young people can impact positively where the young person is seen not just in relation to the offence they committed and the relationship is used as a vehicle to assist them in seeing themselves as more constructive members of society with opportunities for development and success.

Working with young people in youth justice also requires you to understand the emotional context of a young person's life at any given moment in time. Such emotions may range from anger or denial in response to loss or to anxiety or frustration, for instance. It is important to acknowledge how such feelings may impact upon a young person and work through the presenting defence mechanisms. Not all emotions will be openly displayed and being able to read body language is often necessary, as well as being aware of how your behaviour is interpreted by them. Being aware of your feelings is essential if you are to work effectively with the emotions of young people, as you may sometimes feel annoyed or upset by, or irreverent to, them. Realising why and ensuring that the young person is not aware of your feelings, let alone affected by them, is all part of developing your own self-awareness or emotional intelligence.

In order to work effectively with users of social work services you need to develop the skills to work in partnership with young people and their families. As Trevithick (2005, p228) states:

Positive practice must involve service users if it is to achieve agreed objectives (empowerment and personal responsibility) and that within this process, service users must be seen not only in terms of the 'problems' they bring, but also as whole people who have an important contribution to make in terms of their knowledge and perception of the situation, personal qualities and problem-solving capabilities.

As Le Fevre identifies (2010) young people are only likely to share their conflicting feelings and thoughts if they have confidence that their worker can hear, contain and make sense of these. Practitioners who are kind, supportive, warm, empathic, respectful and accepting are more likely to make them feel safe and cared for and consistent, available and reliable behaviour should help in building trust. She cites the work of Morgan (2006) whose research identified that children and young people wanted social workers to be approachable, outgoing, not too formal, able to get on with children and young people, capable of understanding the 'ways and thoughts of kids', able to keep promises, be good listeners, have a sense of humour, good at calming others when they are upset and not judging, but trying to listen and understand (Morgan, 2006 p12, cited in Le Fevre, 2010, p32–3).

Effective practice with young people who offend

The YJB guidance, *Key elements of effective practice: Engaging young people who offend* (2008) identifies the fact that most research undertaken into effective practice with young people who offend focuses on the types of interventions provided and how effective these are in reducing offending behaviour. As such there is a dearth of knowledge to inform why some interventions work better than others, and what makes a difference when interventions are delivered in practice. Mason and Prior (2008) were commissioned to undertake a review of research into effective practice in relation to techniques of engagement using established principles and procedures for systematic review, however, as very little research has been undertaken into techniques of engagement, such a review was not possible. Prior and Mason (2010, p213) refer to the conclusions drawn from various systematic reviews and meta-analyses which suggest that:

Effectiveness at the level of intervention or programme is more likely when certain factors are present: careful assessment; use of a risk and protective factors framework; a cognitive skills element; a coordinated multi-modal design; an element of reparation; implementation in accordance with design ('programme integrity'); and long-term engagement and contact time, particularly for persistent and more serious offenders.

Hagell (2003, pp5–6), in a Department of Health briefing for Quality Protects, identifies a number of characteristics of successful programmes to change behaviour:

- *They should be based on a clear theoretical model of how they are meant to change behaviour.*

- *There needs to be a clear focus for all the activity involved in the programme. Everyone should know what the outcome will be, and this should be specific and measurable.*

- *They last for a reasonable length of time. Six months is usually necessary if they are to have a chance of making a difference.*

- *They need to have reasonably frequent contact with the young people. As a rule of thumb this is often suggested to be around twice a week although it depends very much on the type of work being done and the needs of the child.*

- *The programme should be focusing on rewarding positive behaviour rather than on meting out punishment.*

- *Following through the intervention with some aftercare also seems to be beneficial.*

Examples of programmes with positive outcomes include social skills training, cognitive behavioural programmes, parent training programmes and multi-modal interventions such as multi-systemic therapy. Such suggestions are generally based on the findings of a large number of studies, through meta-analysis (Smith, 2005), where programmes deemed as the most effective in changing behaviour are those directly addressing behaviour problems *by using a social learning approach, teaching social and interpersonal skills and helping young people to perceive and think about their own and other people's behaviour in a different way* (Smith, 2003, p188).

Some of the cognitive behavioural techniques used with offenders include:

- *Pro-social modelling* – Modelling positive behaviour and rewarding and reinforcing pro-social behaviour in young people.

- *Motivational interviewing* – Working with young people to encourage them to be motivated to making changes in their lives and a belief in their capacity to learn.

- *Problem solving* – Offending is reduced by enhancing problem-solving skills, often using case scenarios and requiring young people to identify problems and solutions and develop consequential thinking skills.

- *Social skills training* – Improving young people's skills in social situations which may include role play and assertiveness training.

- *Moral reasoning* – Giving young people a range of moral dilemmas to discuss and make decisions about.

Because the research into effective practice often focuses on new, 'flagship' programmes where resources are invested heavily and motivation is high among those delivering the programmes, Smith (2003) suggests they are not representative of what is delivered to most young offenders. He concludes that t*hese findings illustrate the danger of using the 'what works' evidence as a platform for extending the scope and activity of the juvenile justice system* and that *widening the scope of intervention to include many adolescence-limited offenders will dilute the effectiveness of efforts to help the core group of life-course persistent offenders* (Smith, 2003, p193). Goldson also cautions against the acceptance of effective practice research stating that:

> *The lives of young offenders are complex and reliance on a single theory of 'reasoning and rehabilitation' or a discrete form of cognitive intervention is unlikely to produce good results. We cannot expect, nor should we expect, to discover law-like universals.*

> (Goldson, 2001, p83)

Prior (2005) reviewed evaluations of youth justice interventions and found only minimal evidence that they are effective in reducing youth offending, suggesting that those involved in youth justice should exercise caution when approaching new initiatives. He maintains that applying a critical approach and being prepared to adapt programmes to meet the needs of the specific population being worked with are essential.

One of the problems with the evidence-based practice movement adopted by policy makers, including the YJB, is that it has tended to favour research from a positivist, quantitative perspective with the randomised controlled trial (RCT) being seen as the 'gold standard'. This has meant that much of social work research that adopted more qualitative, interpretivist methods of inquiry, often of much smaller scale, have been negated or dismissed as adding value to the 'what works' debate. Cooper and Lousada (2010) suggest that:

> In the competition to produce evidence for treatments or interventions, those that have done the best job of playing the scientific game can and do present themselves as 'the best'. Branding, marketing, management, cost, efficiency and public legitimation through science, move in alongside traditionally grounded truth claims about what might really be the best treatment for a particular condition.

> (Cooper and Lousada, 2010, p40)

This contends that psychoanalysis or psychodynamically informed social work has not promoted its value sufficiently in providing evidence of its effectiveness in intervening in work with service users whereas cognitive behavioural therapy, for instance, has promoted its own value much more effectively through the use of research evidence. However, as Briggs (2005) states, the RCT model does not lend itself well to assessing effectiveness in psycho-social interventions, which are complex and ambiguous, not to mention potentially unethical and costly. Nonetheless, there are examples of RCTs that have identified the value of psychoanalytic psychotherapies and Kennedy's systematic review (2004) of psychoanalytic child psychotherapy found strong, if not conclusive, support for the claim that it does 'work'. Briggs (2005) maintains that the effect of research from a psychoanalytic perspective is to enrich the psycho-social space in which social work takes place by bringing another perspective, focus and method.

Despite research evidence providing such a confident identification of effective practice interventions in working with offenders the absence of research that highlights *why* such interventions work meant that Prior and Mason needed to acquire such knowledge from other means as part of their YJB commissioned research. They then drew on practice literature to identify key messages about engagement techniques that produce positive outcomes in work with young people who offend. In doing so they found that central to the literature was the capacity to understand and focus on the lived experiences of young people which requires the ability to communicate and empathise rather than just a technical or formal knowledge of child development. Much of the practice literature has focused on the importance of the relationship and of qualities such as openness, empathy and warmth. This is further consolidated by McNeil (2006) who, writing in relation to the wider realm of psychological interventions than youth justice, suggests that common factors likely to be conducive to effecting positive change include empathy, genuineness, establishing a working alliance and a person-centred approach. He suggests that critical to the success of an intervention are, more importantly, the relationship and the social and material contexts of the young person's life than the programme itself.

In order to attempt to redress the absence of research into how youth justice practitioners can effectively engage young people in different interventions, the YJB commissioned a piece of research (Ipsos MORI, 2010) focusing on the views of YOT practitioners about how to engage young people and the barriers to successful engagement. This also involved seeking the views of young people about their own engagement with services. The research also found that the main factors in relation to successful techniques of engagement were:

- The relationship between a young person and their worker which was dependent on the ability of staff to be 'firm but fair' in their approach; achieving a mix of friendliness coupled with appropriate boundaries within which rules can be enforced where necessary. Consistency was also seen as important to the young people as change can be unsettling. Many young people also identified having someone to talk to as positive.

- The skills and qualities of the worker were deemed as important in developing a positive relationship with young people and in directly engaging them in interventions. These included excellent communication skills and demonstrating an interest in the young person as an individual. Being humorous or approachable is important as is being flexible, creative, having the ability to develop mutual respect and to inspire trust, being persistent and prepared to go the extra mile with young people.

- The need for clarity in relation to enforcement at the outset of the order so that young people are clear about what is expected of them and are able to take responsibility for their own actions was also identified.

- Pro-social modelling was acknowledged as important in terms of achieving both clarity and consistency for the young people in terms of keeping appointments and expecting the same of the young people, thereby encouraging good behaviour.

- The need to view young people in the context of their wider circumstances and involving families is vital and should be attempted as much as possible however difficult this may be to achieve.

Table 7.1 identifies other techniques that were identified as good practice in the research.

Table 7.1

Behaviour of young person	Method most highly perceived by practitioners in the online survey to be successful in engaging young person
Those who fail to engage from the start of the order.	Practitioners suggest liaising with their family, friends or peers to encourage engagement. Breaching for non-compliance where necessary is an option.
Those whose attendance is poor.	Collecting the young person where possible is advocated by YOT workers in this instance.
Young people are not fully participating, but are engaging with the YOT to some extent.	Involving young people in their intervention plan is important in this circumstance to try to get their 'buy-in'. For example, where young people turn up but fail to fully participate, YOT workers think this is essential – as is the use of creative ideas to try to encourage participation.

Continued

Table 7.1 continued

Behaviour of young person	Method most highly perceived by practitioners in the online survey to be successful in engaging young person
Where the young person has a good relationship with their worker, but still fails to fully participate with their order.	Practitioners advocated involving the young person in the planning of the intervention/supervision session. Also important to ensure clear objectives are set from the start of the order.
Young person is participating but not fully engaging with YOT staff.	The YOT/young person relationship could be explored in more detail, and possible allocation of a different worker could be considered.

Source: (Ipsos MORI, 2010, p66)

While this research attempts to begin to address the lack of knowledge and evidence about what are effective techniques for engaging young people, this is still a significantly under-explored area of practice. Until additional research is commissioned to contribute to this picture, knowledge from the practice literature will continue to be the main source to which students and practitioners will need to refer.

Working with difference

In Chapter 1 we looked at values and ethics and how these might impact on your work as a social worker within youth justice and considered the over-representation of young men and ethnic minorities in the youth justice system. How you practise an anti-discriminatory and anti-oppressive approach will also help determine your success in engaging young people. How you treat young people as service users and demonstrate acceptance of them as individuals in spite of their offending will also contribute to this process of engagement. It is also important to bear in mind that much of the research identifying positive outcomes with offending young people is based on studies involving white males from western countries such as the USA and how much applicability these have in relation to working with young people from ethnic minority backgrounds or girls/young woman is questionable.

ACTIVITY 7.2

Based on your assessment of Jermaine in Activity 6.3, he has been sentenced to a 12-month YRO. Draw up an intervention plan to address the identified needs. Would anything different need to be taken into account if the young person was a newly arrived asylum seeker?

COMMENT

The intervention plan should be informed by the areas in which the assessment rated Jermaine highly in terms of the likelihood of reoffending. You may have considered it important to focus on family relationships, his education and leisure, particularly given his interest in football, in order to draw on protective factors. You probably identified the need for one-to-one or group work sessions to focus on his offending behaviour – specifically driving-related offences as well as reparation.

Given that you will be working with young people from a range of cultural, racial, religious and social backgrounds, of different ages, sexualities and with a range of physical disabilities and learning difficulties, you will need to develop skills and competence in working with difference. It is not possible to be an 'expert' in working with difference and complacency or in relation to this continually emerging area will not assist in developing effective ways of working with young people. Some basic principles should assist in starting to build a relationship:

- Demonstrating respect for all young people.

- Actively listening to what they say and ensuring you are understood.

- Not making assumptions.

- Showing an interest in other cultures, religions, etc. by asking young people to talk about this and what it means to them in terms of how they want you to work with them.

- Identifying if they have any specific needs that you need to be aware of.

- Enabling young people to define their identity and to explore their experiences of discrimination and oppression.

Planning your work with young people

The YJB's *Key elements of effective practice: Assessment, planning, interventions and supervision* guidance referred to in Chapter 6 (YJB, 2002a) provides the framework that YOT practitioners should follow in their work with young people. The main aim of this guidance is to impress upon practitioners the importance of ensuring that any assessment of a young person should be clearly linked to a plan of intervention that responds to the identified risks and needs in order to reduce their likelihood of re-offending. This is where knowledge of relevant criminological and social work theories will need to be applied as a way of identifying appropriate methods to meet assessed needs and risks. Plans should also take into account both risks and positive factors in the young person's life so that these can be incorporated in the intervention programme and so appropriate sequencing of intervention takes place. Focusing on strengths and not only criminogenic factors here may be one way to secure engagement with a young person at the start of an order.

Planning is an activity that underpins all social work practice and is not unique to youth justice; however, different areas of social work will use a different framework or planning process. The Asset assessment should be completed to determine the key areas for intervention and planning should focus on the sections with the highest ratings; identifying positive factors and incorporating these into the plan to promote and sustain progress; and identifying mediating factors that may need to be managed if the young person is going to be able to complete the order successfully, such as health or literacy difficulties (YJB, 2003a, p60). Important in all planning is partnership with the service user. The purpose of a plan is to identify how the needs or risks identified will best be met, with tasks and timescales allocated to specific people who should carry out the tasks. The young person needs to agree with the plan and to participate in its formulation if it is to be effective, and a process of negotiation may be necessary. This can serve as part of the relationship-building exercise. Plans will also include other people such as specialist YOT workers, parents or carers and mentors and should also integrate any other plans such as a care plan or pathway plan if the child is looked after or a protection plan if the child is known to childrens services as a child in need or at risk of harm. When a young person does not acknowledge an identified problem from the assessment, you will need to work with them, using a technique such as motivational interviewing, in order to help them recognise why you have identified this as an issue and to encourage them to address it.

YJB National Standards (2010d) state that a YOT practitioner should prepare the intervention plan within 15 working days if sentenced to a YRO and ensure that a healthcare plan is completed alongside this as appropriate.

In order for plans to be meaningful they should be SMART (Talbot, 1996, cited in YJB, 2003c, p68):

- Specific

- Measurable

- Achievable

- Realistic

- Time-limited.

From the plan, therefore, it should be clear to the young person, you the social worker, parents/carers and any other workers involved, what the purpose of the objectives are. They should be clearly conveyed, agreed by both the young person and the worker and reviewed regularly. We will return to reviews later.

Types of intervention

The type of intervention that you, and others, undertake with a young person will depend on their assessed needs and risks, their age, sex, stage of development and learning styles/ needs, as well as the type and length of order and availability of resources to you and the service. Remember, as discussed in Chapter 6, plans should always seek to harness and strengthen protective factors. The *Key elements of effective practice* guidance states that in deciding on a specific intervention, the following factors should also be addressed:

Offender *classification and differential supervision*, both of which are linked to the level/ intensity of service provided to a particular young person (Risk). In terms of reoffending, the key principle is that the type and intensity of interventions should depend on the assessment of individual risk, need and circumstances. Practitioners need to be sufficiently flexible to adapt to this. Asset produces an overall score that can be used to classify young people into groups in relation to their likelihood of reoffending. Generally, the higher the overall score the higher the likelihood of reoffending. Young people with higher scores should normally receive more intensive levels of supervision. However, decisions about the level and intensity of programmes of supervision should not be taken automatically.

Intervention *planning*, which covers the targeting of particular offending-related needs within the boundaries of appropriate intensity of service (Need). Intervention plans should reflect the assessment on which they are based. Targets should be related to the high scoring sections of Asset *and* Onset. The specific content of interventions and methods used should reflect what is recorded in 'evidence boxes' associated with those high scoring areas, and take account of protective factors that can be built upon. An understanding of wider contextual issues is essential to the planning and sequencing of interventions to ensure that they are delivered in a way that an individual young person is able to respond to, and therefore benefit from. For example, some issues, such as accommodation problems or debilitating substance use, might need to be addressed first so that they do not hinder engagement in offence-focused work. It is therefore important to encourage the young person to take part in the development of intervention or training plans to ensure that their perspective and life experience is taken into account.

Delivering supervision so that interventions are more likely to have a positive impact (Responsivity). Enforcement is necessary to promote public confidence in community penalties, but there can be a tension between this and encouraging programme completion by offenders. Compliance will be enhanced if interventions are matched to an individual's risks and needs, and barriers to engagement are taken account of when agreeing the intervention/supervision plan. Responses to interventions are as individualised as the interventions themselves. Since enforcement may be the end result of non-compliance, at the outset of any work with an individual, the practitioner needs to be clear about:

- what requirements or behaviours the young person is expected to comply with;
- what will happen if they do or don't comply (realistic rewards or sanctions);
- how they can help that particular young person to comply and complete their order;
- how they will review progress and compliance.

(YJB, 2008, pp15–17)

One of the greatest challenges you will come across will be working with young people who have no interest in working with you or for whom motivation levels are very low. Hopefully, if you ensure the basic factors discussed in developing a relationship are followed, you will at least have something to work with. There are various approaches, methods or models of intervention that you can use in your work. Some of these are discussed in this chapter, and some useful sources are recommended in Further Reading at the end of the chapter.

Casework/case management

As discussed, establishing a good working relationship early on is essential as this will enable you to continually assess and update the existing assessment, in relation to the young person's strengths, motivations and difficulties. This is important particularly when you start referring them to other specialist workers in the YOT or to other organisations. One of the difficulties for YOT practitioners is that it takes time for relationships to develop, especially the trust element, and many practitioners want to get to know the young person before they start referring them elsewhere. However, as National Standards require more contact at the start of an order, referring the young person to YOT specialist workers or a group work programme is one way of utilising resources in order to manage the workload. This can result in a young person being in contact with a number of different YOT staff at the start of the order and this can be detrimental to the development of this relationship. Research by Burnett and Appleton (2004) found that the case-management model with its disjointed involvement of different workers made it more difficult for the allocated worker to gain the trust of young people and prevented the relaxed communication that comes with familiarity.

However, as YOT caseloads have increased, with more available sentencing options for early stage offenders, the abolition of continued cautioning and the revised National Standards, case management as a model has become the norm. Despite this, Burnett and Appleton concluded that staff *continued to regard the development of a supervisory relationship as the necessary foundation for any other work: for achieving accurate and in-depth assessment; for engaging their interest in interventions and activities; and for motivating the young person to change their behaviour* (2004, p35).

One of the challenges you will face as a YOT social worker is managing to build a good relationship with young people before they start having to meet with other workers within and outside of the team, sustaining this as your contact reduces and ensuring that you liaise with all the other professionals involved so that you are able to keep a firm grasp of the case and the young person's progress.

Group work with young people

A common type of intervention for young people receiving services from a YOT is a group work programme focusing on a particular aspect of offending such as anger management of victim awareness or offence specific such as knife crime or driving related offences. Thus a sound knowledge of group work in terms of theory and skills is an important requisite. Payne (2005) cautions that it is important for group workers to understand how they work and behave *in* groups in order that they can understand how they are working *with* a particular group.

In determining whether group work as an intervention will be an appropriate course of action you must consider whether a young person is suitable to participate in a group setting in terms of their emotional and social development is required. Putting someone in a group setting who is already of low self-esteem may be damaging for them. Assessing their speech, language and communication needs as identified in Chapter 6 is vital as group work may be difficult for some young people who have difficulties in expressing themselves. However, if managed well it can be more beneficial than 1:1 work which may be too intense for some young people. Other issues which need to be taken into account are the age and gender of other group participants and whether they are assessed as high or low risk of offending to avoid mixing people of significantly different ages or risk together. Placing a small number of girls with a larger group of boys would also be inappropriate. Indeed many YOTs run separate groups for male and female offenders. Before referring a young person to a group programme it is important that you:

- Assess the suitability of the programme for the young person, taking into account the factors discussed above.

- Assess the young person's level of motivation and work with them to ensure that they are sufficiently motivated, particularly as non-attendance may result in you having to enforce breach proceedings.

- Explain the purpose of the programme, its requirements and expectations of the young person so that they are clear about what to expect before starting.

Once these important issues have been addressed, there are many benefits to group working with young people:

- *The provision of a potentially fertile learning environment.*

- *Features of group life, such as negotiation, performing tasks, sharing thoughts and feelings, contain potential for personal development.*

- *Being with others with similar experiences reduces isolation and increases support.*

- *Supporting people to create change for themselves.*

- *Raising consciousness.*

- *Learning that there are many things that can only be achieved by co-operating with others.*

    (Payne, 2005, pp127–8)

However, such positive changes will only be realised provided the group is facilitated and managed well. Chapman (2005, p173) claims that effective group work requires:

- *A common purpose.*

- *A process or set of tasks designed to achieve the purpose.*

- *Relationships between members which facilitate progress towards the achievement of that purpose.*

- *Effective facilitation.*

If you are facilitating a group work programme, it is vital that you are familiar with theories and processes of group work so that you are 'in tune with the stages of development known as forming, storming, norming, performing and adjourning' originally outlined by Tuckman and Jenson (1977), and a final stage, mourning, added later, cited in Lindsay and Orton (2011). It is also important to be aware of the unconscious processes taking place in a group setting. These are explored by Preston-Shoot (2007) in a text on effective groupwork. Facilitating group work with young people who offend can be a very difficult and challenging experience. Chapman suggests a number of principles for workers when dealing with problematic behaviour in a group setting (2005, p178):

- *Try to understand before making judgements.*

- *Avoid taking sides – focus on the problem in relation to group progress.*

- *Affirm strengths and any sign of motivation.*

- *Ensure the group feels safe, respected and supported.*

- *Move at a pace appropriate to each group member.*

- *Ensure that negative behaviour is not allowed to attract more attention than positive behaviour.*

- *Regularly review progress with the group in relation to objectives and purpose.*

- *Use supervision to explore their own feelings and perceptions, and to develop a skills base which contains a repertoire of responses.*

Restorative justice

A central element to the Labour government's reforms to the youth justice system is ensuring that young people take responsibility for their actions and face up to the consequences of their offending by, in part, encouraging reparation to victims. This was to be achieved by the introduction of restorative justice into the youth justice provisions, already outlined in Chapter 4. Restorative justice has a particular philosophical base which sees offending within a wider, societal context and seeks to bring about restoration to the victim and the community affected by offending behaviour. Restorative justice has been defined as *a process whereby the parties with a stake in a particular offence come together to resolve collectively how to deal with the aftermath of the offence and its implications for the future* (Marshall, 1996, cited in Crawford and Newburn, 2003). Elements of restorative justice are identified as being the inclusion of each stakeholder, the importance of participatory processes and the emphasis on restorative outcomes (Crawford and Newburn, 2003, p22).

As part of a police reprimand or final warning, or part of a referral order, reparation order or YRO, reparation has to be addressed. This can take a number of forms: direct reparation, such as victim–offender mediation, family group conferencing, restorative conferencing or Youth Offender Panel meetings (for referral orders); or indirect reparation, which can involve community reparation or shuttle mediation where the victim and offender communicate via a third party. There are concerns about whether community reparation is restorative in nature as it may happen without the victim being consulted. However, Masters (2005) suggests that it is *the process through which it is achieved that defines an activity as restorative* (2005, p183) and that providing the young person is able to acknowledge the harm they have caused and feels obliged to do something to remedy this, community reparation is sufficient when the victim is unwilling to engage or the offence is victimless.

One of the most important things to bear in mind in restorative justice work is how emotive bringing together victim and offender can be. You need to prepare the young person very well for any meeting and support them in what may be a very challenging, intimidating and anxiety-provoking event. The victim needs to be equally well briefed and supported if the meeting is to be successful.

The inclusion of restorative justice approaches within the youth justice system in England and Wales has been criticised as they are ineffectively incorporated into a punitive, justice-based system which is at odds with the philosophy of restorative approaches. Research presents a mixed picture of the effectiveness of restorative justice interventions with some studies showing benefits in terms of reoffending rates or repairing the harm to victims. Sherman et al. (2008) provide a review of the evidence base in the source document accompanying the YJB KEEP for restorative justice.

Review

Within youth justice a framework for review is provided, or even prescribed by, National Standards and the *Key elements of effective practice* (KEEP). The purpose of review is to identify if an intervention has achieved what it set out to do, to assess the progress a young person is making and to identify additional aspects of the intervention that still need to be delivered in order for it to be effective. Intervention plans are required to be reviewed every 12 weeks or any time there has been significant change in a young person's circumstances. The review process should be an opportunity for the young person to provide feedback on how the intervention programme is working for them and to identify any problems or difficulties they may be experiencing with it, and as a result of a review it may be necessary to make changes. If cases are not reviewed an intervention may be inappropriate, ineffectual or even damaging to a young person as well as cost-ineffective.

Thinking back to the SMART objectives, the review process should consider if each objective set has been achieved and if not, the reasons for this, such as a particular group work programme not running. During the review you should consider the positive successes achieved as well as the difficulties or areas where things have not gone to plan. These may be down to the young person, to you or to external factors. The review process may be carried out between you and the young person, or it may be chaired by your manager with the young person's parent/carer also present. Asset must also be looked at and possibly updated as a result of this. Depending on the length of the programme of intervention, there may be a number of reviews over the course of your involvement with a young person. The YJB (2003a, p87) stresses the importance of the final review as 'very important'; and continues:

> Cases should be closed in a positive way. It is a chance for young people to express their views on the work that has been done, and for successes, even small ones, to be celebrated and encouraged for continuation in the future. Remember that re-offending does not automatically mean that an intervention has been a failure.

Should the objectives in the plan be completed and no further reoffending by the young person has taken place, the option of returning the case back to court for early discharge of an order is possible.

Endings

Whatever the reason for the ending of a relationship – successful completion of an order, transfer to another team or resentencing of the young person, it is important that, where possible, the ending of the professional relationship is fully planned and prepared for. It is possible to manage the process of ending using psychodynamic theory and theories of loss to enable the complexities involved to be understood by the social worker and young person. Given the importance of the relationship in social work effectiveness, as discussed earlier in this chapter, the impact of the ending of this relationship can be enormous for the young person. Due to the fact that both social workers and young people may invest a lot of energy, time, commitment and effort into a relationship, its end may be viewed as a loss or a crisis, raising previous experiences of loss. For many young people whose emotional needs have not been met by the adults in their lives, being able to tolerate the intense feelings evoked by the pain and loss of a relationship ending may be too much leading to the unconscious adoption of defence mechanisms, such as denial and projection in order to cope with the pain. Clow (1998) suggests that the *flavour and significance of each individual ending will depend on the investment in the relationship, the nature and extent of the transference and the individual's learned responses to loss and change* (p131).

Coulshed and Orme (2006, pp287–8) suggest a good model of ending as incorporating the following:

- *Clarification in the first meeting that contact will be time-limited.*

- *Using the experience of termination as a learning opportunity rather than a painful separating experience.*

- *Using a fixed time limit purposefully, using time as a therapeutic agent.*

- *Deciding on certain objectives to achieve in the ending phase.*

- *Beforehand, exploring a person's feelings about the end of a relationship.*

- *Introduce the new worker if there is to be one and talk about feelings of endings in the meeting.*

- *Help the person construct a helping network in the community.*

- *Explore your own feelings. Demonstrate that you will remember the person; have confidence in his or her ability to manage without you.*

- *In some contexts a ritual or ceremonial ending could mark the occasion.*

- *Write a closing record, together, if appropriate.*

ACTIVITY 7.3

You have been working with Jermaine now for over a year. He has completed his 12-month supervision order and apart from a theft, for which he received a community punishment order, he has not committed any other offences. Think back to your assessment of Jermaine and the intervention plan that you completed. You are now carrying out the final review of the order. What factors would you want to address and how would you use this as part of the process of ending your relationship?

COMMENT

You may have decided it is important to focus on the objectives in the Intervention Plan in order to identify if they have been met and if not, why this was. You may have thought it useful to include his mother and step-father in the review process as well as inviting his school and football coach, or at least obtaining feedback from them. You could review Asset and determine whether the risk of his reoffending has reduced, high-lighting the positive improvements Jermaine has made as well as any continuing areas of risk and looking at strategies he can employ to mitigate against these. Giving praise and recognition for his achievements may also be part of the review.

Evaluation

As mentioned earlier, reviewing your practice on a regular basis is crucially important in social work and prescribed by YJB guidance and National Standards for those practising in youth justice settings. Therefore, it could be argued that we are constantly and consistently evaluating our practice. Certainly, part of the review process is to consider how relevant, effective and cost-effective an intervention is in relation to an individual service user. Evaluation is more than this, though. It is also about being aware of how research can inform, enhance and complement your practice. Your degree course will instigate an approach that encourages you to be research-minded so that you are aware of studies that are relevant to the area you practise in as well as to develop your own research skills. You need to be competent in evaluating your own practice and able to make the necessary changes in order that you are constantly striving to progress it. You need to be confident that the work you are doing with young people is effective in relation to the stated aims and objectives.

Part of evaluation means obtaining feedback from those in receipt of the services you are providing, namely the young people and their families. The ways that this can be achieved within youth justice include the regular review process. It is your responsibility to ensure that all the young people and their parents are provided with the opportunity to give honest feedback during the intervention and after it, and that they know that their comments will be taken seriously. It may also be useful for YOTs to obtain feedback from other users of services, for instance the courts who might provide information on the quality of pre-sentence reports or bail supervision assessments. It is important to ensure that the process for providing feedback is open and transparent and that the mechanisms enable reliability.

Evaluation is a 'must do' part of the job that should not be ignored because you do not have the time or it is low on the list of priorities. As Thompson says:

> Evaluation is a fundamental part of good practice, as it provides us with a platform from which to continue to improve. No matter how skilled, experienced or effective we are, there are, of course, always lessons to be learned, improvements to be made and benefits to be gained from evaluating our practice. (2005, p65)

Evaluation is therefore a tool you must be competent in using as part of your commitment to reflective practice, thus ensuring your positive growth and development as a practitioner.

CHAPTER SUMMARY

This chapter has looked at the importance of building a relationship with young people, focusing on issues such as the initial contact, working within a welfare approach and working with difference. We have also looked at the process of working with young people, commencing with planning – something that should be done in conjunction with the young person, using a strengths-based approach that acknowledges their strengths and protective factors. Various types of interventions have been considered within the context of effective practice, such as the traditional casework approach, and restorative justice. We have emphasised the essential component of reviewing practice, the significance of endings and the fundamental concept of evaluation.

FURTHER READING

Trotter, C (2006) *Working with involuntary clients: A guide to practice*, 2nd edition. London: Sage.

This book outlines a range of approaches for working with difficult and reluctant clients including problem-solving and pro-social modelling.

Crawford, A and Newburn T (2003) *Youth offending and restorative justice: Implementing reforms in youth justice*. Cullompton: Willan.

Provides an exploration of the introduction of restorative justice into the youth justice system and the implementation of the referral order. It examines the difficulties of trying to marry principles of restorative justice into the UK's existing adversarial youth justice system.

Salzberger–Wittenberg, I (1970) *Psychoanalytic insight and relationships*. Hove: Routledge and Kegan Paul Ltd.

Provides an understanding of Kleinian psychoanalytic concepts and their application to social work through the use of case material.

Chapter 8

Looking forward: Developing your career and proposed youth justice reforms

Paul Dugmore and Jane Pickford

Part one: Developing your career

Paul Dugmore

Introduction

This chapter will examine key areas relating to ensuring you continue to practise effectively once you have qualified as a youth justice social worker. These are: requirements with regards to maintaining your social work registration; engaging in continued professional development; and emerging future legislative and policy changes in the youth justice arena. In both social work and youth justice the legislative and policy frameworks are subject to frequent change. In order to face the challenges associated with fast paced developments within a professional context, it is vital to keep abreast of primary and secondary legislation, guidance, contemporary policy debates, reports, reviews, proposals and relevant research evidence. This can be achieved by reading academic journals, relevant websites, quality newspapers and joining organisations such as BASW, the National Association of Youth Justice and the newly established College of Social Work. Alongside this, it is important that practitioners continue to develop their skill and knowledge base and perhaps take a lead on developing knowledge and skills in relation to a specialist area of practice.

Social work often receives a bad press and you are likely to be subjected to negative opinions about the profession from service users, other professionals, the media and the general public. It was hoped that introducing registration to the profession and protecting the title of social worker would help improve the standing of social work. However, the death of Peter Connelly in Haringey led to a huge attack on the profession in 2008 by the media and the government. This led to the establishment of the Social Work Taskforce (2009) which carried out a major review of social work and made 15 recommendations to the then Labour government, all of which were accepted. One of the recommendations was the establishment of the Social Work Reform Board in 2010 to continue the work of the Taskforce and steer through the reforms. Another was the establishment of an independent national college of social work in order to act as a powerful voice for the profession and provide strong leadership. The College of Social Work will be fully established by 2012. One of the proposals of the Taskforce was to strengthen arrangements for continued professional development and the Reform Board has published a series of proposals in relation to this which include the closure of the existing post-qualifying framework for social work. The College of Social Work will take the lead on the development of this once it is established.

Other significant developments in relation to social work include the *Munro Review of Child Protection* (2011) which was commissioned by the Coalition government in 2010 and which reported back in May 2011 with a further 15 recommendations. The Coalition government has also proposed to abolish the General Social Care Council in 2012, following the passing of the Health and Social Care Bill (2011) currently progressing through parliament. This intends to transfer the functions of regulation of the social work qualifying degree and the process of registration to the Health Professions Council, to be renamed the Health and Care Professions Council (HCPC) when the GSCC closes in 2012.

Within the context of these changes it is important that social workers have confidence and pride in their practice and abilities and are able to challenge some of the stereotypes that exist about social workers. Some of the ways of assisting with this are engaging in continued professional development and becoming members of professional bodies such as the College of Social Work.

Continuing professional development (CPD)

Once qualified, social workers are required to attend training or participate in a range of learning activities in order to develop, refresh and update their knowledge and skills further. Part of the GSCC Code of Practice requires social workers to:

> *Be accountable for the quality of their work and take responsibility for maintaining and improving their knowledge and skills.*

> (GSCC (2002) Code of Practice for Social Care Workers)

This means that it is your responsibility as a professional as well as that of your employer, to ensure that you are able to carry out the roles and responsibilities required of you in terms of being equipped with the necessary skills and knowledge.

As a social worker it is extremely important that you are registered with the registering body (GSCC/HCPC) as this confirms that you are qualified and registered to practice as a social worker. Part of this professional registration requires that all social workers evidence that they have undertaken CPD related activity each year. Currently this is five days per year or fifteen days over the current three year registration period, however, this is liable to change once registration transfers to the HCPC. Failure to demonstrate to the registering body that you have undertaken the required amount of CPD means that your registration will not be renewed. As such, it is important that you keep a record of any CPD related activity that you undertake during any period of registration. CPD is widely interpreted and may include:

- Shadowing the work of a colleague in a related team or profession.

- Negotiating protected time to research latest policy and good practice developments in your field of practice.

- Undertaking a piece of research related to your practice.

- Completing a formal post-qualifying programme of study as approved/endorsed by the GSCC/College of Social Work.

As mentioned, the GSCC currently has responsibility for overseeing the post-qualifying training of social workers and in 2007 a new post-qualifying framework was introduced. The demise of the GSCC and the transfer of the responsibility for leading on CPD to the College mean that changes to the existing post qualifying (PQ) framework are inevitable. The recently published proposals are:

- *The College will take on the proposals for a new CPD framework and further develop mechanisms and guidance to support social workers in achieving high professional standards.*

- *The framework will be aligned with the relevant levels of the professional capabilities framework (PCF) and linked to the career structure.*

- *The framework will support social workers to maintain and develop core standards for re-registration set by HCPC.*

- *Social workers will be supported by employers and expected to take professional responsibility for developing their skills to a high professional level, through undertaking learning and development activities over and above core standards required for re-registration with the HCPC.*

- *A wide range of learning and development activities should be promoted. Space for critical reflection, learning from others and opportunities for access to research should be valued alongside more structured training.*

- *There is an aspiration that social workers should have the opportunity to achieve PQ awards at Masters' level, through modular programmes. Guidance will be made available, by the College building on examples of good practice across the country.*

- *Learning and development needs will be identified, planned for and monitored through annual appraisal cycles and supervision.*

- *Mechanisms for recognising and recording CPD activities will be established to provide clarity of process, and portability across the country.*

- *Employers will be encouraged to develop learning opportunities working in partnership with other local employers and HEIs.*

(Social Work Reform Board, 2011)

In addition to this the Munro Review (2011) recommends that the new Professional Capabilities Framework (PCF) being introduced by the Social Work Reform Board (2011) should include the following capabilities for child and family social work:

Knowledge

- *knowledge of child development and attachment and how to use this knowledge to assess a child's current developmental state;*

- *understanding the impact of parental problems such as domestic violence, mental ill health, and substance misuse on children's health and development at different stages during their childhood;*

- *knowledge of the impact of child abuse and neglect on children in both the short and long term and into adulthood.*

Critical reflection and analysis

- *ability to analyse critically the evidence about a child and family's circumstances and to make well-evidenced decisions and recommendations, including when a child cannot remain living in their family either as a temporary or permanent arrangement; and*

- *skills in achieving some objectivity about what is happening in a child's life and within their family, and assessing change over time.*

Intervention and skills

- *recognising and acting on signs and symptoms of child abuse and neglect;*

- *purposeful relationship building with children, parents and carers and families;*

- *skills in adopting an authoritative but compassionate style of working;*

- *skills to assess family functioning, take a comprehensive family history and use this information when making decisions about a child's safety and welfare;*

- *knowledge of theoretical frameworks and their effective application for the provision of therapeutic help;*

- *knowledge about, and skills to use and keep up to date with, relevant research findings on effective approaches to working with children and families and, in particular, where there are concerns about abuse or neglect;*

- *understanding the respective roles and responsibilities of other professionals and how child and family social workers can contribute their unique role as part of a multi-disciplinary team; and*

- *skills in presenting and explaining one's reasoning to diverse audiences, including children and judges.*

(Munro, 2011, p96)

While these relate specifically to social workers within a child and family setting there is clear overlap with social workers working with children and young people in other settings such as youth justice and all social workers who work with children and young people have a responsibility to safeguard their welfare. Munro recommends this PCF should explicitly inform postgraduate professional development and it is likely that the College of Social Work will adopt this recommendation once it takes over responsibility for the CPD framework for social workers.

Studying a GSCC/College of Social Work-approved certificated post-qualifying course, can also be used as evidence towards meeting the post-registration training and learning requirements.

With so many changes pending it is important that newly qualified and more experienced social workers keep themselves updated so it is important to be aware of the full options open to you at post-qualifying level. This will help ensure that you are not only aware of current evidence-based, research-led, best practice but also that you are contributing to the development of such knowledge as a practitioner. It will also ensure you are able to reflect critically on your practice so that it retains a clear social work focus: young people are receiving a high quality service that meets their needs and you are still finding your work satisfying and rewarding, or if not, that you are able to identify an alternative change based on your existing knowledge and skills.

ACTIVITY *8.1*

What skills and knowledge have you already acquired and which ones would you like to develop?

Can you identify gaps in your learning/experience?

Which type of CPD do you think might be useful to address these?

Part two: Reforming youth justice: Future youth justice legislation

Jane Pickford

In this section we consider the various proposals for youth justice practice that have been put forward by the Coalition government. This includes analyses of two consultation papers (Ministry of Justice, 2010; Home Office, 2011) detailed below and an outline of subsequent draft legislation in the form of the Legal Aid, Sentencing and Punishment of Offenders Bill 2011 (introduced into Parliament in June 2011).

The review of proposals below will enable you to be forewarned of the probable changes to youth justice practice that are arguably forthcoming. Keep your eyes on the quality newspapers and the Ministry of Justice's website. It may also be worth checking the Youth Justice Board's website, though from April 2011 the Coalition government has moved most of the YJB's responsibilities to the Ministry of Justice.

Breaking the cycle: Effective punishment, rehabilitation and sentencing of offenders (Ministry of Justice, 2010)

In December 2010, Ken Clarke, the Lord Chancellor and Secretary of State for Justice in the Coalition government, published a consultation/green paper entitled *Breaking the cycle: Effective punishment, rehabilitation and sentencing of offenders* (Ministry of Justice, 2010a). The paper seeks to address *how an intelligent sentencing framework, coupled with more effective rehabilitation, will enable us to break the cycle of crime and prison which creates new victims* (ibid. p1).

Chapter 5 of the document specifically sets out proposals in relation to juveniles, citing statistics indicating that 75 per cent of young offenders leaving the secure estate and 68 per cent of those completing community sanctions re-offend within 12 months. The overall goal of these proposals is to address the issue of recidivism and to *stop the young offenders of today becoming the prolific adult offenders of tomorrow* (ibid. p67). Five bold aims of the reforms are trumpeted as follows:

- *prevent more young people from offending and divert them from entering into a life of crime, including by simplifying out-of-court disposals;*

- *protect the public and ensure that more is done to make young offenders pay back to their victims and communities;*

- *ensure the effective use of sentencing for young offenders;*

- *incentivise local partners to reduce youth offending and re-offending using payment by results models; and*

- *develop more effective governance by abolishing the Youth Justice Board and increasing freedoms and flexibilities for local areas.*

    (ibid. p67)

Bearing in mind that this green paper was a consultation paper that invited interested members of the public, professionals and academics to contribute feedback on the ideas by March 2011 (and some recommended changes are arguably present in the final Bill) it is useful to examine each of the five aims in turn and then provide some commentary on the overall package of proposed reforms to youth justice.

Preventing offending by young people and paying back to victims and communities

In order to address the first two aims (which are discussed together in the paper) the government proposed a three-pronged attack, namely to:

- *encourage Youth Offending Teams to improve the quality of work with parents including through greater use of parenting orders where parents will not face up to their responsibilities;*

- *simplify out-of-court disposals;*

- *increase the use of restorative justice.*

    (ibid. p67).

Citing academic evidence linking high crime volume adult offenders with early-age first time offending, the government advocate early intervention into the lives of those children and young people who pose the highest risk of developing a pattern of prolific offending. They suggest a localised approach to identifying problematic young people, with youth offending teams playing a pivotal role in liaising with other key professional bodies in their area (police, probation, education, health, social services, etc.) to this end. Once identified, intervention should be planned and targeted appropriately. Mental health and family support services are mentioned as being pivotal to this approach. Further, the paper encourages the robust use by youth offending teams of parenting orders where it is assessed that parents/guardians are not fulfilling their responsibilities (indeed, Chapter 6 of the paper gives further details of cross-government plans to deal with *families with complex problems*).

In relation to pre-court disposals, the paper asserts that the current system is too rigid and that more flexibility is needed. To remedy this apparent problem, the government proposes to give the police and crown prosecution officers (working with local agencies e.g. youth offending teams) more discretion when dealing with first-time and low-level young offenders, putting their *trust in professionals* who are working with juvenile offenders. It is envisaged that this *could involve reparation or interventions such as a referral to mental health provision to tackle offending behaviour* (ibid. p69). Moreover, the government states that it will review anti-social behaviour legislation and the use of juvenile penalty notices of disorder (PNDs) as part of its evaluation of pre-court measures.

With regard to first-tier disposals, the paper indicates a review of the rules regarding the issuing of referral orders, though there are no details given of any concrete proposals for such a change. However, it invites suggestions while stating that the current conditions that can be imposed in a referral order by a youth offending panel can consist of *onerous requirements*, asserting that orders need to be made *more flexible*. Further, the paper advocates for greater use of reparative measures within referral order contracts where victims are willing to cooperate.

Effective sentencing for young offenders

The government proposes that custody is targeted effectively at those who pose the greatest risk, but is restricted, so that it does not continue to be used inappropriately, against *young people whose offences are not the most serious and whose behaviour does not pose a risk to the public* (ibid. p70). Their five proposals for addressing this issue include:

- *addressing the extensive use of remands to custody in the youth justice system;*
- *introducing a single remand order for all under 18s making local authorities gradually responsible for the full cost of court ordered secure remand;*
- *amending the Bail Act 1976 to remove the option of remand for young people who would be unlikely to receive a custodial sentence;*
- *proposing that Youth Offending Teams establish new compliance panels to support young people in complying with their sentences;*
- *addressing breach of detention and training orders by returning young people who breach to custody, even if their detention and training order has expired.*

    (ibid. p70)

While the government does not propose any amendments presently to the generic youth community sentence of the youth rehabilitation order (YRO) (though they state that they are reviewing its operation) they assess that practices for breaching the YRO are inconsistent between local jurisdiction areas. Their proposal to remedy this involves youth offending teams setting up 'compliance panels' to review breaches within their area and suggest an appropriate response.

Addressing the issue of secure remand, the paper states that currently there are several frameworks in place relating to different rules according to age of suspects and funding of placements. To simplify the system, they propose introducing a single framework for 10 to 17 year olds entitled 'youth remand order' funded by local authorities.

Funding and payment by results

The government wish to test how payment by results might be a means of providing incentives for reducing youth (and adult) offending. They hope to:

- *test how we can enable local areas to share in financial savings and risks resulting from the use of youth custody;*

- *test how financial incentives to local areas can be used to reduce demand on the criminal justice system;*

- *explore how Youth Offending Teams and secure accommodation providers could move to a payment-by-results model.*

  (ibid. p72)

The paper argues that the current system of costs for custody being borne centrally has meant *that local agencies lack the incentive, and the opportunity, to develop effective alternatives to custody for young people* (ibid. p73). Funding will be placed on the shoulders of local youth offending teams, in the belief that this will incentivise them to reduce offending and re-offending rates and provide successful community sentence and remand interventions. These initiatives will be tested in a 'small number' of pilot schemes. In short, the government is, *exploring how we could apply a payment by results approach to Youth Offending Teams and custodial providers. This would link the funding we give them to the outcomes that they deliver* (ibid. p74).

Effective governance and flexibility

The government wishes to reform management and accountability within the youth justice system via:

- *clearer accountability structures at national level for youth justice;*

- *increasing freedom and flexibility to Youth Offending Teams, focusing support on areas that need it most;*

- *giving communities greater involvement in youth justice services in their area.*

  (ibid. p75)

To achieve these aims, it proposes that the independent Youth Justice Board is scrapped and that the Ministry of Justice take over their duties (albeit, probably scaled-down). The transfer of powers to the Ministry of Justice commenced in the spring of 2011. Their rationale for this abolition is that youth justice teams are now firmly embedded and no longer require 'oversight'. However, with regard to performance management of youth offending teams, the paper asserts that there is an intention to *move towards a lighter touch performance monitoring capability which supports a more risk based inspection programme and increases professional discretion* (ibid. p75). This pared down oversight will focus on reducing first-time offenders, re-offending and the use of custody. It is acknowledged that practitioners ideally should be able to spend more time working with young offenders and less time glued to their computers. The paper also encourages the development multi-agency initiatives (e.g. in the area of resettlement) local transparency and further use of volunteers within the youth justice system.

Commentary on the proposals

The consultation paper outlined above includes several proposals relating to youth justice that merit further discussion.

- The proposed introduction of greater flexibility in pre-court disposals for young offenders, including a reform of the current system of reprimand and final warning, appears to be a move back to the system of multiple pre-court disposals (then called 'cautions') that existed in the 1980s and early 1990s. As noted in Chapter 2, over this period the Home Office encouraged the use of multiple cautions for low level young offenders as a diversionary tactic to avert non-serious youthful law breakers away from the full rigors and detrimental impact of a court appearance. This practice was restricted after the Bulger case in 1993 and eventually replaced by the rigid procedure of reprimands and final warnings, introduced by the Crime and Disorder Act 1998.

- The consultation paper envisages that ideally police officers should consult local agencies such as youth offending teams when exercising their new discretion in relation to pre-court diversion. However, the actual levels of consultation might not be consistent across all boroughs.

- The loosening of erstwhile rigorous rules for the issuing of pre-court measures could lead to divergent practices across police areas and is based on the idea of trusting professionals to act fairly. As any lawyer who specialises in judicial review would attest, discretionary decisions are fraught with legal difficulties and open the door to unjustifiable and inconsistent outcomes.

- The review of the current referral order due to them containing the opportunity for allegedly 'onerous requirements', needs further explanation. For example, the consultation document states that the Government wishes to make the order 'more flexible' – but surely this will only generate a greater risk of 'onerous requirements' being imposed on a young person?

- The paper calls for more victim targeted restorative justice input in relation to referral orders. However, as Earle (2005) has noted, victims are largely reluctant to attend youth offending panels and only a minority accept the offer to meet their offender.

- There is a proposal to convene compliance panels in all youth offending teams to deal with the issues of developing consistent breach procedures within teams – but how would consistency between teams be ensured?

- In relation to Detention and Training Orders, the consultation paper states that there needs to be *change to ensure that if a young offender has breached the supervision requirement of the order they can still be returned to custody even if the DTO has expired* (ibid. p70). It is not clear whether this section should say *even if the detention part of the DTO has expired*, because it is hard to envisage how a young person could be returned to custody for 'breach' if the whole of the order had expired (what would there be to breach?).

- Regarding the proposed transfer of the total cost (including commissioning costs) of all youth remands to local authorities (covering those costs currently shouldered by the Youth Justice Board) – local councils might find this burden difficult, especially given central government's cuts to local councils that commenced in the financial year 2011/12. This financial yoke will be made heavier by the proposed inclusion of 17 year olds into the new arrangements for remand (currently an anomaly exists whereby 17 year olds are treated as adults regarding remand procedures).

- Local authorities will also be wary of the proposals to 'incentivise' them by introducing a payment by results scheme, as this might result in the transfer of the costs of risk of youth offending to local councils. Further, some local council officers, members of crime teams or youth offending teams might feel slighted by the implication that the rate of youth custodial remand in their area is of little concern to them presently because their local council does not pick up the bill for it – or that they are not interested in creating alternatives to secure remands for the same reason!

- It is notable that the paper proposes to increase professional discretion within the work of youth offending team officers. As Fionda (2005) and Bateman (2009) have implied, the loss of professional discretion has been a feature of a culture of actuarialism within youth justice which was witnessed in the Crime and Disorder Act 1998 and reached a nadir with the introduction of the scaled approach to risk assessment in November 2009. Perhaps the tide is beginning to turn and youth justice officers might be allowed to utilise their professional judgment more in the future and not continue to feel like form filling, risk calculating automatons!

- Finally, one of the most controversial proposals is the abolition of the Youth Justice Board. The paper states that youth offending teams no longer need a 'separate' organisation for oversight and proposes to move the (albeit reduced) powers of oversight to the Ministry of Justice. Responding to criticisms of the ad hoc and inconsistent nature of youth justice management within local authorities made by the Audit Commission in 1996, the Board was established following the Crime and Disorder Act 1998 with the task (among others) of standardising and overseeing youth offending teams. The Board has been pivotal in setting standards, targets and management procedures within youth offending teams as well as producing vital research and supervising custodial placements. However, some academics welcome the move. Rod Morgan, former Chair of the Board who resigned over unacceptable levels of youth custody in 2007 states that abolition might be *part of a radical, positive change of policy direction* and that the momentum of cuts should be siezed to propose new ways of dealing with young offenders based on more pre-court diversions, a greater use of community rather than costly custodial disposals and agrees with the move to incentivise local authorities to provide viable alternatives to custody (Guardian, 26 October, 2010).

Proposed reforms to anti-social behaviour legislation

In February 2011, the Coalition government published a consultation paper relating to anti-social behaviour legislation entitled *More effective responses to anti-social behaviour* (Home Office, 2011). In what they assert will amount to a 'radical streamlining' of existing procedures, the following major amendments to the present system are proposed:

- abolition of the current anti-social behaviour order and associated orders;
- creation of three new 'tools', namely
  - *The criminal behaviour order* – that can be made at the time of a criminal conviction
  - *The crime prevention injunction* – targeted towards addressing low-level anti-social behaviour with the aim of stemming its escalation
  - *The community protection order* – to address problems in particular localities
- strengthening deterrents to breaching new measures by providing further penalties (e.g. losing social housing);
- consolidation of current powers of dispersal that police officers have into a single power to direct people to move away from a location;
- promotion the ideals of rehabilitation and restoration when dealing with anti-social behaviour incidents;
- empowerment of communities by allowing them to issue a community trigger, to prompt local agencies to address problematic anti-social behaviour in their area.

It is useful to provide some further details and commentary (below) on the three key proposals that will have particular implications for youth justice issues.

Criminal behaviour order

This order would be a civil order that would be available to be made against any person aged 10 or above who has been found guilty of a criminal offence. It could be made if the person had behaved *in a manner that caused or was likely to cause harassment, alarm or distress* or if such an order was necessary for protection of the public.

In essence, the order could be used in addition to a criminal conviction. It would allow the court to impose a range of restrictions on the individual and/or require them to take positive measures to address their anti-social behaviour. If the subject of the proposed order is under sixteen, a report should be prepared which investigates the current care situation of the young person, with appropriate information about possible remedial intervention (e.g. a compulsory parenting order or voluntary support via family intervention projects). It is envisaged that details of the order could be published locally.

In relation to duration of these orders, discussions about maximum and minimum terms are part of the consultation process. However, there are indications that a non-prescriptive maximum might be preferable in that it would give aurthorities greater flexibility to deal with anti-social behaviour. Breach of the order would result in a criminal conviction with a maximum sanction of five years custody.

We have referred to the ethical problems with such measures in Chapter 4. The proposed repacement of the anti-social behaviour order with a new criminal behaviour order does nothing to address the problems academics have expressed concerns about, namely that they are predominantly aimed at the most socially and economically vulnerable in society (the so-called 'underclass'); that young people are disproportionately targeted; that there are civil liberty implications relating to civil orders for which breach results in a criminal conviction; that they lead to criminalisation via a 'back door' route; that the probable adoption of no maximum but a movable time limt for completion of the order will suffer from all the civil rights implications of indeterminate sanctions (which were reserved in criminal law for the most serious sexual and violent offences); and, they result in an unjustified level of state control measures being focused on those who are least able to stand up to the might of state power. Further, the new order would be called a 'criminal' behaviour order, even though it is a civil order – the unfaimess of this needs no further explanation!!!

Crime prevention injunction

This would be a purely civil order (with civil law consequences for breach) that would replace the non post-conviction anti-social behaviour order, the anti-social behaviour injunction, intervention orders and individual support orders (outlined in Chapter 4). The authority applying for the injunction would have to show that it is more likely than not (on the balance of probabilities) that the individual had engaged, was engaging or likely to engage in anti-social behaviour. The injunction could include restrictions but also positive requirements to assist the person to desist from the behaviour that led to the injunction being made.

The test to be used for imposition of the proposed injunction is an issue that is open for consultation – whether it should be a test of 'harassment, alarm or distress' or the less stringent test of 'nuisance or annoyance'. The preferred option of the Home Office is clear when they indicate that the latter test would give authorities greater prevenative flexibility. Though there is discussion about the appropriate court venue for crime prevention injunction hearings, it is clear that the injunction would be available from the age of ten. Police/local authorities or social housing providers who apply for an injunction against someone under 18 should consult with the local youth offending team, who would provide a report for under 16 year olds, noting the family situation and any recommended parenting interventions.

Similar to the proposals for the criminal behaviour order, time limits of these injunctions are to be part of the consultation process, but flexibility is probably preferred. Breach by an under 18 year old could result in a supervision order (similar to breach of a gang injunction – see Chapter 4) including the possibility of a detention requirement for serious and/or persistant breach(s). The proposals reassure us that these are civil sanctions. However, it's a very unusual civil sanction that could result in locking-up youngsters!!!

Direction powers

This would enable a police officer (or PCSO) to direct a person aged 10 or above away from a specific area and require them not to return within 48 hours. The power can be used where the individual has caused, is causing or about to cause crime, disorder or anti-social conduct and the direction is necessary to prevent the continuation of such behaviour. The officer could also confiscate items related to the situation (e.g. alcoholic beverages). An unaccompanied young person under 16 can be accompanied home by the officer. Under the current dispersal order (see Chapter 4) refusal to disperse can result in a criminal offence. While the Home Office wishes to retain this power, they requested feedback during the consultation period about the implications of this power for young people and views regarding appropriate consequences of refusal.

The Legal Aid, Sentencing and Punishment of Offenders Bill 2011

Following consultations, this Bill was introduced to Parliament in June 2011 and is currently in its Report Stage in the House of Commons (November 2011). The Bill includes several changes in relation to youth justice. These include:

- introducing penalties for breach of Detention and Training Order – even when the Order has been completed;

- amending rules relating to Referral Orders to provide more flexibility in addition to discretionary powers relating to their repeated use;

- introducing new custodial remand procedures for under 18 year olds. Previous divergent rules in relation to age and sex are removed and a stricter test for remand to youth detention is to be imposed;

- introducing a new youth caution and increasing the flexibility of youth conditional cautions.

These provisions are referred to in outline only, immediately prior to the publication of this book. You should consult www.parliament.uk and www.justice.gov.uk for detail and updates.

ACTIVITY *8.2*

Check the Ministry of Justice and Home Office websites for updates and outline the reforms that are likely to occur in youth justice. Which changes are likely to have the most significant impact on practice? Will the proposed measures lead to a re-orientation in youth justice theory?

CHAPTER SUMMARY

In this chapter we have examined the skills you will develop as a youth justice practitioner and analysed their transferability to other professional contexts. We have also stressed the importance of continuing your professional development once in situ as a practitioner and outlined the various options in relation to that. Finally we have examined recent government proposals relating to potential changes to the youth justice system. Perhaps one of the things most evidenced throughout this book is what a fast-changing and evolving environment the youth justice system is, with frequent legislative reform. The impact such frequent changes can have on practitioners should not be underestimated and some of the skills you will need to develop in order to survive will be change management and resilience skills!

In order to stay up to date in the three areas of skills, continuing development and legislation, the following sources will be useful:

Ministry of Justice (2010) *Breaking the cycle: effective punishment rehabilitation and sentencing of offenders*. London: Ministry of Justice.

Home Office (2011) *More effective responses to anti-social behaviour*. London: Home Office. Proposals to change anti-social behaviour legislation.

Keen, S, Gray, I, Parker, J, Galpin, D and Brown, K (2009) *Newly qualified social workers: A handbook for practice.*

www.justice.gov.uk

The Ministry of Justice website for information on the youth justice system and any pending legislation proposals.

www.parliament.co.uk

For information on the progress of legislative proposals.

www.nacro.org.uk

National Association for Care and Resettlement. See especially their youth crime section for briefings on changes, legislation and research.

www.homeoffice.gov.uk

Home Office website for information about crime and policing.

www.communitycare.co.uk

Community Care website for news and updates for social care professionals.

www.thenayj.org.uk

The website for the National Association of Youth Justice.

www.gscc.org.uk

The General Social Care Council website has information on the Code of Practice and the revised post-qualifying framework.

Conclusion

This book has sought to introduce you to social work practice within the field of youth justice by considering the different aspects of the youth justice system and the work undertaken by social workers in Youth Offending Teams. We have looked at social work practice by considering case studies of young people at differing stages of involvement in youth justice as a way of exploring some of the issues.

One of the themes running through this book is the fact that as a social worker practising in youth justice, you will encounter many practice dilemmas when working with young people involved in offending behaviour. In order to ensure that you approach these professionally, the importance of supervision and reflective practice as tools to deal with this complex area of practice have been discussed as well as the frameworks in place to ensure that practice is guided by firm ethical principles. We have tried to emphasise the importance of your practice being grounded in values that support, empower, respect, include and enable young people to make desisions, achieve and flourish, together with those values that challenge prejudice, injustice, stigma and inequality in society. All of these are enshrined in the Code of Practice for Social Care Workers and the National Occupational Standards, and are crucial if you are to become a well-rounded reflective practitioner.

The book has also introduced you to the conventional theoretical debates and highlighted the tensions between the justice and welfare philosophies of youth justice as well as an array of contemporary analyses of philosophical approaches and their applicability to contemporary practice. Your practice should now be grounded in criminological theory giving you an insight into the causational factors behind criminal behaviour. It is vital for youth justice practitioners to have some knowledge of mainstream criminological explanations of crime, because you will have to analyse causational triggers and risk factors relating to criminal behaviour with the young people you work with. Indeed, an analysis of these factors is necessary as part of risk assessment and is an integral part of pre-sentence reports. As well as being up-to-date with theoretical approaches to your work, it is essential that you are aware of the legislative and policy changes that impact on youth justice, and you should now be fully aware of how often such changes are implemented.

This book has focused on the mutli-agency system that you will be a part of and emphasised the importance of your understanding all aspects of the large and complex system as well as respecting the many professional disciplines involved. We have aimed to help you to consider your role as a social worker within a team of practitioners who may have undertaken different training from you and, therefore, have divergent philosophies and attitudes towards offending young people.

Finally, we hope the book has enabled you to understand the skills and knowledge required by social workers in relation to the preparation, assessment, planning, intervention and reviewing of young people involved in criminal activity. You should now be fully aware of the transferable skills and knowledge you should possess as a social worker within the youth justice context and how these need to be continually updated, post-qualifying, in order for you to maintain and develop further competence. You will also appreciate that it is necessary to be able to respond to or positively challenge proposed reform as an effective and confident practitioner.

As this book has shown, working with young people involved in offending behaviour brings together many different aspects of social work practice. Primarily, we have encouraged you to gain an understanding of the legal and theoretical framework in which you will be practising and the areas of assessment, intervention and working with others within youth justice. We hope that this has enabled you to develop some sound skills and the knowledge required for good social work practice with young people who offend as a foundation for a long and rewarding social work career in youth justice. You will undoubtedly be qualifying and practising as a social worker in times of uncertainty and change but offering many opportunities for you as a professional. We wish you well in your social work career.

Appendix:
Subject Benchmark
for Social Work

Subject knowledge, understanding and skills

Subject knowledge and understanding

5.1 During their degree studies in social work, honours graduates should acquire, critically evaluate, apply and integrate knowledge and understanding in the following five core areas of study.

5.1.1 Social work services, service users and carers, which include:

- the social processes (associated with, for example, poverty, migration, unemployment, poor health, disablement, lack of education and other sources of disadvantage) that lead to marginalisation, isolation and exclusion, and their impact on the demand for social work services;

- explanations of the links between definitional processes contributing to social differences (for example, social class, gender, ethnic differences, age, sexuality and religious belief) to the problems of inequality and differential need faced by service users;

- the nature of social work services in a diverse society (with particular reference to concepts such as prejudice, interpersonal, institutional and structural discrimination, empowerment and anti-discriminatory practices);

- the nature and validity of different definitions of, and explanations for, the characteristics and circumstances of service users and the services required by them, drawing on knowledge from research, practice experience, and from service users and carers;

- the relationship between agency policies, legal requirements and professional boundaries in shaping the nature of services provided in interdisciplinary contexts and the issues associated with working across professional boundaries and within different disciplinary groups.

5.1.2 The service delivery context, which includes:

- the complex relationships between public, social and political philosophies, policies and priorities and the organisation and practice of social work, including the contested nature of these;

- the issues and trends in modern public and social policy and their relationship to contemporary practice and service delivery in social work;

- the significance of legislative and legal frameworks and service delivery standards (including the nature of legal authority, the application of legislation in practice, statutory accountability and tensions between statute, policy and practice;

- the current range and appropriateness of statutory, voluntary and private agencies providing community-based, day-care, residential and other services and the organisational systems inherent within these;

- the significance of interrelationships with other related services, including housing, health, income maintenance and criminal justice (where not an integral social service).

5.1.3 Values and ethics, which include:

- the nature, historical evolution and application of social work value;

- the moral concepts of rights, responsibility, freedom, authority and power inherent in the practice of social workers as moral and statutory agents;;

- the complex relationships between justice, care and control in social welfare and the practical and ethical implications of these, including roles as statutory agents and in upholding the law in respect of discrimination;

- aspects of philosophical ethics relevant to the understanding and resolution of value dilemmas and conflicts in both interpersonal and professional contexts;

- the conceptual links between codes defining ethical practice, the regulation of professional conduct and the management of potential conflicts generated by the codes held by different professional groups.

5.1.4 Social work theory, which includes:

- research-based concepts and critical explanations from social work theory and other disciplines that contribute to the knowledge base of social work, including their distinctive epistemological status and application to practice;

- the relevance of sociological perspectives to understanding societal and structural influences on human behaviour at individual, group and community levels;

- the relevance of psychological, physical and physiological perspectives to understanding personal and social development and functioning;

- social science theories explaining group and organisational behaviour, adaptation and change;

- models and methods of assessment, including factors underpinning the selection and testing of relevant information, the nature of professional judgement and the processes of risk assessment and decision-making;

- approaches and methods of intervention in a range of settings, including factors guiding the choice and evaluation of these;

- knowledge and critical appraisal of relevant social research and evaluation methodologies, and the evidence base for social work.

5.1.5 The nature of social work practice, which includes:

- the nature and characteristics of skills associated with effective practice, both direct and indirect, with a range of service-users and in a variety of settings;

- the factors and processes that facilitate effective interdisciplinary, interprofessional and interagency collaboration and partnership;

- the place of theoretical perspectives and evidence from international research in assessment and decision-making processes in social work practice;

- the integration of theoretical perspectives and evidence from international research into the design and implementation of effective social work intervention, with a wide range of service users, carers and others;

- the processes of reflection and evaluation, including familiarity with the range of approaches for evaluating service and welfare outcomes, and their significance for the development of practice and the practitioner.

Subject-specific skills and other skills

5.4 Social work honours graduates should acquire and integrate skills in the following five core areas.

Problem-solving skills

5.5 These are sub-divided into four areas.

5.5.1 Managing problem-solving activities: honours graduates in social work should be able to plan problem-solving activities, ie to:

- plan a sequence of actions to achieve specified objectives, making use of research, theory and other forms of evidence;

- manage processes of change, drawing on research, theory and other forms of evidence.

5.5.2 Gathering information: honours graduates in social work should be able to:

- gather information from a wide range of sources and by a variety of methods, for a range of purposes. These methods should include electronic searches, reviews of relevant literature, policy and procedures, face-to-face interviews, written and telephone contact with individuals and groups;

- take into account differences of viewpoint in gathering information and critically assess the reliability and relevance of the information gathered;

- assimilate and disseminate relevant information in reports and case records.

5.5.3 Analysis and synthesis: honours graduates in social work should be able to analyse and synthesise knowledge gathered for problem-solving purposes, ie to:

- assess human situations, taking into account a variety of factors (including the views of participants, theoretical concepts, research evidence, legislation and organisational policies and procedures);

- analyse information gathered, weighing competing evidence and modifying their viewpoint in light of new information, then relate this information to a particular task, situation or problem;

- consider specific factors relevant to social work practice (such as risk, rights, cultural differences and linguistic sensitivities, responsibilities to protect vulnerable individuals and legal obligations);

- assess the merits of contrasting theories, explanations, research, policies and procedures;

- synthesise knowledge and sustain reasoned argument;

- employ a critical understanding of human agency at the macro (societal), mezzo (organisational and community) and micro (inter and intrapersonal) levels;

- critically analyse and take account of the impact of inequality and discrimination in work with people in particular contexts and problem situations.

5.5.4 Intervention and evaluation: honours graduates in social work should be able to use their knowledge of a range of interventions and evaluation processes selectively to:

- undertake practice in a manner that promotes the well-being and protects the safety of all parties.

Communication skills

5.6 Honours graduates in social work should be able to communicate clearly, accurately and precisely (in an appropriate medium) with individuals and groups in a range of formal and informal situations, i.e. to:

- make effective contact with individuals and organisations for a range of objectives, by verbal, paper-based and electronic means;

- communicate effectively across potential barriers resulting from differences (for example, in culture, language and age).

Skills in working with others

5.7 Honours graduates in social work should be able to work effectively with others, ie to:

- act cooperatively with others, liaising and negotiating across differences such as organisational and professional boundaries and differences of identity or language;

- develop effective helping relationships and partnerships with other individuals, groups and organisations that facilitate change;

- act with others to increase social justice by identifying and responding to prejudice, institutional discrimination and structural inequality.

Skills in personal and professional development

5.8 Honours graduates in social work should be able to:

- advance their own learning and understanding with a degree of independence;

- reflect on and modify their behaviour in the light of experience;

- identify and keep under review their own personal and professional boundaries;

- manage uncertainty, change and stress in work situations;

- understand and manage changing situations and respond in a flexible manner;

- challenge unacceptable practices in a responsible manner;

- take responsibility for their own further and continuing acquisition and use of knowledge and skills.

References

Allen, R (1996) *Children and crime: Taking responsibility*. London: Institute of Policy Research.

Allen, G and Langford, D (2008) *Effective interviewing in social work and social care: A practical guide*. Basingstoke: Palgrave Macmillan.

Andrews, DA, and Dowden, C (2006) Risk principle of case classification in correctional treatment: A meta-analytic investigation, *International Journal of Offender Therapy and Comparative Criminology*, 50(1), pp88–100.

Andrews, DA, Bonta, J, and Hoge, R (1990) Classification for effective rehabilitation: Rediscovering psychology, *Criminal Justice and Behaviour*, 17(1), pp19–52.

Annison, J (2005) Risk and protection, in Bateman, T and Pitts, J (eds) *The RHP companion to youth justice*. Lyme Regis: Russell House Publishing.

Ashworth, A (1994) Abolishing the presumption of incapacity: C v DPP, *Journal of Child Law*, 6(4): 174.

Ashworth, A (2000) *Sentencing and criminal justice*, 3rd edn. London: Butterworths.

Audit Commission (1996) *Misspent youth: Young people and crime*. London: Audit Commission.

Audit Commission (2004) *Youth justice 2004: A review of the reformed youth justice system*. London: The Stationery Office.

Bailey, R and Williams, B (2000) *Inter-agency partnerships in youth justice: Implementing the Crime and Disorder Act 1998*. Sheffield: University of Sheffield Joint Unit for Social Service Research.

Baker, K. (2004) Is asset really an asset? Assessment of young offenders in practice, in Burnett, R and Roberts, C (eds) *What works in probation and youth justice: Developing evidence-based practice*. Cullompton: Willan.

Baker, K, Jones, S, Roberts, R and Merrington, S (2003) *Asset – The evaluation of the validity and reliability of the Youth Justice Board's assessment for young offenders*. London: Youth Justice Board.

Baker, K, Jones, S, Merrington, S and Roberts, C (2005) *Further development of asset*. London: Youth Justice Board.

Baker, K, Kelly, J and Wilkinson, B (2011) *Assessment in youth justice*. Bristol: Policy Press.

Ball, C (2004) Youth justice? Half a century of responses to youth offending, *Criminal Law Review*, March: 167–80.

Bandalli, S (2005) The legal framework for youth justice and its administration, in Bateman, T and Pitts, J (eds) *The RHP companion to youth justice*. Lyme Regis: Russell House Publishing.

Banks, S (2001) *Ethics and values in social work*, 2nd edn. Basingstoke: Palgrave.

Barry, M (2000) The mentor/monitor debate in criminal justice: 'What works' for offenders, *British Journal of Social Work*, 30: 575–95.

Barrett, G and Keeping, C (2005) The process required for effective interprofessional working, in Barrett, G Sellman, D and Thomas, J (eds) *Interprofessional working in health and social care*. Basingstoke: Palgrave.

Bateman, T (2003) A state of affairs that shames us all, *Safer Society*, 18.

Bateman, T (2005) Court reports, in Bateman, T and Pitts, J (eds) *The RHP companion to youth justice*. Lyme Regis: Russell House Publishing.

Bateman, T (2008) 'Target Practice': sanction detection and the criminalisation of children, *Criminal Justice Matters*, 73.

Bateman, T (2009) *Community care*, 30 November. communitycare.co.uk

Bateman, T and Pitts, J (eds) (2005) *The RHP companion to youth justice*. Lyme Regis: Russell House Publishing.

Beccaria, C (1963, first published 1764) *On crimes and punishments*. New York: Bobbs Merrill.

Becker, H (1963) *Outsiders: Studies in the sociology of deviance*. New York: Free Press.

Bercow, J (2008) *Review of services for children and young people (0–19) with speech, language and communication needs*. London: Department for Children, Schools and Families.

Bevan, D (1998) Death, dying and inequality, *Care: The Journal of Practice and Development*, 7(1).

Blueprint Project (2005) *Start with the child, stay with the child*. London: National Children's Bureau.

Borum, R, Fein, R, Vossekuil, B and Berglund, J (1999) Threat assessment: Defining an approach for evaluating risk of targeted violence, *Behavioural Sciences and the Law*, 17, 323–37.

Bottoms, A and Dignan, J (2004) Youth justice in Great Britain, in Tonry, M and Doob, A (eds) *Crime and justice*, vol 31: Chicago: University of Chicago Press.

Bower, M (2005) *Psychoanalytic theory for social work practice: Thinking under fire*. London: Routledge.

Braithwaite, J (1989) *Crime, shame and reintegration*. Cambridge: Cambridge University Press.

Braithwaite, J (2003) Restorative justice and a better future, in McLaughlin, E, Fergusson, R, Hughes, G and Westmarland, L (eds) *Restorative justice: Critical issues*. London: Sage.

Briggs, S (2005) Psychoanalytic research in the era of evidence-based practice, in Bower, M (ed) *Psychoanalytic: theory for social work practice: Thinking under fire*. London: Routledge.

Briggs, S (2008) *Working with adolescents and young adults: A contemporary psychodynamic approach*. Basingstoke: Palgrave.

British Association of Social Workers (BASW) (2002) *Code of ethics*. Birmingham: British Association of Social Workers.

Burnett, R and Appleton, C (2004) *Joined-up youth justice: Tackling crime in partnership*. Lyme Regis: Russell House Publishing.

Case, S (2007) Questioning the 'evidence' of risk that underpins evidence-led youth justice interventions, *Youth Justice*, 7: 91–105.

Case, S and **Haines, K** (2009) *Understanding youth offending: Risk-focused research, policy and practice*. Cullompton: Willan.

Chapman, T (2005) Group work with young people who offend, in Bateman, T and Pitts, J (eds) *The RHP companion to youth justice*. Lyme Regis, Russell House Publishing.

Christie, N (1977) Conflicts as property, *British Journal of Criminology*, 17: 1–19.

Clarke, J and **Newburn, J** (1997) *The managerial state*. London: Sage.

Cleaver, H and **Walker, S** with **Meadows, P** (2004) *Assessing children's needs and circumstances: The impact of the assessment framework*. London: Jessica Kingsley Publishers.

Clow, C (1998) Managing endings in practice teaching, in, Lawson, H (ed) *Practice teaching – Changing social work*. London: Jessica Kingsley.

Cloward, R and **Ohlin, L** (1960) *Delinquency and opportunity: A theory of delinquent gangs*. Chicago: Free Press.

Cohen, A (1955) *Delinquent boys: The culture of the gang*. Chicago: Free Press.

Cohen, S (1973) *Folk devils and moral panics: The creation of mods and rockers*. London: Paladin.

Committee on the Rights of the Child (49th Session). *Consideration of reports submitted by States parties under article 44 of the Convention. Concluding observations; the United Kingdom of Great Britain and Northern Ireland*. CRC/C/GBR/CO.4.

Cooper, A and **Lousada, J** (2010) The shock of the real: Psychoanalysis, modernity, survival, in, Lemma, A and Patrick, M (eds) *Off the couch: Contemporary psychoanalytic approaches*. Hove: Routledge.

Coulshed, V and **Orme, J** (2006) *Social work practice*, 4th edn. Basingstoke: Palgrave Macmillan.

Council of Europe Commission for Human Rights (2008) *Rights of the child with focus on juvenile justice*, memorandum by Thomas Hammarberg, Commissioner for Human Rights of the Council of Europe.

Crawford, A and **Newburn, T** (2002) Recent developments in restorative justice for young people in England and Wales: Community participation and representation, *British Journal of Criminology*, 42: 476–95.

Crawford, A and **Newburn, T** (2003) *Youth offending and restorative justice: Implementing reform in youth justice*. Cullompton: Willan.

Crawford, K and **Walker, J** (2010) *Social work and human development*, 3rd edn Exeter: Learning Matters.

Cross, N, Evans, J and **Minkes, J** (2003) Still children first? Developments in youth justice in Wales, *Youth Justice*, 2(3): 151–62.

de Winter, M, and **Noom, M** (2003) Someone who treats you as an ordinary human being . . . homeless youth examine the quality of professional care, *British Journal of Social Work*, 33.

Dennis, N (1993) *Rising crime and the dismembered family*. London: Institute of Economic Affairs.

Dennis, N (1997) *Zero tolerance: Policing a free society*. London: Institute of Economic Affairs.

Dennis, N and **Erdos, G** (1992) *Families without fatherhood*. London: Institute of Economic Affairs.

Department for Children, Schools and Families (2008) *The youth taskforce action plan*. London: Department for Children, Schools and Families.

Department for Children, Schools and Families (2011) *Working together to safeguard children: A guide to inter-agency working to safeguard and promote the welfare of children*. London: Stationery Office.

Department of Education (2010) Youth crime: Young people aged 10–17 receiving their first reprimand, warning or convictions, six-monthly figures to September 2009. *Statistical Bulletin*, June. London: Department of Education.

Department of Health (2000) *Framework for the assessment of children in need and their families*. London: The Stationery Office.

Department of Health / Home Office (2003) *The Victoria Climbié inquiry: Report of an inquiry by Lord Laming*. London: The Stationery Office.

Department of Health (2011) *Health and social care bill*. London: HMSO.

Downes, D and **Rock, P** (2003) *Understanding deviance*, 4th edn. Oxford: Oxford University Press.

Durkheim, E (1893, republished 1964) *The division of labor in society*. New York: Free Press.

Durkheim, E (1895 republished 1964) *The rules of sociological method*. New York: Free Press.

Durkheim, E (1897, republished 1952) *Suicide: A study in sociology*. London: Routledge and Kegan Paul.

Earle, R (2005) The referral order, in Bateman, T and Pitts, J (eds) *The RHP companion to youth justice*. Lyme Regis: Russell House Publishing.

Egan, G (2002) *The skilled helper: A problem-management and opportunity approach to helping*, 7th edn. California: Brooks/Cole.

Farrington, D P (1992) Explaining the beginning, process and ending of antisocial behaviour from birth to adulthood, in McCord, J (ed) *Facts, frameworks and forecasts: Advances in criminological theory, Vol 3*. New Brunswick, NJ: Transaction.

Farrington, D P (1995) Teenage antisocial behaviour, in Rutter, M (ed) *Psychosocial disturbances in young people, challenges for prevention*. Cambridge: Cambridge University Press.

Farrington, D (2007) Childhood risk factors and risk-focussed prevention, in Maguire, M, Morgan, R and Reiner, R (eds) *The Oxford handbook of criminology*, 4th edn. Oxford: Oxford University Press.

Feeley, M and **Simon, J** (1992) The new penology, *Criminology*, 30 (4): 449–74.

Ferrell, J, Hayward, K, Morrison, W and **Presdee, M** (Eds) (2004) *Cultural criminology unleashed*. London: Cavendish.

Fionda, J (2005) *Devils and angels: Youth policy and crime*. Oxford: Hart.

Garland, D (1996) The limits of the sovereign state: Strategies of crime control in contemporary society, *British Journal of Criminology*, 36 4: 445–71.

Garland, D (2002) Of crimes and criminals: The development of criminology in Britain, in Maguire, M, Morgan, R and Reiner, R (eds) *The Oxford handbook of criminology*, 3rd edn. Oxford: Oxford University Press.

Gibson, B (1994) *The youth court: One year on*. Winchester: Waterside.

Goldblatt, P and Lewis, C (eds) (1998) *Reducing offending*, Home Office Research Study 187. London: Home Office.

Goldson, B (2000) 'Children in need' or 'young offenders'? Hardening ideology, organisational change and new challenges for social work with children in trouble, *Child and Family Social Work*, 5: 255–65.

Goldson, B (2001) A rational youth justice? Some critical reflections on the research, policy and practice relation, *Probation Journal*, 8 (2): 76–85.

Goldson, B (2002) *Vulnerable inside: Children in secure and penal settings*. London: The Children's Society.

Goldson, B (2006) Penal custody: Intolerance, irrationality and indifference, in Goldson, B and Muncie, J (eds) *Youth crime and justice*. London: Sage.

Goldson, B (2009) Fatal injustice: Rampant punitiveness, child-prisoner deaths and institutional denial – a case for a comprehensive independent inquiry in England and Wales, in Goldson, B and Muncie, J (eds) *Youth Crime and Justice*. London: Sage.

Graham, J and Bowling, B (1995) *Young people and crime*, Home Office Research Study 145. London: Home Office.

GSCC (2002) *Code of practice for social care workers*.

Hagell, A (2003) *Quality protects research briefing no 8: Understanding and challenging youth offending*. London: Department of Health.

Haines, K and Drakeford, M (1998) *Young people and youth justice*. Basingstoke: Macmillan.

Hall, S and Jefferson, T (eds) (1976) *Resistance through rituals: Youth subcultures in post-war Britain*. London: Hutchinson.

Hall, S, Critchner, C, Jefferson, T, Clarke, J and Robert, B (1978) *Policing the crisis: Mugging, the state and law and order*. Basingstoke: Macmillan.

Hardy, J (ed) (1999) *Achieving health and social care improvements through interprofessional education*. Conference Proceedings. Institute of Health and Community Studies: Bournemouth University.

Hebdige, D (1979) *Subculture: The meaning of style*. London: Methuen.

Hendrick, H (2002) Constructions and reconstructions of British childhood: An interpretive survey, 1800 to the present, in Muncie, J, Hughes, G and McLaughlin, E (eds) *Youth justice: Critical readings*. London: Sage.

Hendrick, H (2006) Histories of youth crime and justice, in Goldson, B and Muncie, J (Eds) *Youth crime and justice*. London: Sage.

Her Majesty's Inspectorate of Probation (2006) *Joint inspection of youth offending teams: Annual report 2005–6*. London: HMIP.

Hester, R (2000) Community safety and the new youth justice, in Goldson, B, *The new youth justice*. Lyme Regis: Russell House Publishing.

Hill, M (1999) What's the problem? Who can help? The perspectives of children and young people on their well-being and on helping professionals, *Journal of Social Work Practice*, 13(2).

Holdaway, S, Davidson, N, Dignan, J, Hammersley, R, Hine, J and Marsh, P (2001) *New strategies to address youth offending: The national evaluation of the pilot youth offending teams*. London: Home Office.

Hollis, F (1972) *Casework: A psychosocial therapy*, 2nd edn. New York: Random House.

Home Office (1927) *Report of the departmental committee on the treatment of young offenders* (Moloney Committee) Cmnd 2831. London: Home Office.

Home Office (1960) *Report of the committee on children and young persons* (Ingleby Report) Cmnd 1191. London: Home Office.

Home Office (1964) *Report of the committee on children and young persons* (Kilbrandon Report) Cmnd 3065. London: Home Office.

Home Office (1965) *The child, the family and the young offender*, Cmnd 2742. London: Home Office.

Home Office (1985) *The cautioning of offenders*, Circular 14/1985. London: Home Office.

Home Office (1988) *Punishment, custody and the community*. London: HMSO.

Home Office (1990) *Crime, justice and protecting the public*. Cmnd, 965. London: HMSO.

Home Office (1991) *Safer communities: The delivery of crime prevention through the partnership approach* (Morgan Report). London: Home Office.

Home Office (1994) *The cautioning of offenders*. Home Office Circular 18/1994 London: Home Office.

Home Office (1997a) *Community safety order*. London: Home Office.

Home Office (1997b) *Getting to grips with crime*. London: Home Office.

Home Office (1997c) *New national and local focus on youth crime*. London: Home Office.

Home Office (1997d) *No more excuses: A new approach to tackling youth crime in England and Wales*. London: Home Office.

Home Office (1997e) *Preventing children offending*. London: Home Office.

Home Office (1997f) *Tackling delays in the youth justice system*. London: Home Office.

Home Office (1997g) *Tackling youth crime*. London: Home Office.

Home Office (2002) *Justice for all*. London: Home Office.

Home Office (2003a) *Every child matters*. London: Home Office.

Home Office (2003b) *Important changes to referral orders from 18 August 2003. Supplementary guidance for courts, Youth Offending Teams and Youth Offender Panels*. London: Home Office.

Home Office (2003c) *Youth justice – The next steps*. London: Home Office.

Home Office (2003d) *Respect and responsibility: Taking a stand against anti-social behaviour*. London: Home Office.

Home Office (2004a) *Restorative justice: The government's strategy. Responses to the consultation document*. London: Home Office.

Home Office (2005b) *Crime in England and Wales 2004/5*. London: Home Office.

Home Office (2005c) *'Safe Week': Schoolchildren urged to 'Keep it safe – keep it hidden' to cut street crime*. London: Home Office.

Home Office (2005d) *Statistics on race and the criminal justice system – 2004*. London: Home Office.

Home Office (2005e) *Youth matters*. London: Home Office.

Home Office (2006a) *Protecting the public and reducing re-offending*. London: Home Office.

Home Office (2006b) *Respect taskforce and action plan*. London: Home Office.

Home Office (2011) *More effective responses to anti-social behaviour*. London: Home Office.

Home Office/Youth Justice Board (2002) *The final warning scheme – Guidance for the police and youth offending teams*. London: HMSO.

Home Office, Youth Justice Board and Department for Constitutional Affairs (2004) *Joint Home Office/DCA/Youth Justice Board circular: Parenting orders And contracts for criminal conduct or anti-social behaviour*. London: Home Office, Youth Justice Board and Department for Constitutional Affairs.

Hough, M and **Roberts, JV** (2004) *Youth crime and youth justice*. Bristol: Policy Press.

Howard League for Panel Reform (2008) *Growing up, shutting up*. www.howardleague.org/fileadmin/howardleague/user/pdf/Press/Press2008/Growingupshutup 2 July 2008/30/7/11

Howe, D (1996) Surface and depth in social work, in Parton, N (ed.) *Social theory, social change and social work*. London: Routledge.

Hudson, A (2002) 'Troublesome girls': Towards alternative definitions and policies, in Muncie, J, Hughes, G and Mclaughlin, E (eds) *Youth justice: Critical readings*. London: Sage.

IFSW/IASSW (2004) *Ethics in social work, Statement of principles*. www.ifsw.org/cm_dataEthics_in_Social_Work_Statement_of_Principles_-_to_be_publ_205.pdf.

Ipsos MORI (2010) A review of techniques for effective engagement and participation. London: YJB. www.yjb.gov.uk/Publications/Resources/Downloads/A%20Review%20of%20Techniques%20for%20Effective%20Engagement%20and%20Participation.pdf

Jacobson, J, Bhardwa, B, Gyateng, T, Hunter, G and **Hough, M** (2010) *Punishing disadvantage: A profile of children in custody*. London: Prison Reform Trust.

Jenks, C (1996) *Childhood*. London: Routledge.

Johns, R (2011) *Using the law in social work*, 5th edn. Exeter: Learning Matters.

Johnson, S, Blum, WR, Giedd, J (2009) Adolescent maturity and the brain: The promise and pitfalls of neuroscience research in adolescent health, *Policy Journal Adolescent Health*. 45(3), 216–21.

Jones, D (2003) *Communicating with vulnerable children: A guide for practitioners*. London: Gaskell.

Kalunta-Crumpton, A (2005) Race crime and youth justice, in Bateman, T and Pitts, J. (eds) *The RHP companion to youth justice.* Lyme Regis: Russell House Publishing.

Kemp, V, Sorsby, A, Liddle, M and **Merrington, S** (2002) *Assessing responses to youth offending in Northhamptonshire.* Research Briefing 2. London: NACRO.

Kennedy, E (2004) *Child and adolescent psychotherapy: A systematic review of psychoanalytic approaches.* London: North Central Strategic Health Authority.

Kondrat, DC (2010) The strengths perspective, in Teater, B, *An introduction to applying social work theories and methods.* Maidenhead: Open University Press.

Koprowska, J (2010) *Communication and interpersonal skills in social work,* 3rd edn. Exeter: Learning Matters.

Labour Party (1996) *Tackling youth crime, reforming youth justice.* London: Labour Party.

Laming, H (2003) *The Victoria Climbié inquiry report,* Cmnd 5730. London: The Stationery Office.

Laming, H (2009) *The protection of children in England: A progress report.* London. The Stationery Office.

Lea, J and **Young, J** (1984) *What is to be done about law and order?* London: Penguin (2nd edn, London: Pluto Press, 1993).

Le Fevre. M (2010) *Communicating with children and young people: Making a difference.* Bristol: Policy Press.

Lemert, E (1951) *Social pathology.* New York: McGraw-Hill.

Leonard, E (1982) *Women, Crime and Society.* New York: Longman.

Liddle, M and **Solanki, A** (2002) *Persistent young offenders: Research on individual backgrounds and life experiences.* London: NACRO.

Lindsay, T and **Orton, S** (2011) *Groupwork practice in social work,* 2nd edn. Exeter: Learning Matters.

Lowenkramp, CT and **Latessa, EJ** (eds) (2004) *Residential community corrections and the risk principle: Lessons learned in Ohio.* Columbus: Ohio Department of Rehabilitation and Correction.

Lyon J, Dennison, C and **Wilson, A** (2000) *Tell them so they listen: Messages from young people in custody.* Research Study 201. London: Home Office.

Mannheim, H (ed) (1960) *Pioneers in criminology.* London: Stevens.

Mantle, G, Fox, D and **Dhami, K** (2005) Restorative justice and three individual theories of crime, *Internet Journal of Criminology,* **www.internetjournalofcriminology.com**

Marlow, A (2005) The policing of young people, in Bateman, T and Pitts, J (eds) *The RHP companion to youth justice.* Lyme Regis: Russell House Publishing.

Marshall, T F (1996) The evolution of restorative justice in Britain, *European Journal on Criminal Policy and Research,* 4(4): 21–43.

Martinson, R (1974) What works? Questions and answers about prison reform, *The Public Interest,* 35: 22–54.

Masters G (2005) Restorative justice and youth justice, in Bateman, T and Pitts, J (eds) *The RHP companion to youth justice*. Lyme Regis: Russell House Publishing.

Matza, D (1964) *Delinquency and drift*. New York: Wiley.

Matza, D and **Sykes, G** (1957) Techniques of neutralisation: A theory of delinquency, *American Sociological Review*, 22: 664–70.

Matza, D and **Sykes, G** (1961) Juvenile delinquency and subterranean values, *American Sociological Review*, 26: 712–19.

McLaughlin, E and **Muncie, J** (1996) *Controlling crime*. London: Sage.

McNeil, F (2006) Community supervision: Context and relationships matter, in Goldson, B and Muncie, J (eds) *Youth crime and Justice*. Lodon: Sage.

McNeill, F and **Whyte, B** (2007) *Reducing reoffending: Social work and community justice in Scotland*. Cullompton: Willan.

Merton, R (1938) Social structure and anomie, *American Journal of Sociology*, 2: 577–602.

Middleton, L (1997) *The art of assessment*. Birmingham: Venture Press.

Miller, W (1958) Lower class culture as a generating milieu of gang delinquency, *Journal of Social Issues*, 15: 5–19.

Milner, J and **O'Byrne, P** (2009) *Assessment in social work*, 3rd edn. Basingstoke: Palgrave Macmillan.

Ministry of Justice (2008) *Youth crime action plan*. London: Ministry of Justice.

Ministry of Justice (2009) *The Youth Rehabilitation Order and the Youth Justice Provisions in the Criminal Justice and Immigration Act 2008, Circular 2009/3*. London: Ministry of Justice.

Ministry of Justice (2010) *Breaking the cycle: Effective punishment, rehabilitation and sentencing of offenders*. London: Ministry of Justice.

Ministry of Justice/YJB (2011) *Strategy for the secure estate for children and young people in England and Wales, plans for 2011/12 – 2014/5*. London: Ministry of Justice/YJB.

Monaghan, G (2005) Human rights and youth justice, in Bateman, T and Pitts, J (eds) *The RHP companion to youth justice*. Lyme Regis: Russell House Publishing.

Morgan, R (2006) *About social workers: A children's views report*. Newcastle upon Tyne: Commission for Social Care Inspection.

Morris, A and **Giller, M** (1987) *Understanding juvenile justice*. London: Croome Helm.

Morrison, T (2007) Emotional intellegence, emotion and social work: Contexts, characteristics, complications and contribution, *British Journal of Social Work*, 37, 245–63.

Moseley, D, Clark, J, Hall, E, Miller, J, Bannfield, V, Gregson, M, Spedding, T, Blanch, G and **Elliot, J,** (2006) *The impact of ESB oral communication courses in HM Prisons – an independent evaluation in developing oral communication and productive thinking skills in HM Prisons*. London: Learning and Skills Research Centre.

Muncie, J (2009) *Youth and crime*, 3rd edn. London: Sage.

Muncie, J and **Hughes, G** (2002) Modes of governance: Political realities, criminalisation and resistance, in Muncie, J, Hughes, G, and McLaughlin, E (eds) *Youth justice: Critical readings*. London: Sage.

Munro, E (2011) *Munro review of child protection: Final report. A child-centred system*. London: Department for Education.

Murray, C (1984) *Losing ground*. New York: Basic Books.

Murray, C (1988) *In pursuit of happiness and good government*. New York: Simon and Schuster.

Murray, C (1990) *The emerging British underclass*. London: Institute of Economic Affairs, Health and Welfare Unit.

Murray, C (1994) *Underclass: The crisis deepens*. London: Institute of Economic Affairs.

NACRO (1999) *Facts about young offenders in 1997*. London: NACRO Youth Crime Section.

NACRO (2003a) Implications of youth justice – The next steps. Companion to the green paper every child matters. *Youth Crime Briefing*. December. London: NACRO.

NACRO (2003b) *Youth Crime Briefing*. Some facts about young people who offend – 2003. London: NACRO.

NACRO (2003c) Some facts about young people who offend – 2001. *Youth Crime Briefing*, March. London: NACRO.

NACRO (2005) *Reducing offending by looked after children*. London: NACRO.

NACRO (2008) *Children's human rights and the youth justice system*. Youth Crime Briefing. London: NACRO.

NACRO (2009) Some facts about children and young people who offend – 2007. *Youth Crime Briefing*, March. London: NACRO.

NACRO (2010) *The use of custody for children and young people*. Policy position paper. London: NACRO.

Newburn, T, Crawford, A, Earle, R, Goldie, S, Hale, C, Masters, G, Netten, A, Saunders, R, Sharpe, K and **Uglow, S** (2001) *The introduction of referral orders into the youth justice system*, RDS Occasional Paper 70. London: Home Office.

Newson, J and Newson, E (1989) *The extent of parental physical punishment in the UK*. London: Approach.

Oliver, C (2010) *Children's views and experiences of their contact with social workers: A focussed review*. Leeds: CWDC.

O'Mahony, P (2009) The risk factors prevention paradigm and the causes of youth crime: A deceptively useful analysis?, *Youth Justice*, August, (9)2.

Park, R (1936) Human Ecology, *American Journal of Sociology*, 42(1) July: 15.

Park, R and Burgess, E (eds) (1925) *The City*. Chicago: University of Chicago Press.

Parker, J and Bradley G (2010) *Social work practice: Assessment, planning, intervention and review*, 3rd edn. Exeter: Learning Matters.

Paylor, I (2010) The scaled approach to youth justice: A risky busines, *Criminal Justice Matters*, September.

Payne, M (2005) Working with groups, in Harrison, R and Wise, C (eds) *Working with young people*. London: Sage.

Pearson, G (1983) *Hooligan: A history of respectable fears*. London: Macmillan.

Perry, AE, Gilbody, S, Akers, J and Light, K (2008) *Mental health: Source document*. London: YJB.

Pickburn, C, Lindfield, S and Coleman, J (2005) Working with parents, in Bateman, T and Pitts, J (eds) *The RHP companion to youth justice*. Lyme Regis: Russell House Publishing.

Pickford, J (2000) *Youth justice: Theory and practice*. London: Cavendish Publishing.

Pickford, J (2008) in Goldson, B (ed.) *A dictionary of youth justice*. Cullompton: Willan. Various entries.

Piper, C (2004) Assessing assessment, *Family Law Journal*, 34: 736–40.

Pitts, J (2001) Korrectional karaoke: New Labour and the zombification of youth justice, *Youth Justice*, 1(2).

Pitts, J. (2003) *The new politics of youth crime: Discipline or solidarity?* Lyme Regis: Russell House Publishing.

Pitts, J (2008) *Reluctant gangsters: The changing face of youth crime*. Cullompton: Willan.

Pratt, J (1989) Corporatism, the third model of youth justice, *British Journal of Criminology*, 29(3): 236–54.

Preston-Shoot, M (2007) *Effective groupwork*. Basingstoke: Palgrave Macmillan.

Preston-Shoot, M and Agass, D (1990) *Making sense of social work: Psychodynamics, systems and practice*. Basingstoke: Macmillan.

Prior, D (2005) Evaluating the new youth justice: What can practitioners learn from research?, *Practice*, 17(2).

Prior, D and Mason, P (2010) A different kind of evidence? Looking for 'what works' in engaging young offenders, *Youth Justice*, 10(3).

Quality Assurance Agency for Higher Education (QAA) (2001) *Social policy and administration and social work subject benchmark statements*. London: QAA.

Quinney, A (2006) Collaborative social work practice. Exeter: Learning Matters.

Quinney, R (1970) *The social reality of crime*. Boston: Little, Brown.

Reder, P and Duncan, S (2004) Making the most of the Victoria Climbié inquiry report. *Child Abuse Review*, 13: 95–115.

Redhead, S (1993) *Rave off: Politics and deviance in contemporary youth culture*. Aldershot: Avebury.

Reiner, R (2000) *The politics of the police*, 3rd edn. Oxford: Oxford University Press.

Ritchie, J (1994) *Report of the inquiry into the care and treatment of Christopher Clunis*. London: HMSO.

Roberts, C, Baker, K Merrington, S and Jones, S (2001) *Validity and reliability of Asset: Interim report to the Youth Justice Board*. Oxford: Centre for Criminological Research.

Rogers, C (1976) *Client-centred therapy*. London: Constable and Robinson.

Rutherford, A (1992) *Growing out of crime: The new era*. Winchester: Waterside.

Rutherford, A (2002) *Growing out of crime: The new era*. Winchester: Waterside Press.

Rutter, M, and Garmezy, N (1983) Developmental psychopathology, in Hetherington, E M (ed) *Handbook of child psychology, Vol 4, social and personality development*. Chichester: Wiley.

Rutter, M, Giller, H and Hagell, A (1998) *Antisocial behaviour by young people*. Cambridge: Cambridge University Press.

Safer Society (2003) *No. 18*.

Salzberger–Wittenberg, I (1970) *Psychoanalytic insight and relationships: A Kleinian approach*. London: Routledge.

Schon, D (1983) *The reflective practitioner*. New York: Basic Books.

Sentencing Guidelines Council (2009) *Overarching principles – sentencing youths: Definitive guideline*.

Shaw, C (1931) *The natural history of a delinquent career*. Chicago: University of Chicago Press.

Shaw, C and McKay, H (1942) *Juvenile delinquency and urban areas*. Chicago: University of Chicago Press.

Sheldrick, C (1999) 'Practitioner review: The assessment and managament of risk in adolescents, *Journal of Child Psychology and Psychiatry*, 40(4): 507–18.

Sheppard, M, Newstead, S DiCaccavo, A and Ryan, K (2001) Comparative hypothesis assessment and quasi triangulation as process knowledge assessment strategies in social work practice, *British Journal of Social Work*, 31(6): 863–85.

Sherman, LW and Strang, H with Newberry-Birch, D (2008) *Restorative justice*. London: Youth Justice Board.

Smale, G and Tuson, G. With Brhal, N and Marsh, P (1993) *Empowerment, assessment, care management and the skilled worker*. London: National Institute for Social Work.

Smith, D (2005) The effectiveness of the juvenile justice system, *Criminal Justice*, 5(2): 181–95

Smith, J (2003) *The nature of personal crime*. London: HMSO.

Smith, R (2007) *Youth justice: Ideas, policy, practice*. Cullompton: Willan.

Social Work Reform Board (2011) *Building a safe and confident future: One year on – progress report from the social work reform board*. London: Department of Education.

Social Work Taskforce (2009) *Building a safe, confident future: The final report of the social work task-force*. London: Department for Children, Schools and Families.

Stokes, E (2000) Abolishing the presumption of doli-incapax: reflections on the death of a doctrine, in Pickford, J (ed.) *Youth justice: Theory and practice*. London: Cavendish.

Souhami, A. (2007) *Transforming youth justice: Occupational identity and cultural change*. Cullompton: Willan.

Sumner, C (1994) *The sociology of deviance: An obituary*. Buckingham: Open University Press.

Talbot, C (1996) *Realising objectives in the probation service – A workbook*. London: Home Office Probation Unit.

Talbot, J (2010) *Seen and heard: Supporting vulnerable children in the youth justice system*. London: Prison Reform Trust.

Taylor, I, Walton, P and Young, J (1973) *The new criminology*. London: Routledge and Kegan Paul.

Teli, B (2011) *Assessment and planning interventions: Review and design. Statement of intent – proposed framework*. London: Youth Justice Board.

Thane, P (2009) Childhood in History, in Goldson, B and Muncie, J (eds) *Youth crime and justice*. London: Sage.

Thompson, N (2001) *Anti-discriminatory practice*. Basingstoke: Palgrave Macmillan.

Thompson, N (2005) *Understanding social work: Preparing for practice*, 2nd edn. Basingstoke: Palgrave Macmillan.

Thompson, N (2006) *People problems*. Basingstoke: Palgrave Macmillan.

Thrasher, F (1927) *The gang: A study of 1,313 gangs in Chicago*. Chicago: University of Chicago Press.

TOPSS England (2002) *Statement of expectations from individuals, families, carers, groups and communities who use services and those who care for them*. London: TOPSS England.

Trevithick, P (2005) *Social work skills: A practice handbook*. Maidenhead: Open University Press.

Tuckman, B W and Jenson, M A C (1977) Stages of small group development revisited, *Group and Organisation Studies*, 2 (4): 419–27.

Uglow, S (2002) *Criminal justice*, 2nd edn. London: Sweet and Maxwell.

United Nations (1966) *International covenant on civil and political rights* (New York).

United Nations (1985) *The United Nations standard minimum rules for the administration of juvenile justice* (New York).

United Nations (1989) *The United Nations convention on the rights of the child* (New York).

United Nations (1990a) *The United Nations guidelines for the prevention of juvenile delinquency* (New York).

United Nations (1990b) *The United Nations rules for the protection of juveniles deprived of their liberty* (New York).

United Nations (2008) *The United Nations committee on the rights of the child* (New York).

Utting, D, Bright, J and Henricson, C (1993) *Crime and the family: Improving child rearing and preventing delinquency*. London: Family Policy Studies Centre.

Walker, M, Barclay, A, Malloch, M, McIvor, G, Kendrick, A, Hunter, L and Hill, M (2006) *Secure accommodation in Scotland*. Edinburgh: SEED.

Walker, S and Beckett, C (2003) *Social work assessment and intervention*. Lyme Regis: Russell House.

White, S and Featherstone, B (2005) Communicating misunderstandings: multiagency work as social practice, *Child and Family Social Work*, 10: 207–16.

Wilson, D and Moore, S (2004) *Playing the game: The experiences of young black men in custody.* London: The Children's Society.

Wilson, J, Q and Kelling, G (1982) 'Broken windows', *Atlantic Monthly*, March, 29–38.

Wilson, K, Ruch, G, Lymbery, M and Cooper, A (2008) (eds) *Social work: An introduction to contemporary practice.* Harlow: Pearson Education Limited.

Wirth, L, (1928) *The ghetto.* Chicago. University of Chicago Press.

Wirth, L (1964) Human ecology, in Wirth, L and Reiss, A, *On cities and social life.* Chicago: University of Chicago Press.

Whyte, B (2009) *Youth justice in practice.* Bristol: Policy Press.

Yelloly, M and Henkel, M (1995) *Learning and teaching in social work: Towards reflective practice.* London: Jessica Kingsley.

Young, J (1971) *The drugtakers.* London: Paladin.

Young, J (1994) Incessant chatter: Current paradigms in criminology, in Maguire, M, Morgan, R and Reiner, R (eds) *The Oxford handbook of criminology.* Oxford: Oxford University Press.

Youth Justice Board (2001a) *Good practice guidelines for restorative work with victims and young offenders.* London: Youth Justice Board.

Youth Justice Board (2002a) *Key elements in effective practice: Assessment, planning, intervention and supervision.* London: Youth Justice Board.

Youth Justice Board (2002b) *Key elements of effective practice: Parenting.* London: Youth Justice Board.

Youth Justice Board (2003a) *Assessment, planning and supervision: A reader for the professional certificate in effective practice.* London: Youth Justice Board.

Youth Justice Board (2003b) *Gaining ground in the community. Youth Justice Board annual review 2002/2003.* London: Youth Justice Board.

Youth Justice Board (2003c) *Key elements of effective practice.* London: Youth Justice Board.

Youth Justice Board (2004a) *Differences or discrimination?* London: Youth Justice Board.

Youth Justice Board (2004b) *National standards for youth justice services.* London: Youth Justice Board.

Youth Justice Board (2005a) *Annual statistics 2004/05.* London: Youth Justice Board.

Youth Justice Board (2005a) *Mental health needs and provision.* London: Youth Justice Board.

Youth Justice Board (2005b) *Key elements of effective practice: Mentoring.* London: Youth Justice Board.

Youth Justice Board (2005c) *Risk and protective factors associated with youth crime and effective intervention to prevent it.* London: Youth Justice Board.

Youth Justice Board (2006a) *Asset guidance*. London: Youth Justice Board.

Youth Justice Board (2006b) *Common assessment framework: Draft guidance for youth offending teams*. London: Youth Justice Board.

Youth Justice Board (2006c) *Key elements of effective practice: Quality assurance framework: Guidance for youth offending teams and secure establishments*. London: Youth Justice Board.

Youth Justice Board (2007) *Accomodation needs and experiences*. London: Youth Justice Board.

Youth Justice Board (2008) *Key elements of effective practice: Engaging young people who offend*. London: Youth Justice Board.

Youth Justice Board (2009a) *Custody*. London: Youth Justice Board.

Youth Justice Board (2009b) *Dangerous offenders – Guidance on multi-agency public protection arrangements*. London: Youth Justice Board.

Youth Justice Board (2010a) *Repairing the harm*. London: Youth Justice Board.

Youth Justice Board (2010b) *The Youth Rehabilitation Order and other Youth Justice Provisions of the Criminal Justice and Immigration Act 2008: Practice guidance for youth offending teams*. London: Youth Justice Board.

Youth Justice Board (2010c) *Youth justice: The scaled approach*. London: Ministry of Justice.

Youth Justice Board (2010d) *National standards for youth justice*. London: Youth Justice Board.

Youth Justice Board/Ministry of Justice (2011) Youth justice statistics 2009/10 England and Wales. *Statistical Bulletin*, January. London Youth Justice Board/Ministry of Justice.

Youth Justice Trust (2003) *On the case:* Survey of 1000 children and young people under supervision by Youth Offending Teams in Greater Manchester and W. Yorkshire. Manchester: Youth Justice Trust.

Index

Added to a page number 'f' denotes a figure and 't' denotes a table.

U

V

W

Y